The News Media in National and International Conflict

Also of Interest

Information, Economics, and Power: The North-South Dimension, edited by Rita Cruise O'Brien

Information Technology in the Third World: Can I. T. Lead to Humane National Development? William James Stover

Toward International Tele-Education, edited by William Blume and Paul Schneller

War of Ideas: The U.S. Propaganda Campaign in Vietnam, Robert Chandler

Paths to Conflict: International Dispute Initiation, 1816–1976, Zeev Maoz

Social Conflicts and Third Parties: Strategies of Conflict Resolution, Jacob Bercovitch

† *Conflict Regulation,* Paul Wehr

† Available in hardcover and paperback.

A Westview Special Study

The News Media in National and International Conflict
edited by Andrew Arno and Wimal Dissanayake

Ironically, as telecommunications technology—the embodiment of modernity—advances, bringing people in different nations into more direct contact during conflict situations, traditional cultural factors become increasingly important as differing ways of thinking and acting collide. The mass media can be seen as a factor in the creation of international conflict; they also, claim many scholars, are the key to control and resolution of those problems. Whichever side of the coin one chooses to look at—mass communication as cause or cure of conflict—there is no doubt that the news media are no longer peripheral players on the global scene; they are important participants whose organizational patterns of behavior, values, and motivations must be taken into account in understanding national and international conflict.

In this volume, a distinguished group of authors explores the variety of ways the news media—newspapers, radio, and television—are involved in conflict situations. Conflicts between the United States and Iran, India and Pakistan, and the United States and China are examined, and national-level studies in Sri Lanka, Iran, Hong Kong, and the United States provide varied contexts in which the authors look at the complex interrelationships among government, news media, and the public in conflict situations.

Dr. Andrew Arno is a former research associate at the East-West Center. He holds advanced degrees in social anthropology and law and has taught at the City University of New York and the University of Rhode Island. **Dr. Wimal Dissanayake** is a research associate at the Institute of Culture and Communication (formerly the Communication Institute) and coordinator of the Humanities Forum at the East-West Center. He is the author of *Communications Research and Cultural Values* (1982) and *Continuity and Change in Communication Systems* (in press) and is consulting and contributing editor to the *Journal of Communication*.

Published in cooperation
with the East-West Center,
Honolulu, Hawaii

The News Media in National and International Conflict

edited by Andrew Arno
and Wimal Dissanayake

Westview Press / Boulder and London

This is a Westview reprint edition, manufactured on our own premises using equipment and methods that allow us to keep even specialized books in stock. It is printed on acid-free paper and bound in softcovers that carry the highest rating of NASTA in consultation with the AAP and the BMI.

A Westview Special Study

Published in 1984 in the United States of America by Westview Press, Inc., 5500 Central Avenue, Boulder, Colorado 80301; Frederick A. Praeger, President and Publisher

Library of Congress Catalog Card Number: 84-50130
ISBN: 0-86531-776-3

Composition for this book was provided by the East-West Center
Printed and bound in the United States of America

5   4   3   2

CONTENTS

THE NEWS MEDIA IN INTERNATIONAL CONFLICT

CONTENTS

NATIONAL LEVEL CONFLICT AND THE MEDIA

ACKNOWLEDGMENTS

This volume is the product of an East-West Communication Institute project called The Role of Communication Systems in Consensus Generation and Conflict Management, led by Andrew Arno. Except for Chapters 2 and 3, the contributions were written specifically for this volume and were read as papers at an East-West Center conference in the fall of 1981. The editors would like to thank George E. Marcus and Majid Tehranian, visiting fellows at the East-West Communication Institute for the summer of 1981, for their help in planning the conference and the book. Other colleagues whose ideas are represented in the conceptualization of the problem addressed by this book are A. I. Nnaemeka, Godwin Chu, and Jack Lyle. We would also like to express appreciation for the efforts of Joyce Gruhn, project secretary, who prepared the manuscript.

Andrew Arno
Wimal Dissanayake

INTRODUCTION

CHAPTER 1

COMMUNICATION, CONFLICT, AND STORYLINES: THE NEWS MEDIA AS ACTORS IN A CULTURAL CONTEXT

Andrew Arno

Conflict is a state or quality of ongoing relationships among social entities, such as persons, groups, or nations. It results from a lack of agreement over an issue and is expressed in words or actions. In form and character, conflict is as highly variable as the social relationships of which it is a property, but in every case, like other dimensions of such relationships, it is created, maintained, and abolished through the exchange of messages. Communication and conflict, therefore, are intimately related, and certain institutionalized pathways of communication are associated strongly with conflict-related exchanges. With regard to conflicts at national and international levels, the news media are among the most important of such channels.

But modern news media are not just passive channels. Dramatic advances in communications technology are resulting in wider and faster dissemination of news, with a related growth in the potential of world and national public opinion as a political force. The media, in fact acting through the ephemeral, intermittent, but explosively powerful coming together of news sources, print or broadcast organizations, and both mass and specialized audiences, are partially autonomous parties to the relationships in which conflict situations exist. The news media are unusual, volatile entities, different in some ways from individuals or organized, stable groups. To the extent that they do not merely transmit, but also frame and interpret messages, however, they must operate within contexts of shared cultural meaning just as other social actors do. Turning the reality of conflicts into stories, which then become part of the reality, media organizations necessarily observe social and cultural conventions, and cultural patterns are essential determinants of the roles that the news media take during conflicts.

Systematic, purposive involvement in conflict situations is the most immediately salient feature of the anatomy and behavior of the news media in relation to other contemporary social entities. They insert themselves or are drawn into virtually every kind of conflict because, in a basic sense, conflict is news.

CONFLICT AS NEWS

Reports of conflicts fill the news media. Neighborhood controversies are ventilated in local papers while newspapers and television broadcasts that reach wider audiences deal with correspondingly more generalized conflict issues. The most cursory examination of a front page or an evening's news show will confirm that conflict is the stuff of the news. The dramatic formula of A vs B is manifested in a thousand different versions, but the structure is there, nearer or further from the surface of the story. Disasters and accidents are portrayed as examples of the primordial conflict of the human struggle against nature and, perhaps just as ancient, against the malfunctioning of human inventions. Social conflicts occur at all levels. Nations confront one another, as do all manner of groups and categories defined by differences along economic, political, religious, and ethnic lines. Such conflicts attract the attention of all those who perceive their interests to be represented by one side or the other as well as those not directly involved who see the fact of conflict itself as a potential threat. Even crime stories, which in one sense represent a conflict between two individuals, the victim and the perpetrator, are followed widely because people identify with the primary parties, normally with the victim, one would hope.

I would go so far as to assert that news is defined by its conflict focus and that there is nothing deplorable about the fact. It is sometimes argued that the predominance of conflict stories in the news gives a distorted picture of the world, but people do not read or watch the news to gain a picture of the world that is "undistorted," where what is good and positive is portrayed in realistic proportion to what is evil and dangerous. Counterbalancing information about nonconflictual topics is available in other formats, and to the extent that a newspaper is filled with recipes, gardening hints, or serialized fiction, for example, it is not functioning as a news medium. Newspapers and television may properly provide material to educate and entertain, but people also want accurate information about conflicts and problems. When it is not supplied by the conventional, they are apt to seek it from alternative channels.

The human disposition to find alarming reports more stimulating than stories about what is right with the world probably accounts in part for the persistence of the species. The farmer who pays more attention to the observation of a single Mediterranean fruit fly in his vicinity than to reports that describe the thousands of healthy plants in his fields is more likely than one otherwise inclined to reap a good harvest. This is not to claim that *any* amount of conflict is good in itself, but a problem, implying some sort of conflict, that is known about is better than a problem that is neglected. This is not always the case, as Coser points out in Chapter 2, but often it is. Left to themselves, many problems grow worse, and what gives conflict its bad name is its potential, if not controlled or managed, to escalate and become destructive.

In a structural sense, social conflict may at times be useful, as when it increases solidarity and cooperation within a group that is in conflict with some outside force. Elevated levels of conflict can also be a temporary part of constructive social change. Before civil rights efforts began to change patterns of racial segregation in southern U.S. towns, for example, there was relative stability and absence of expressed conflict in such matters as seating on buses and service in restaurants. Today, there is again little open conflict about these issues, but the racial segregation and integration patterns themselves are quite different. In the transition from one pattern to the other, public controversy and conflict were highly elevated, and the mass media played an important role in the process.

Even so, conflict can be dangerous and destructive if it gets out of control and escalates to the point of destroying necessary or desirable relationships. Conflict management is the social process of allowing conflict to run its course and perform its beneficial functions in society without becoming destructive to basic structural relationships. Communication has always been a central part of the management process, especially when parties to a conflict have attempted to generate consensus for their own positions through persuasion. In modern, large-scale societies as in international relations, the mass media have become an essential part of the process, and their content is an indicator of the importance of their roles.

A basic question is how communication about conflict is related to the actual conflicts that exist in and among societies. It is often argued that communication about certain kinds of issues can actually create or intensify conflict. At the interpersonal level, rumor and gossip are condemned on such grounds, and in many nations political leaders and government officials have periodically denounced the press and electronic media for their alleged roles in creating conflict. On the other hand, one can maintain, as have many journalists and media philosophers, that by supplying information about conflict issues to a wide audience, the press and television constitute an essential part of a "court of public opinion" and thereby help to contain social conflict by assisting in the solution of underlying community problems.

Both arguments agree that media content does not merely reflect the level of conflict in the society but has a functional relationship to it: it either intensifies or diminishes it. A basic position suggested from a variety of viewpoints by the authors in this volume is that there is truth to both assertions, depending on how and in what circumstances the media become involved in public controversies. The conflict issue may have a starting point; a period of definition during which it is shaped into a form that can be recognized by the parties and the media; a crescendo of evaluation, analysis, and information; and finally some kind of resolution, however temporary it might be. During such a process, the media may at times play the role of intensifying controversy and at other times diminishing it.

In national conflict situations, it is important to consider more than just single elements of a nation's communication system in isolation. The various media, such as newspapers and television, are interrelated in the process of conflict management because they can reach different sectors of the society with the same message, or the same sectors with different messages, on a particular issue. The nature of the issue will make a difference as to which media or interpersonal networks are most salient, and in different cultural contexts the same kinds of media may play different roles.

CULTURE, CONFLICT BEHAVIOR, AND THEORIES OF THE NEWS

Every cultural tradition has evolved or adopted certain dominant modes of dealing with specific kinds of conflicts, be they interpersonal or intergroup, private, legal, or political in nature; family, local community, or national in scope. It is in the context of such cultural patterns that conflict-related behavior, from the use of violence to formal apology, takes its meaning, and media reports of such actions are interpreted according to culturally recognized models. Cultural patterns are never static, and new communications technology can powerfully influence the way conflict behavior is expressed and interpreted.

In comparing the way conflict issues are treated in the communication systems of different nations, it is essential to distinguish differences that derive from the substantive positions the countries might take from differences in the structures of their conflict management processes. In this book, attention will be focused on the *way* conflicts are treated in the national communication systems, not the substantive positions that may be taken. For example, in the United States, community-level political conflict is often expressed in confrontational ways, and proponents of either side of an issue may be expected to use the media to persuade the public. In this adversarial process, the media often assume an objective stance, presenting the arguments of both sides. Access to the media is not overtly limited by social standing, and conflicts are often portrayed in individual rather than structural terms. As an aspect of individualism, the presumption of potential legitimacy is accorded all parties, with a consequent disposition toward compromise and negotiation as a path toward consensus. Small minorities and eccentric splinter groups are therefore allowed access to the media through the staging of dramatic "media events."

In contrast, other nations may have dominant modes of conflict management that are nonconfrontational, that portray conflict more in structural than individual terms, and that restrict access to media because of the idea that there can be only one legitimate view to be presented. Users of media in such contexts may learn to read between the lines to deduce the unvoiced positions. Alternative media may also be available to support partisan arguments.

The purpose of this volume is to examine the proposition that the media in various social settings are themselves actors in the conflict situations they report. They, as individual media organizations and as industries, have their own interests, motives, and behavior patterns. In some cases, they may have a stake in the issue at controversy. Very often, however, their interests are concerned with the process of conflict behavior in general—how it is played out on the public stage—rather than with the particular issues.

Discovering the nature and characteristics of news media as actors in national and international conflict scenarios is a complex project, and the result will be a description of something not quite like other social actors with which we are acquainted. Still, as Max Black (1962) has suggested, every scientific venture begins with metaphor, and it helps to clarify one's assumptions by thinking about the basic metaphors that may be applicable. I have already suggested that the news media are actors, but what kinds of parts do they play? Are they merchants of information, or would it be better to think of them as priests of information? Perhaps information is not quite the right concept, and it would be better to think of media organizations as storytellers.

With regard to their actions, do media organizations, like lawyers, act as the mouthpieces of some particular individuals, groups, classes, or sectors of society? And, as professionals, do they also serve their own interests and ideals, which are not totally coincident with those of other social entities? How do the media see themselves, and how are they seen by their users? How are they linked to the political, economic, and social structures of communities, nations, and the world, and what are the effects of these linkages on their natures and functions? It is against these dimensions of reality that the proposed metaphors must be measured.

The short answer to the questions I have posed, of course, is that it all depends on the particular news organization, the particular issue with which the news item is concerned, and the social and cultural context in which the medium operates. The problem of discovering a coherent set of descriptions of the media as actors, although very complex, is not quite so intricate as it would seem at first because all possible combinations of the many salient characteristics are not found. Whether as a matter of logic or simply historical fact, certain constellations of features are associated in a few distinct traditions of journalism, and these traditions are parts of larger sociocultural complexes. In other words, ideas of news and processes of news gathering, explication, and dissemination are cultural artifacts, and they exhibit a certain functional and symbolic consistency both internally and as parts of larger social contexts. The main traditions and their many variations are what Wilbur Schramm,* building on his classic studies of the press (Siegert et al. 1956), has recently called theories of news.

These conceptualizations of news as a social process are theories in the anthropological sense. They are guides to understanding activities in which we are all to some extent participants, and they draw upon the ideas, conceptual models, and explanations of the people who are most directly involved, as well as upon regularities of behavior revealed by scientific observation. The perspective is holistic and includes a range of cross-cutting value orientations and interinstitutional linkages that bind the news media to their social contexts.

Majid Tehranian (1982) has presented seven metaphorical characterizations of media organizations as they play various roles throughout the world. According to the point of view of the observer and the social context in which the media operate, they are described as "selfless revolutionaries," "fearless truth-seekers," "responsible agenda setters," "benign gatekeepers," "development promoters," "hidden persuaders," and "sinister manipulators." Some of these labels are consistent with one another and could be parts of a single theory of news, and others are incompatible. Each of them illuminates a part of the complex role that any media organization plays depending on the relationships it has to the community it serves and the issue it reports. I should like to propose another characterization, namely, the media as storytellers. This perspective emphasizes the cultural contexts of the media and focuses on differentiation among world media organizations.

HOW STORYLINES SHAPE THE NEWS

The role of a newspaper or television production unit as a storyteller has interesting historical roots. Schudson (1978), in his recent account of the

---

*Comments in the East-West Communication Institute seminar, 1981.

historical development of the press in America, provides a lucid account of newspapers' concern with "story," especially at the height of the yellow journalism era in the nineteenth century, and the evolution of the now-dominant concern with providing objective information instead. This has long been a topic of controversy, and journalists and their critics have often remarked on the necessity for a balance between the two, because uninter-preted facts can easily be as misleading and subject to manipulation as groundless stories.

A story, especially in fiction but also in other writing contexts, is true if it portrays some situation or makes some point that is accepted as accurate by readers. A great novel tells a good deal of truth about human nature and the social conventions of the time and cultural tradition in which it is set. Such a work is true to life, so to speak, and if the facts it sets out are true in this sense, it does not matter at all that they never happened. It is pretty well settled at present, however, that in U.S. newspapers imaginary facts are not acceptable. In 1981, a Pulitzer Prize was accepted and then re-turned when the "facts" in a story turned out to be fictional. This case, which involved a news story about an imaginary eight-year-old heroin ad-dict in Washington, D.C., illustrates the reaction against treating facts as subordinate to the story, but it also illustrates the attraction that this style of writing can have for journalists whose main concern is the effect the story will have. The critical point, however, is that the story is an inevitable part of journalism even when the facts are solid.

It is important to consider how stories are evaluated and why one has more impact than another. A story is an abstracted, simplified scenario of social action, and as such it can only make sense within the agreed conven-tions of social understanding and behavior appropriate to a particular cul-ture. Stories are measured against the reader's own experience and under-standing of how society and human psychology work. In its own way, the story is analytical, and it gives the reader an insight that, if he has never thought of before he will immediately recognize as just, and if he has no-ticed himself he will welcome as confirmation of his own astuteness. Little storylines or agreed conventional scenarios of social action operate at all levels of generality. If everyone knows that a certain person has particular characteristics or traits, stories that reinforce that impression are plausi-ble, while others ring false. At a deeper level, if the conventional opinion is that human nature is thus and so, stories that rely on that understanding seem accurate and realistic, although if some such truism is the point of the story, it may be condemned as banal. Such conventions go on and on, and they are as much a part of communication as language. Any writer, whether of fiction or news, must respect these little scenarios just as he must respect the rules of grammar and usages of vocabulary. They do change, of course, the superficial ones very quickly and the more profound ones slowly, but they must be taken into account. Some writers challenge them, but most use them to get their messages across.

An example of a superficial storyline in the U.S. press was the treatment of President Ronald Reagan's handling of the air controllers' strike of 1981. Early on, long before the likely outcome could be discerned, a very consistent pattern emerged, based partly on Reagan's then current series of notable political triumphs in Congress, of treating the strike story as one more in a string of victories for a somewhat unlikely "champ." Since the situation was rather ambiguous—it was not at all clear that a major air disaster or a colossal traffic tie-up would not vitiate the government's position—the evolving storyline rather than the facts seemed to have determined the treatment of the event in the news. It was not impossible, but it was difficult then, given his recent victories, to portray the president as a loser, just as it would have been hard to write about former President Gerald Ford as a physically graceful person after many stories had detailed instances of his stumbling or falling down; it is not clear that any one of such instances should have been considered newsworthy in itself, but after the scenario had become established, the storyline and not the facts dictated the play that each would receive.

Superficial storylines can be changed rapidly by dramatic events, but more profound ways of looking at social action are harder to modify. When the U.S. hostages returned from Iran, for example, the newspapers and television networks portrayed the large-scale and emotional greeting demonstrations that followed as celebrations in honor of returning heroes. A columnist or an editorial writer here and there complained that the American people were acting foolishly because the hostages were in no sense true heroes, but in reality the confusion may have lain mostly with the press coverage. The facts did not fit a "returning heroes" scenario very well, but none other seemed appropriate in view of the enthusiastic welcome. What may have happened is that the public's concept of hero had changed. The astronauts and Vietnam War veterans, in different ways, strained the old definition so much that it finally gave way. In the hostages, the American public may have seen a chance to assert a new kind of scenario to fit conditions that are becoming more prevalent than those that defined heroism in the past. Before, public rituals of welcome and recognition were mobilized for individuals who, by virtue of superior personal qualities, had gone beyond the normal range of performance to secure some benefit for the group. Now, it seemed, the meaning was quite different. It did not matter that the hostages did not "win" in Iran, and it did not matter that they were totally ordinary individuals and had behaved as such. The community turned out to welcome them in warm fashion as hapless victims of rather impersonal forces and unfathomable events and who, having suffered, were returning to the family circle. In a way, it was probably a kind of ritual postscript or afterthought to Vietnam.

The press did not really know how to play the event. It was not clear in what mold it could be cast. The words were there, but the story wasn't. Even in this kind of case, however, the scenario of action and meaning is fairly close to the surface and easy to comment on. I would argue that such structures also exist on a much deeper and more fundamental level. Being simpler and more general, the basic storylines are capable of being employed in a great variety of instances, but there is a limit to their flexibility. Inevitably, they operate to cast news writing, no matter what the facts, into certain molds; therefore they are important to the understanding of news as a social process. Elemental storylines are cultural artifacts. One might even define them as the real essence of cultural differences around the world, because they are very much tied up with basic definitions of social entities and motivations and because by their very generality they are resistant to change. It is hard to call them into question, because it is seldom that they cannot be used to cast events and situations into meaningful form.

Because news may be defined as stories about conflict, the elemental scenarios that most concern the task of constructing theories of news are those that come into play when conflict is being described. The basic scenarios of conflict situations vary from one cultural tradition to another, and when a journalist writes about conflict or portrays it in visual form, I would argue, the necessity of being intelligible to his audience forces him to rely on these inherent, elemental storylines. Conflict is a universal of human experience, of course, so in many ways the patterns of conceptualizing and describing conflict situations may have much in common from one cultural context to another. The area that needs research is that area of nonoverlap that may exist between one cultural tradition, such as that of the United States, and another, such as Japan or Iran. Such areas account in part for the differences in the roles of media organizations as storytellers concerned with conflict in their societies.

Some of the specific questions that might be asked, probably through the medium of content analysis, would include the following:

- How are parties to conflicts identified as a rule?
- Are they usually individuals or are they groups?
- Are group interests emphasized, as opposed to individual interests, as the basis for conflicting claims?
- Are issues seen as specific and contractual, or are they subsumed in some sort of encompassing body of obligations that defines a total relationship?
- Is the aim of conflict management retribution, restitution, or reconciliation?
- What role does open confrontation between the parties play?

- How are rational and sentimental values weighted?
- What is the role of abasement and apology?
- What procedures of conflict management are preferred, and what is the role of third parties, if any?
- If a number of different types of conflict scenarios are recognized, how are they distributed according to kinds of parties and kinds of issues?

EVOLVING PATTERNS OF WORLDWIDE CONFLICT PROCESSES

There may be a variety of models, including distinctive elemental story-lines as well as structural arrangements, that explain how communication systems function as parts of conflict management processes in specific nations. Each one may be quite effective in its own social context, and yet persons used to the role of media in one may not understand the role they play in another. This lack of understanding—not on the part of experts, but among the ordinary users of mass media—becomes a problem when one national media system becomes involved in the conflict management processes of another nation.

In some cases, participants in a national conflict situation may want to use external media exposure to exert pressure in an internal problem. For example, in a media event staged in 1980 by U.S. women's groups to express opposition to what they considered a shift toward militarism by the government, a chant familiar from an earlier radical protest era was used. After staging a mass demonstration, with elaborate visual and sound effects to attract television news coverage, the group chanted, "the whole world is watching," as some of their number blocked an entrance to the Pentagon and were carried away bodily by armed guards. Also in 1980, in China the "gang of four" trial, in which former leaders were condemned and punished for the excesses of the Cultural Revolution, included the provision of videotapes to outside media. Meanwhile, during the early stages of the movement in Poland to establish independent labor unions there were examples of the use of mass media to reach audiences in other countries. In examples of this kind, the participants in the conflict process acted as though segments of a world audience would, actively or passively, influence the outcome. The parties to a national conflict, then, may be conceptualized to include dispersed multinational interest groups who can exert some degree of influence on the outcome through economic, political, or other channels. It is especially through modern communications technology that such rudimentary, unformalized systems of social control can exist.

Another situation in which national communication systems interact in conflict situations involves international rather than national conflict. When nations are themselves parties to a conflict, the content of one nation's media systems sometimes becomes part of the content in the media system of the other nation. In the hostage crisis between the United States and Iran, for example, the mass media became a significant forum for information exchange. The information in this case may have been less about objective facts than about the moods, emotional reactions, and subjective states of public opinion in the two nations. Communication directly between governments is still of primary importance, but public participation through mass media is becoming more and more an important factor in international conflict management. In former times, primary contacts were restricted to trained diplomats who developed an international subculture of their own to assure a common understanding of the process. They in turn could inform the people of their countries about the issue. The contact is more direct now, and it probably will become more so. Under the circumstances, understanding the role of communication systems in national and international conflict is a crucial problem.

In previous analyses, such as Davison's classic book on mass communication and conflict resolution (1974), the news media were seen primarily as conduits for the messages of government leaders. Recent studies have also begun to explore the critical approach that sees the media as inextricably tied to the social and cultural status quo at a deeper level, further clouding the press's claims to objectivity. In the present volume, the media are treated not only as tools that are used by participants in conflict situations, but also as actors in their own rights, neither more nor less tied to their culturally defined means of expression than other actors. The media themselves are significant participants in many conflicts, and their characteristic patterns of behavior derive from the ways they are organized and the roles they perform.

The question—crucial to the evolution of supranational conflict management systems—of how widely theories of news may be shared by media organizations throughout the world is complicated by several powerful but opposing factors. In support of a trend toward growing uniformity is a sense of professionalism among media practitioners. Being in contact with one another more and more on personal and professional bases, they come to have similar standards of work, ideals, and prejudices. Journalists with newspapers or television stations in many countries, to the extent that they deal with foreign-produced copy or material on a daily basis and at times send their own work abroad, are perhaps more likely than members of other professions to see themselves as part of a peer group that spans national boundaries. The potential is there, given the frequency and the nature of interaction patterns, for the development of a global subculture.

Another factor tending to produce uniformity of behavior in the news field is the advance of new technology. Technology, although to a major extent controlled by the values of its users, also imparts its own inherent values to those who employ it. Television is a good example of a tool that brings along with it certain values; as the use of the tool becomes universal, so do the values. These values are related to production, not to the substance of conflicts that are reported on television news. Becoming involved with television does not make people conservative, liberal, pro this or anti that in any obvious way. In analyzing the role of a party in conflict situations, however, it is important to distinguish between the substantive issues of the controversy and the techniques that govern how the issues are presented and dealt with. Production values deal with this latter set of factors. Values that directly follow the adoption of television include technical standards of picture quality, judgments about the visual impact of footage, and decision standards for the allocation of time. If one makes the assumption that under certain structural conditions, which in fact are inherent in the sociology of conflict situations, a party's predispositions to one side or the other in matters of substance become divorced from and subordinated to a concern for techniques of presentation and procedure, it becomes clear that values of this kind can make the difference between a particular piece of material's being included in or deleted from a broadcast. When the broadcast is put on the air, the link between technique and substance is made. In other words, the decision to put together a segment in form A rather than form B may be made on purely technical grounds—with regard to production values rather than political or social values—and yet form A may have a slightly different substantive impact than form B.

While professionalism and production values, two closely related factors, exert a homogenizing effect on world media systems, there are also countervailing tendencies that operate to make media organizations in various countries different from one another. In certain political contexts, the professionalism of the media practitioners is minimized in its effect on final products because political or social values are reasserted in the decision-making process and ultimately have the greater weight. Differences among forms of government then may show up as differences in the behavior of media organizations in conflict situations. Another more subtle factor that works toward differentiation is the cultural context in which the media organization operates. In a certain sense, of course, the more obvious political values and practices, such as those reflected in degrees of government ownership and control of the media as well as in degrees of political participation accorded to different social sectors, are parts of a society's culture. But the much more basic and deeply rooted patterns that govern social interactions, ways of conceptualizing and symbolizing social entities and situations, and the hierarchies of rules and precepts that constitute prevailing systems of morality or ethics—all factors that delineate elemental storylines in news reporting and analysis—also make a difference in the ways a society's media organizations become involved with various kinds and levels of conflicts.

Ironically, as telecommunications technology—the embodied essence of modernity—advances, traditional cultural factors in international conflict become more important. In the U.S.-Iran conflict, for example, television allowed the American public to observe Iranian conflict behavior more or less directly. In order to effectively interpret the nightly footage from Iran, Americans would have needed an understanding of traditional Iranian ways of dealing with conflict as well as an idea of how Iranians conceptualize and use the mass media. Needless to say, such intercultural awareness has lagged behind the means of communication. Too often, national and international conflict processes have been considered largely from a U.S. or Western perspective. In this book, both the examples and the authors represent a balance between Western and non-Western, First and Third worlds. While the case studies represent only the United States and Asia geographically, the issues that are raised have significance in all parts of the world. It would be instructive, for example, to examine the role of the British Broadcasting Corporation during the Falklands War in comparison with its role in the Iranian and Sri Lankan conflicts discussed in chapters that follow.

GOALS OF THIS VOLUME

Conflict, as Lasswell (1948) said about power, is not "a brick that can be lugged from place to place," but rather a situation existing between or among social actors. Given the ways we talk about such concepts in everyday conversation, however, it is difficult not to think of them as things in themselves—power as a thing possessed by the powerful, and conflict as a malevolent force looking for places to "break out."

Specialized usage, on the other hand, also presents difficulties because ideas, layered with the intellectual accretions of years of discussion in subfields of sociology, political science, and anthropology, tend toward reification in another sense. They become objects of study that derive meaning as much from technical literature as from concrete experience. Narrowly defined in a variety of different senses to serve as elements of formal hypotheses, a single basic concept can be transformed into a multitude of bricks for use in the construction of disciplinary mansions—as well as the walls and fortifications between disciplines.

Disciplinary boundaries have never really been respected in the important, emerging field of peace research and conflict study, however, and one might argue that it will never develop into a discipline itself (Schellenberg

1982). One reason might be that the reality of national and international conflict is too pressing. Real life intrudes itself too much into the discussion, and real life is never describable in terms of a single discipline. In this volume, accordingly, conflict as an organizing concept is broadly defined. Treated this way, conflict enters into virtually every human activity, and although individual chapters of the book may present hypotheses and use narrow definitions, the collection does not add up to a sharply delimited theoretical statement about conflict or conflict resolution. The primary object of the book is not to look at conflict from the point of view of sociological or psychological theory but to examine the roles of the news media in day-to-day operations, and this requires the consideration of a wide range of conflict situations.

In fact, if conflict is conceptualized as a situation or a relationship state, an essential part of understanding it in a general sense is to identify the characteristic participants and map out their motivations and ranges of behavior. This volume, therefore, represents an initial exploration of the nature of news media as perennial conflict participants. At this point in the inquiry, the goals are those of preliminary description, conceptualization of the problems involved, and the indication of likely paths for more precisely focused studies to be undertaken later.

Reflecting the dialectic between broad conceptualization and minute observation characteristic of the beginning stages of this kind of discourse, the chapters that follow include both philosophical essays and empirical studies. A certain amount of mental gear-shifting will be required of the reader, with the inevitable tension between stimulation and distraction, but for the most part the "think pieces" are grouped together in the section on perspectives on communication and conflict, and the empirical case studies fall into the sections on national and international levels of conflict. The division is not strict, of course, because each contribution contains argument and explanation as well as concrete observation.

Several themes emerge from the chapters of this book and give it an overall unity, despite the diversity of the cases and illustrations that are cited. One major theme is that media organizations, viewed metaphorically as actors in societal dramas, are storytellers who must operate within given technological limitations and cultural conventions. Another major theme, addressed in the concluding chapter, concerns the role of the news medium as the third party to a conflict. The issue of the autonomy of the news media is seen as central to their potential in both such roles. Degrees of press autonomy vary not only with different ideologies of news held by particular societies but also with the structural character of the conflict involved. In any case, media, like all social actors, are never completely autonomous but are meshed into interdependent relationships with other groups and sectors of society. If they were totally autonomous, they would lose access to information as well as rapport with audiences, but if they became totally identified with a party to a conflict they would cease to function, in that conflict situation, as news media. The media tread the line between these structural extremes.

REFERENCES

Black, Max. 1962. *Models and Metaphors: Studies in Language and Philosophy.* Ithaca: Cornell University Press.

Davison, W. Phillips. 1974. *Mass Communication and Conflict Resolution.* New York: Praeger.

Lasswell, Harold D. 1948. *Power and Personality.* New York: W. W. Norton.

Schellenberg, James A. 1982. *The Science of Conflict.* New York: Oxford.

Schudson, Michael. 1978. *Discovering the News.* New York: Basic Books.

Siegert, Fred S., Theodore Peterson, and Wilbur Schramm. 1956. *Four Theories of the Press.* Urbana: University of Illinois Press.

Tehranian, Majid. 1982. "International communication: A dialogue of the deaf?" *Political Communication and Persuasion* 2(1):21–46.

PERSPECTIVES ON
COMMUNICATION AND CONFLICT

CHAPTER 2

SALVATION THROUGH COMMUNICATION?
Lewis A. Coser

OPEN COMMUNICATION: A PANACEA?

Most discussions on communication processes in recent decades have been premised explicitly or implicitly on the idea that the clearer the message between the parties, the less distorted it is by irrelevant "noise," the greater the chances of full understanding between the parties and the higher the probability that they will be able to develop a common perspective and overcome parochial or idiosyncratic interests and outlooks. In this view, open channels of communication enhance the chances of shared modes of thought and minimize the effects of particularistic concerns and interests. It is assumed that the better people understand each other, the easier they will find it to arrive at common solutions to mutual problems. Eased communication is hence viewed wittingly or unwittingly as a prime solvent of human predicaments on the interpersonal, the interorganizational, and the international plane.

This basic orientation can be seen at work in a variety of scholarly endeavors of different degrees of sophistication. At its most naive this premise influenced much writing on international relations in the late forties and fifties. Such widely read popularizers as Stuart Chase (1951), for example, argued that if we could only succeed in destroying the stereotypes that informed the views of Russia held by most Americans, and the reciprocal views of America held by most Russians, the "roads to agreement" between the two nations would be easy. Similarly, the preamble to the constitution of UNESCO (United Nations Educational, Scientific and Cultural Organization) states that "since wars begin in the minds of men, it is in the minds of men that the defenses of peace must be constructed." UNESCO sponsored a survey of research by Otto Klineberg (1952), entitled *Tensions Affecting International Understanding*, which was devoted

17

mainly to an examination of national stereotypes, personality factors, attitudes, or hostilities that were assumed to block and interfere with rational communication, thus impeding international dialogue and ultimate concord among the nations of the world.

Such naive approaches were not limited to international affairs. Much of the research of the human relations school of management of Elton Mayo and his associates (e.g., Mayo 1946) was based on similar premises. Conflicts in industry, these authors argued, could be traced largely to misunderstandings between management and labor. Counterposing what they called a logic of facts ("the logic of cost and the logic of efficiency") that guided managerial decisions, against the "logic of sentiments" allegedly governing the conduct of workers, these researchers argued that once workers were weaned from their dysfunctional sentiments through better communication systems, the road to agreement was open, and each side could deal with the other to maximize efficiency and reduce costs to mutual benefit.

Social psychologist Kurt Lewin argued in a similar vein in his writings in the late forties, particularly in his influential book *Resolving Social Conflicts* (1948). Social conflicts, he stated, are invariably dysfunctional and disintegrating, so that it is a prime task for the social scientist to contribute to their reduction and eradication. "On whatever unit of group life we focus," Lewin wrote, "whether we think of nations and international politics; of economic life, of race or religious groups, of the factory and relations between top management and the worker, we find a complicated network of conflicting interests" (1947, 7). Social management and social engineering, he felt, must be enlisted to reduce such tensions and conflicts by opening channels of communication between antagonists. This school of thought said that as adversaries learn to put themselves in the role of the other and as they are enabled through open communication channels to learn about the motivation and springs of action of their antagonists, they will be able to acquire the flexibility to arrive at common solutions through mutual enlightenment.

These works written in the forties and fifties are no longer as influential as they were then, but in the sixties and early seventies another set of writings, emerging from a different tradition, has followed in their footsteps, albeit in a more sophisticated vein.

The work of Juergen Habermas (1971), the most notable member of the second generation of the Frankfort School of Sociology and probably the most important contemporary sociologist in the German-speaking world, is representative in this respect. Habermas was schooled in the Marxian tradition in which conflicts of class interests preempt the scene and in which the processes of communication are mainly examined only with respect to their impact on the strengthening or weakening of class solidarity.

But under the impact of his experiences in the postwar world of relative affluence, Habermas seems gradually to have lost his belief in class conflict as the road to salvation and the associated belief that the proletariat was the "universal class" on whose victory hinged the further destinies of humankind.

Refusing to accept the technocratic vision of his contemporary Niklas Luhmann, who argued that the prevalent societal drift could be overcome by strengthening the political steering system manned by managerial elites (cf Habermas and Luhmann 1971), Habermas searched for a model of enlightened citizen participation in societal guidance. He turned to psychoanalysis, more precisely to the processes of therapeutic psychoanalytic practice, in an effort to find analogies to the participatory mode of societal guidance for which he was searching. Neurotic disturbances, he reasoned, be they in speech or in conduct, are largely brought about through "distorted communication." The therapist trying to overcome the patient's personality defects works with him or her in bringing into consciousness the impact of traumatic events that have brought the distortions into being. The communicative interaction between patient and therapist is meant to increase the self-awareness of the patient gradually. In the measure that patients increase their self-awareness, they can participate in an equal communicative intercourse with the analyst. Their communicative interchange is now cleared of distortions due to past traumas. In the same manner, Habermas argues, in society at large, the unenlightened and distorted communication patterns that are the residues and legacies of previous forms of human exploitation, ignorance, and repression can be overcome through enlightened forms of discourse in rational source inquiry:

> Just as in the clinical situation, so in society, pathological compulsion itself is accompanied by the interest in its abolition. Both the pathology of social institutions and that of individual consciousness reside in the medium of language and of communicative action and assume the form of a structural deformation of communication. That is why for the social system, too, the interest inherent in the pressure of suffering is also immediately an interest in enlightenment, and reflection is the only possible dynamic through which it realizes itself (1971, 288).

Habermas in effect is preaching the gospel of salvation through communication. Even though he admits that the notion of undistorted communication is not yet realizable, that it remains counterfactual, he still sets it up as a theoretical Archimedian point from which it becomes possible to move the entire world.

What seems common in both the earlier and later approaches to conflict analysis is the tendency to disregard realistic sources of conflict rooted in particular interests and to assume that conflicts arise mainly from distortions of communication processes. With realistic sources for contention ruled out, these theorists and researchers can then assume that the sources of conflict are to be found in sentiments that distort relations rather than in the nature of these social relations themselves (cf Coser 1956, 52–53 and passim). As Reinhold Niebuhr once put it with his customary shrewdness: "Educators ... underestimate the conflict of interest in political and economic relations, and attribute it to interested intelligence (1932, 215)." James Rule, a critical commentator on Habermas's work, put the matter well:

> Is Habermas telling us that discourse can resolve even those clashes which entail nothing more rational than zero-sum conflicts over the allocation of limited resources? Could the method, for example, point to a solution which both labor and management could accept as "rational" for distributing available resources between profit and wages? How do we distinguish between those disputes which turn on "generalizable interests" and hence presumably admit of "rational" solution, and those which do not?" (1978, 134).

It would be foolish to deny that better communication, reduction of the "noise" of affect and sentiment, might in some cases foster a more rational solution of differences. The real question, however, is not whether affect-laden distortions might at times impede rational solutions, but whether many, if not most, conflicts involve realistic confrontations over scarce resources such as status, power, and economic advantages. An examination of the record of human affairs strongly suggests the latter to be the case (Coser 1956). If this is so, exclusive concern with communication processes and their distortions is likely to be counterproductive when it concerns the amelioration of human affairs. As long as there are large inequalities among human beings, as long as there exist sharp asymmetries in power and structurally induced discrepancies in access to resources, it seems unlikely that the potential for conflict will be successfully minimized, no matter what channels may be available for undistorted communication. It well may be that both parties in a conflict will find it to their advantage to formulate their divergent interests clearly so that the other side harbors no doubts about them. In such cases, however, the communicative interaction, far from eliminating conflict, only serves to conduct it in a rational manner.

IS LESS COMMUNICATION BETTER?

The remainder of this chapter focuses attention on one particular contention of the salvation-through-communication theorists, namely, the assertion that by reducing ignorance among contenders it is possible to facilitate agreement between them and to enhance their respective interests. Arguments to the contrary are based largely on pioneering papers by

Wilbert Moore and Melvin Tumin (1949) and Louis Schneider (1962). Both works conclude that ignorance, far from being always dysfunctional, may instead subserve definite functions in social relationships. If that is indeed the case, the reduction of ignorance, far from being a blessing, may under specifiable conditions be a curse.

James Rule, in the work referred to earlier, makes this point with considerable force when he writes:

> Ignorance of or lack of attention to potentially contentious issues may in fact confer stability and ensure peace. Thoroughgoing discussion, in which such things as habits of acquiescence, custom and power relations are ignored, may have the opposite effect. Perhaps the only certain result, if all social relations were indeed subjected to "rational discussion" by their participants, would be the outbreak of conflict and controversy in the place of apathy and acquiescence (1978, 136).

Ignorance, in other words, may minimize conflict, while full knowledge might enhance it.

An unexamined premise among salvation-through-communication theorists is the belief that if partners would only know each other better they would find it easier to discover grounds of agreement. There is no rational or empirical foundation for such a generalized belief. In fact, there are many instances in which, if we really knew what motivated other persons, we would become much more antagonistic toward them. As the old saying has it, people do not necessarily improve upon acquaintance. Thus, a veil of ignorance may often operate as a means to maintain relations between people where full disclosure would lead to a rupture in relations.

Disputes about whether full self-disclosure in social interaction or a decent veil of ignorance is desirable in human affairs have been a perennial theme in social thought. When Rousseau (1970), for example, attempted in his *Confessions* to disclose his whole private self, both reputable and disreputable parts, to the gaze of the public, he self-consciously laid the foundation for a truly radical assault against traditional culture and its pieties and conventions. Full disclosure of self, he argued, would purify human relations. When he wrote in the *First Discourse* that "the good man is an athlete who loves to wrestle stark naked; he despises those vile ornaments which cramp the use of his power . . . ," he advocated a position of total openness. But he was soon answered by Edmund Burke, who lamented that in the age of the French Revolution,

> . . . all the decent drapery of life is to be rudely torn off. All the superadded ideas, furnished from the wardrobe of moral indignation which [are] necessary to cover the defects of our naked, shivering nature, and to raise it to dignity in our own estimation, are to be exploded as a ridiculous, absurd and antiquated fashion (1855, 348–49).

Burke was arguing, in effect, that civilized living required the restraint of convention and usage to tame the propensities of "natural man." Rousseauian politics of authenticity, he argued, would make civilized intercourse impossible. He held that the masks of custom and convention protect persons from invasion of their private selves.

In recent decades, Erving Goffman (1959) has been the foremost analyst of the strategies that human beings employ to hide portions of their selves from those with whom they deal. He illustrates and analyzes in masterly fashion the complicated ways men and women construct and project images of their selves in encounters with significant others. Our conduct and demeanor, he argues, is shaped by our desire to leave an acceptable impression in the minds of those we deem important to us. We must hide unacceptable aspects of ourselves backstage to present an unblemished impression frontstage. We are forever on stage, Goffman writes, even when we believe that we are most spontaneous and sincere in our responses to others. In other words, the wearing of masks in encounters with others is part of the human condition. Just like actors on the theatrical stage must wear the "masks" their parts require, so human actors on the social scene must put on those masks that correspond to the projected images of their selves. If they were deprived of these masks, their selves would disintegrate. Goffman is arguing in effect that full self-disclosure would make social intercourse impossible. Ignorance on the part of others about our "true selves," he seems to say, is a protective coat we cannot do without.

Though Goffman may exaggerate—indeed many sociologists are not prepared to follow him all the way—it seems nevertheless that most classical as well as contemporary sociologists, by emphasizing the central importance of custom, ceremonial, ritual, and belief systems, agree with him in holding that a full and "authentic" disclosure would tear down some of the basic foundations of social life.

In some instances, it would seem that ignorance actually serves to the advantage of one or both partners in an interaction. Following are some examples:

1. It is often to the benefit of the patient that an unfavorable diagnosis the physician has tentatively established not be brought to the patient's attention. Ignorance in this respect may be therapeutic. Full disclosure may cause a great deal of anxiety and may, in some cases, even act as a self-fulfilling prophecy by helping to bring about a tentatively predicted fatal outcome. Under such conditions, ignorance may indeed be bliss.

2. Many educational or therapeutic efforts may be undertaken with the knowledge on the part of educators or therapists that their efforts have a relatively low chance of being effective. If this poor

prognosis were brought to the attention of student or patient, it might discourage them thoroughly and again result in a self-fulfilling prophecy. In such cases, ignorance seems to maximize chances of successful intervention.

3. Consider a situation of emotional closeness between two human beings — between lovers or friends. One or both in such a relationship may feel that the newly established close relationship has led them to become, as it were, reborn. They have attempted to shed previously established aspects of their selves, which they may now consider unacceptable. If they were forced to bring all aspects of the old selves, all previous experiences they now wish to disregard, to the attention of the partner, they would put an unacceptable burden on the new relationship. To the extent that the new partner has no access to knowledge about the earlier self, the new relationship remains unaffected by a past that could destroy it. Here again, ignorance may well be bliss.

4. If all previous normative violations were known to prospective employers, the chances are high that persons sincerely committed to redeem themselves could not do so. Rehabilitation would become vastly more difficult. More generally, as Moore and Tumin put it, "The security of the individual may depend upon ignorance by others of personal attributes or past experiences that have no intrinsic bearing on his own present status but which would be regarded unfavorably if shown: for example, the technical Negro who is passing for white, the reformed ex-convict, the person below or above the required age for his position, the illegitimate child subsequently adopted" (1949, 790–91).

5. To the degree that people's private records are opened to public scrutiny, they would become vulnerable to manipulation by persons who have access to such information. If credit ratings, health records, bank balances, and police records of everybody were freely available to public agents of control, Orwell's *1984* might become a reality (cf Rule 1974).

6. As Rose Laub Coser has shown, the smooth functioning of organizations is predicated on the fact that certain actions of subordinates in the status hierarchy remain hidden from the observability of superiors at the same time that certain actions of superiors can be insulated from observation by subordinates. She concludes, "The determination of who can hide from whom may be essential to the workings of a social system as determination of who has power over whom" (1961, 38). If there is no place to hide, no curtain safeguarding privacy, if everybody has open access to the total behavioral life space of any individual, people will be unprotected and hence pow-

erless cogs in the bureaucratic machine.

7. In a by now classic paper, Merton (1968) has distinguished manifest functions (those functions of which actors are aware) from latent functions (those functions that are unintended and unrecognized). He argues that the analysis of latent functions is the peculiar domain of the social scientist, and that the discoveries of functions of which people were previously unaware "represent significant increments in sociological knowledge." He refrains, however, in his published writings though not in his lectures, from considering situations in which latent functions have become manifest. This involves problems that Max Weber considered under the general rubric of "the disenchantment of the world." If patients recognize that the physician's bedside manner has the function of reassuring them about their state, they might well no longer be reassured; if ceremony and ritual are perceived by participants as serving to reinforce the collective solidarity of the group, they might no longer serve this purpose. If the heroic actions of great men or women are seen as the result of psychic compulsions, these persons might no longer serve as role models. In these cases, knowing all comes perilously close to undermining the bases for conviction.

CONCLUSION

Rational enlightenment, which has been at the center of most sociological inquiry, is among my own most highly prized values. I believe that the great traditions of sociology are humanistic and that the calling of sociology is to contribute to the self-interpretation of humankind. To the extent that the sociologist lives up to the ancient injunction to "know thyself," he or she cannot afford to cut loose from any sources that enhance enlightenment about the human condition. But commitment to such a vision does not entail the belief that under any and all concrete circumstances full disclosure of information is necessarily the most adequate or humane course of action. To the contrary, concern for those with whom one is engaged in social interchanges may well require withholding certain types of information so as to save the face, the moral integrity, or the sense of self of the other person or of oneself. A dogmatic commitment to truth telling under any circumstances may well involve cruelty and sadistic assaults. Humane concern for the other may dictate a policy of protective withholding of information. Here as in so many other areas of social life, those who are generally committed to enlightenment need nevertheless to tolerate ambiguities and understand that the truth is not enough; in fact it may be counterproductive and inhumane.

Finally, open channels of communication, while they may indeed enhance human understanding in specific circumstances, may not invariably accomplish this. With this the case, it must be realized that there can be no salvation through communication, that communication is *not* the universal solvent to human predicaments. A certain degree of skepticism of all panaceas characterizes all mature sociological thought (cf Wrong, 1976, Prologue). Skepticism does not imply debunking; it emphatically teaches us to be wary and suspicious when it is claimed that this or that particular approach is the key to the riddles of the universe. The ways of the human animal in its interplay with its fellows are too complicated and devious to be susceptible to any monistic explanation.

Sociologists interpreting communication processes always need to be aware of four interrelated questions when assessing communication impacts: (1) Under what circumstances can communication serve useful functions, and under what circumstances is it likely to be counterproductive? (2) What are the structural circumstances that limit the impact and effect of communication? (3) What purpose does such limitation serve? (4) Who is benefited and who suffers harm? When such questions are addressed, the sociology of communication becomes a significant area of research, and communication will no longer be regarded as a panacea.

REFERENCES

Burke, Edmund. 1855. *Reflections on the Revolution in France*, in Works, vol. II. London: Bohn's British Classics.

Chase, Stuart. 1951. *Roads to Agreement.* New York: Harper.

Coser, Lewis A. 1956. *The Functions of Social Conflict.* New York: The Free Press.

Coser, Rose Laub. 1961. Insulation from observability and types of social conformity. *American Sociological Review* 26:28–39.

Goffman, Erving. 1959. *The Presentation of Self in Everyday Life.* New York: Doubleday-Anchor.

Habermas, Juergen. 1971. *Knowledge and Human Interests.* Boston: Beacon.

Habermas, Juergen, and Niklas Luhmann. 1971. *Theorie der Gesellschaft oder Sozialtechnologie.* Frankfort: Suhrkamp.

Klineberg, Otto. 1952. *Tensions Affecting International Understanding.* New York: Social Science Research Council.

Lewin, Kurt. 1947. *The Research Center for Group Dynamics*, Sociometry Monographs No. 17. New York: Beacon House.

Lewin, Kurt. 1948. *Resolving Social Conflicts.* New York: Harper.

Mayo, Elton. 1946. *The Human Problems of Industrial Civilization*. Boston: Graduate School of Business Administration, Harvard University.

Merton, Robert K. 1968. Manifest and latent functions. Chapter 1 in *Social Theory and Structure*, enlarged ed. New York: The Free Press.

Moore, Wilbert E., and Melvin M. Tumin. 1949. Some social functions of ignorance. *American Sociological Review* 14: 787 – 95.

Niebuhr, Reinhold. 1932. *Moral Man and Immoral Society*. New York: Scribner's.

Rousseau, Jean Jacques. 1970. "Discourse on Arts and Sciences," as quoted in Marshall Berman, *The Politics of Authenticity*. New York: Atheneum.

Rule, James B. 1974. *Private Lives and Public Surveillance*. New York: Schocken.

Rule, James B. 1978. *Insight and Social Betterment*. New York: Oxford Univ. Press.

Schneider, Louis. 1962. The role of the category of ignorance in sociological theory. *American Sociological Review* 27:492 – 508.

Wrong, Dennis H. 1976. *Skeptical Sociology*. New York: Columbia Univ. Press.

CHAPTER 3

COMMUNICATION, WORLD ORDER, AND THE HUMAN POTENTIAL: TOWARD AN ETHICAL FRAMEWORK
Hamid Mowlana

APPROACHES TO INTERNATIONAL COMMUNICATION

Four basic assumptions or approaches have characterized the activities of scholars, governments, media practitioners, and individual citizens in the field of international communication over the past half century. The idealistic-humanistic approach characterizes international communication as a means of bringing nations and peoples together and as a power to assist international organizations in exercising their services to the world community. This approach strives toward increasing understanding among nations and people and toward the attainment of world peace. The communication process in this approach is seen in its most idealistic form.

A second approach, sometimes called political proselytization, sees international communication as propaganda, ideological confrontation, advertising, and the creation of myths and cliches. These are usually one-way communications, and they all require central organizing authorities of some kind. They are thus imbued with a certain authoritarian, totalitarian character that makes it possible to manipulate human beings. This approach to international communication has dominated relations between and among states for the past several decades.

A third, increasingly visible, approach is to view information in the international context as economic power. Here its operation is more subtle, the message more subliminal. Overtly respectable international development projects, business ventures, marketing, trade, and technology transfer have been characterized by this approach, and they usually have resulted in the domination of weaker, peripheral nations. "Modernization" of less-developed countries has in fact resulted in their conversion to Western ways and has made them more amenable to control by Western power centers. Since this process, sometimes referred to as "Westoxification," may

27

make its converts want to behave in ways different from their natural ways, it might result in a certain schizophrenic paralysis of creative power.

The fourth approach to international communication is to view information as political power. Information, in the form of news and data, is treated as a neutral, value-free commodity. A study of international mass media, the wire services, literature, cinema, and television programs reveals a concentration of the means of production in a few countries. When information is conveyed from one country to another, the culture of the sources also is conveyed, and that may not always be in the best interests of the recipient.

These four orientations characterize how states, scholars, and media practitioners have described the increasing capacities of international communication over the past five decades. The four approaches are not mutually exclusive and are interrelated to varying degrees. Student exchange, for example, may serve the idealistic-humanistic, political proselytization, or economic power aspects of international communication. Generally speaking, the political proselytization, economic power, and political power approaches are especially closely related.

None of these four approaches has escaped criticism. The idealistic-humanistic approach in particular suffers from certain problems. First, it is impossible to achieve an objective transfer of information and values. Every person's knowledge and value system is unique and reflects the accumulated image of all the messages he or she has received. There are no such things as facts in this world, only a changeable value system and images that are malleable and open to socializing influences. As a result, an individual's objectivity is mercurial, unstable, and subjective. Second, whose ideal of international peace and world community are we talking about? Interpretations vary, and unless there is a consensus on an ideal world, it is impossible for the currently dominant ideas to escape the opposition's accusation of ideological imperialism. Third, there is a certain inherent defect in equating universal agreement with universal good. Human progress springs from individuals who disagree with the norm, who initiate new lines of thought and creative ideas tangential to prevailing opinion. All great truths begin as heresy. When a particular world view or ideological system is proposed as an ideal system, it becomes fossilized as the status quo and resists progressive innovations. This can ultimately result in war, for war is not the extension of dispute, but a refusal to dispute. Fourth, the rational pursuit of human good that idealism demands is an unrealistic expectation from beings whose rational faculty is often overwhelmed by irrationalism and emotion.

If the benign approach of idealism-humanism has been criticized, so too have the three relatively malevolent approaches. International political proselytization has led to a general distrust of international media, whose purpose is assumed, sometimes incorrectly, to be manipulative. The "war of ideas" has been charged with ideological rivalry and fueled by intolerance among nations and hatred among peoples. International communication has been guilty of aiding and abetting international tensions, if not intentionally, then at least by not promoting peaceful solutions and not conferring legitimacy on the peacemakers.

In the arena of economic and political power, with the two approaches described previously, information has assumed its place beside petroleum, strategic metals, and uranium as an international resource to be bartered, boycotted, and blackmailed. Megabit streams of digital data have become the source of power in our information-based society. Information means power, and its manipulation can have far-reaching effects on economic, social, and political development.

But these difficulties should not incapacitate our ability to see international communication as an exciting and challenging area for human growth and potential and for a peaceful world. It is in pursuit of this goal that we must focus our attention and efforts on new frontiers in international communication and mobilize our professional and intellectual resources for new and needed illumination on human potential.

THE UNFINISHED REVOLUTION

It is ironic that for at least the last two decades both the idealist-humanist and the strategist (embracing the three approaches mentioned previously) have emphasized the so-called "communications revolution" as a focus of analysis for their respective schools of thought. The communications revolution that Dordick describes in Chapter 4 has meant the spread of technology, systems innovation, and improvements in the speed and quantity in which messages travel. But the real revolution has been the *communication* revolution, explained in terms of a quest for satisfactory human interaction, rather than a *communications* revolution, viewed through the lens of technological and institutional growth. It is unfortunate that the cultural components of international and human relations have been overshadowed by the political, economic, and technological aspects of the field in recent years. Modern political development, social rebellion, religious resurgence, and contemporary revolutionary movements in both the industrially developed and less-industrialized societies can be better understood if approached from the perspective of human interaction (communication analysis) rather than from a purely politicoeconomic or technological perspective.

Western theories of human development, both Marxist and liberal-democratic, proceed from a shared assumption that the development of societies requires that modern economic and social organization replace traditional structures. Widely accepted in the West (including eastern as well as western Europe) and diffused among the elites of the less-industrialized countries, this assumption includes, among other things, industrialization in the economy; secularization in thought, personality, and communication; the development of a "cosmopolitan attitude"; integration into the "world culture"; and rejection of traditional thoughts and technologies because they dominated the past and thus are not "modern." But contemporary movements around the world, whether of a group, nation, or community, all share an alternative vision of human and societal development. This "third way" eschews both Marxism and liberal democracy. It has its roots in more humane, ethical, traditionalist, anti-bloc, self-reliance theories of societal development. In short, the third way seeks not to promote itself or its ideology. It seeks dignity through dialogue, and that quest underlies the current revolutionary movements around the world.

The French revolution, for all its noble ideas and promises, in the end did not further this quest for dialogue among individuals. On the contrary, it marked the watershed in the rise of the individual vis-à-vis the nation-state. The concepts of freedom, equality, and fraternity, which came to the forefront when individuals began making political and economic demands on the state, have played major roles in revolutions ever since and have led to the rise of modern nationalism. This juncture also can be identified as the point of departure of the individual from his community. No longer was interpersonal communication the main mode of communication. Bureaucracies arose to take care of human needs. Humans communicated with each other more as roles than as individuals. Mass *media* began to *mediate* government-citizen communication. People became alienated from one another as cultures moved inexorably from association (Gemeinschaft) into abstraction (Gesellschaft). The growth of "instrumental" and "functional" communication became paramount in the decline of genuine inter/intrapersonal dialogue.

This preliminary exploration into the inquiry of human communication appears to present few points of controversy. The detrimental effect of modern technological society and its monstrous institutions on the capacity for inter/intrapersonal communication has been well documented, analyzed, and accepted as a fait accompli by countless sociologists, anthropologists, and psychologists. What still begs analysis, however, is the possibility of reversing this trend, of reviving the capacity for human communication among already alienated individuals. Two steps are required. First, we must shift our attention and our emphasis from *communications* (as means) to *communication* (as sharing and trust). Second, we must create a code of ethics and conduct that can stop the deterioration in relations, can protect humans from destroying themselves, and can eventually direct the machinery of communications to explore the human growth and potential.

COMMUNICATION AND THE HUMAN POTENTIAL

Today many scientists in the United States, Japan, the Soviet Union, and elsewhere in Europe agree that humans use a very small fraction—between 6 and 10 percent—of their capacities. For example, the capacity to experience our environment more freely through our olfactory organs remains a potential. Ever since the air became an overcrowded "garbage dump" for industrial wastes and the internal combustion engine, it has become easier for us to turn off our sense of smell than to keep it functioning. In general, by closing ourselves off from both our physical and interpersonal environment, we have reduced our capacity to communicate. Consequently, we perceive less clearly and as a result we feel less. Not only do we shut off awareness of our own feelings, but we are becoming desensitized to how other people feel.

Research in at least a half dozen human potential centers across the United States supports the hypothesis that our capacities are almost infinite. But the question remains: How can we learn to use them when "negative conditioning" limits our confidence and approach to life?

As examples of negative conditioning, let us look at the media and the educational systems—two of the most powerful channels of communication. The excessive focus on violence in television programs and motion pictures, and the emphasis on sensationalism in current American radio and TV news are the result of a narrow, almost brutalizing attitude toward life that is inimical to the development of the human potential. The world is increasingly perceived as a threat as viewers and readers become anxious and lose their reservoir of trust. In many people there slowly grows a conviction that it is safer to withdraw from such a world, to isolate oneself from its struggle, and to let others make decisions. As our self-concept erodes, our "trust factor"—a fundamental element in harmonious social life—diminishes.

Many commentators also have argued that the Western educational system damages creative minds and limits experiences with problem solving rather than effectively teaching necessary skills and fostering diverse abilities. Compartmentalizing information not only makes it more difficult to learn and to retain; it also removes the necessary perspective and practical aspects that a more comprehensive approach would include. Each student has unique needs and abilities that must be taken into consideration when planning a course of study.

The general tendency now is to emphasize the vocational aspect, using a hard-headed businesslike tone of voice. Higher education is represented as an industry, engaged in manufacturing socially needed commodities such as business secretaries, engineers, economists, and even communicators. As usual, the central claim is efficiency, and the logic is that mass education requires mass production methods. To some critics, the result is already clear—"technication," meaning standardization. In the age of cybernetics and our highly technological society, the process of personal orientation and self-discovery is becoming not a luxury but a necessity. On most Western college campuses few students, apart from the few who have a vocation and know exactly where they are going, know enough either about themselves or about the world to make effective choices. Although we are limited by our culture, we must seek alternatives that best suit our political, social, and economic needs. Education is the mainstay of culture, for how one learns is culturally determined, but flexibility and creativity are the keys to positive change and growth.

TOWARD AN ETHICAL FRAMEWORK

I have suggested that the quest for dialogue and the transcendence of alienation through interpersonal communication is an on-going revolution in society and that this must be recognized and studied. The point here is to note a social phenomenon, not to lament the lack of good conversation. This is both a human and societal problem. The suggestion is that the way *people* relate to each other in a world of "internationalized" culture and consciousness may be more important than how *nation-states* relate. On this human level, we must distinguish between the politically "sexy" right to communicate and the more homely yearning, or even need, to communicate.

I am not suggesting that we should abandon our efforts to improve our communication technology, nor am I proposing that organizational, technical, or even politically organized communication should be limited. In an extension of Shakespeare's observation that the world is a stage where all humans are players nestles one of the most powerful tributes to the utility of international communication fora. The United Nations, with all its shortcomings, UNESCO, the International Telecommunication Union, and other international institutions have served as theaters where nation-actors might play out their roles and communicate frustrations that if left unexpressed might lead to violence. The value of this cannot be underestimated in view of the recurrent scenario in world history in which comparatively small countries that feel neglected or unheard set in motion chains of events that climax in catastrophic conflagrations. Another advantage of international fora has been that they have at least partially compelled an end to that long chapter of human history where the strong divided the rest of the world among themselves, literally and figuratively, or set the rules that the weak would follow.

The world scope of the media ultimately must be viewed as a whole. While nations will always retain lifestyle characteristics, maintaining their distinctiveness, it is important to consider the impact a hypothetical global code of ethics might have. After all, the whole idea behind a media entity lies in the effectiveness of its communication. Communication can only occur on interpersonal, local, and national levels for so long. Eventually it transcends national boundaries to blanket other countries' operations, and people gain insight into new and different cultural schemes. Communication also creates an international or global symbolic environment in which international political and economic behavior takes place. It is at this juncture, when the nature of the media coverage crosses cultural lines, that an international code of media ethics, one that hovers above all nations, must be considered. Recent public opinion surveys in the United States and in Europe show dramatic changes in public opinion on such issues as arms expenditure, nuclear war, and allocation of world resources. In the United States, the threat of war has become more real in people's minds, and the support of military spending has increased significantly. Yet, ironically, the same population feels that such expenditures are a waste of available resources. It is perhaps difficult at this point to prove that media coverage has had a major responsibility in this shift of attitude. But the long history of the media's coverage of the arms race and perpetuation of the so-called "threat" perception and arms "gap" cannot be denied, nor can the inability of the media to cover the current religious resurgence and political upheaval around the world be disputed any longer.

This in itself supports the argument that what is needed now is a shift from a manipulative, technology-oriented communication to more interaction, human dialogue, and exchange of ideas. To achieve this we must move to create and promote a set of principles or code of ethics that is not culture-bound but universal, strives for the dignity and potential of human beings, and prevents a catastrophic war and worldwide destruction. Present narrowly defined ethical or professional codes of ethics are irrelevant, inconsistent, and ineffective as tools in creating such an atmosphere of understanding. They do not challenge the technological determinist view of communication, they are acquiescent to the centralized system of management, and they put too much trust in the nation-states and other actors to deliver the goods. A confluence of historical factors has produced this disorder in the moral dimension of our communication process. The utilitarianism that pervades the world and marks various political economies generates a stream of dissenters who consider social choices unjust. Until some synthesis of the moral system is achieved, human conduct at home and abroad will continue to be indecisive. Before we can begin to suggest a better future, however, we need to engage in a dialogue and national debate about the cycle of desire in our own institutions. Prevention of war, respect for human dignity, and recognition of diverse cultural values, religions, and traditions different from our own must be promoted and publicized internationally.

The kinds of principles that an international code of ethics might propose should be designed to apply to a form of behavior that engenders moral, ethical, and thoughtful issue coverage, whether or not there is fertile ground in a given country for it to flourish. Part of the idea of a code of ethics is that it be exactly that—ethical. The concept of ethics does not imply force. It is the study of what ought to be, so far as this depends upon the voluntary action of individuals. While it is still too utopian to hope for countries to feel an ethical duty and obligation in mass media communication, the only way for such a proposition to be sustained would be for professional media organizations, and not governments, to decide on these principles. The ultimate ethical power the media have is to serve the public, and the zenith of serving that public is reached when a medium succeeds in raising a group, a public, or a world, whatever its size, to a higher level of understanding and insight.

In this spirit I propose four basic principles of an international code of media ethics.

AN INTERNATIONAL CODE OF ETHICS

1. **Prevention of war and promotion of peace.** If, as is so often demonstrated, international media can mobilize for war and exacerbate tensions, why can they not do the reverse? International media should take the following actions:

- Increase the amount of information available on peaceful solutions to conflict.
- Break down stereotypes that dehumanize opposing populations.
- Be aware of hidden biases in coverage on controversial issues.
- Serve as early warning devices to bring attention to potential flash points.
- Remind opponents of peaceful solutions to conflicts.
- Confer prestige on the peacemaker.
- Help create a public mood conducive to the spirit of reconciliation.
- Put peacemakers on opposite sides in touch with one another.

2. **Respect for culture, tradition, and values.** No one culture or value system has a monopoly on the truth. Only in the dialogue of adversaries will the truth emerge. International media should work to do the following:

- Promote respect and tolerance for the world's manifold cultures.
- Uphold tradition in the face of "modernization."

- Facilitate the often difficult and distorted communication between cultures.
- Help diverse value systems arrive at definitions for such common goals as peace, integrity, and national sovereignty.
- Point out that deeply ingrained cultural values determine in part a nation's political behavior.
- Strengthen and preserve cultural identities and support cultures in the face of outside domination.

3. **Promotion of human rights and dignity.** Mass media must provide a voice to the dissenter and the downtrodden. Freedom of speech, of the press, and of information are vital for the realization of human rights. International media should promote human rights in the following ways:

- Publicize violations of international conventions such as the International Bill of Human Rights, the Helsinki Final Act, and the United Nations Charter.
- Promote access of individuals to media outlets in the face of domination by elites or majorities.
- Promote the democratization of communication by removing obstacles to the free interchange of ideas, information, and experience among equals.

4. **Preserve human association in the context of the home, family, and community.** International media must attempt to reverse the trend toward alienation, deindividualization, atomization, and anonymity. They should work to do the following:

- Promote interpersonal communication by facilitating more interaction among people rather than narcotizing them through mass-distributed programming.
- Facilitate self-reliance and interdependence by publicizing local, decentralized solutions to common problems.
- Encourage wholesome television and radio programming for children.
- Encourage respect for elders and work toward local solutions for such problems as youth crime and violence.

CHAPTER 4

NEW COMMUNICATIONS TECHNOLOGY AND MEDIA POWER
Herbert S. Dordick

Any examination of the roles of the news media in national and international conflict must take into account the new communications technology that has revolutionized the news industry in the past few decades. Abel (Chapter 6) points out the impact of a variety of new technologies, including the jet plane and electronic newsgathering and dissemination methods, on such a basic operational feature of news organizations as the system of foreign correspondents. This is but one example of the effects of technology on social institutions, and the general topic of such effects has received wide attention from social and political analysts for a number of years.

Improved worldwide communications technology has, it would appear, increased rather than decreased tensions around the globe. For more than two decades, nations north and south, rich and poor, advanced and less developed have searched for a new international economic system that will create some form of order that could lead to equitable development. To this search has now been added a search for a new information order—a search for a means to encourage, not stifle, the flow of information and to decrease the gap between those who have already been labeled as information poor and those who are information rich. This search has led to intense conflict as nations seek to communicate on a common network and find that they cannot agree on how to use that network, let alone what to communicate.

The idea that improvements in communications make communication more difficult, as James Carey (1983) recently put it, may indeed be true. In considering the effects of technology on society, however, we must be careful to account for the social choices that play a part in those effects. Many writers have argued that high technology in itself has both basic and pervasive effects on the culture of the people who create and use it. In a subtle way, technology actually carries with it certain general cultural values, but we must not lose sight of the more obvious and important fact that technology is a tool that may be used any number of ways according to the decisions made by its users.

Increased communication does not necessarily lead to understanding and the reduction of tension, as Coser (Chapter 2) points out. But how can there be understanding without communication? More access to better and more varied means of communication through the new technology *could* lead to more communication and more understanding. If it does not, we cannot blame the technology; we must look to the uses we make of it (see Cherry 1971).

What we must always consider is the impact of culture on technology, as well as the reverse. The use of communications technology in conflict situations is pertinent because it is clear that communication can exacerbate conflict as well as help resolve it. The topic of this book, news media and conflict, is becoming more important precisely because recent scientific and engineering developments in the communications field have magnified the potential for fostering good or ill that communication has always possessed.

How one uses a technology depends to a considerable degree on one's attitudes toward that technology. Fear and apprehension cannot result in the creative use of any technology, and this is especially true of the information technologies. Knowledge of the technologies can go a long way to alleviate inappropriate attitudes.

SATELLITES AND CHIPS

While the origins of the communications revolution go back to the late seventeenth and early eighteenth centuries, two relatively recent technological advances must be given major credit for the extraordinarily rapid developments of the past two decades. The communication satellite has fired the imagination of all nations and aroused hopes for modernization among all peoples on the globe. The satellite knows no national boundaries; it has made possible communications where it had been impossible or extremely difficult before. Some politicians have had the audacity to see in the satellite great hopes for the future of democracy throughout the entire world.

A little more than thirty years ago any domestic telephone system separated from another by more than about 300 miles could only interconnect by the rather limited and unreliable facilities of radio. It was only in 1956 that the intercontinental submarine cable was laid between Europe and North America. Only nine years later, 15 countries had subscribed to Intelsat and were using the satellite for intercontinental communications! Today, there are more than 120 member nations of Intelsat, including the emerging nations of Africa and Southeast Asia and the new nations of the Pacific Basin.

The semiconductor chip, the other great advance in communications technology, has created the potential for every man, woman, and child in the world to be able to talk with every other man, woman, and child in the world. The Venus fly-by, launched by the National Aeronautics and Space Administration of the United States several years ago, had sufficient communications capability for every U.S. citizen and every Soviet citizen to speak with a citizen from the other country. Consider what this might have done for resolving (or exacerbating) conflict.

Let us examine some other figures that illustrate the extent and power of this revolution. Today there are some 400 million telephones in more than 200 countries, and they operate on what is essentially a single global network. This network annually carries a total traffic of about 400,000 million telephone calls—to which we must add telex and data messages. Indeed, data communications are increasing at a rate exceeding 20 percent per year. The global telecommunications network is growing at about 6 percent per year, and by the end of this century we expect that 1,500 million telephones will be generating more than a trillion calls each year.

The combined capacity of Intelsat and the submarine cables has resulted in an almost exponential growth in telephone message traffic between North America and the United Kingdom (UK). Prior to the laying of the first submarine cable, traffic across the Atlantic averaged about 50,000 calls per year, all by often weak and unreliable high frequency radio. Within one month after the laying of the submarine cable, calls between the UK and New York City increased by more than 50 percent and between London and Canada by 100 percent (Pool 1977).

The introduction of Intelsat I in 1965 resulted in an increase in calls to more than 400,000 annually. Today, with Intelsat V in orbit, the annual number of telephone messages is almost 6 million.

The cost of transmission has fallen by a factor of ten over the past forty years and with the addition of optical fibers for the so-called "final mile," (from the earth station to your telephone) we can expect another cost reduction by a factor of ten. Satellite band width costs will be one-twenty-fifth of today's costs by the end of the century. Switching costs also will be reduced by a factor of at least three, and with the new digital coding and multiplexing technologies made possible by the "miracle chip," the cost of transmission will be essentially zero by the end of the century. This means that transmission will be free; processing will cost!

One thing is certain about the future. Much of the basic science for that time is with us today. Because of this, we can forecast the following future applications and trends with a high degree of certainty:

- The demand for telecommunications services will grow at a rate exceeding 10 percent per year.
- International network capacity will increase at about the same rate.
- There are no obvious physical limitations or impediments to growth.
- There are many kinds of organizational difficulties.

Expansion can be achieved with relatively modest use of material, energy, and labor per unit. For example, in transmission the real cost per unit has been falling steadily, and this is occurring also in switching and data processing units. As a result, we can expect some technological unemployment, especially in nations that might not be able to accommodate the industrial expansion created by the information and communications technologies. In addition, international conflict will occur over the broadcast spectrum and the geo-stationary orbital spectrum. In the long run, however, pressure and conflict will be reduced by the use of higher frequencies, the reuse of frequencies, and the introduction of digital time division multiplexing and very large band width cables and optical fibers.

There are many uncertainties about the nature of user needs, of national administrations, and of existing bureaucracies that must be altered, if not replaced, due to increased technology (Berting et al. 1980, Rada 1980). Questions to be answered include: How creative can society become to make the best use of these remarkable capabilities? Will society be able to tolerate and eventually eliminate possible excesses? How will nations avoid the price of productivity—high unemployment? How will users of the media handle the double-edged sword of these new telecommunications channels? How will the emerging nations match their resources with their international and national political and economic objectives?

COMMUNICATIONS TECHNOLOGIES AND CONFLICT

Communications technologies of one sort or another have always been important in the management of international conflict. Messengers carried word of the outcome of battles, of the maiden's cry for rescue, of insults that led to more conflict, or of proposals for peace. Was it not the Rothschild family that profited so well from the early news of the outcome at Waterloo? And if Lenin had not had a telephone or telegraph connection between Berlin and Petrograd (as well as the sealed railroad car), his return to the Finland station would have been less than nation-shattering. We are well acquainted with the success of the Ayatollah Khomeini's use of the audio cassette to pave the way for his successful return to Iran. The national broadcast station has become an early target of every revolutionary as a means to inform the citizens of his presence and his progress and also to initiate a resolution of the conflict. A recent coup attempt in Thailand was almost entirely initiated and resolved by radio. Indeed, it is often referred to as the Radio Coup.

The dual nature of the media, as creators of conflict and as means to resolve that conflict, is clearly evident. How this duality emerges can be seen best in the hopes and realities for the ubiquitous telephone that we take so much for granted. The telephone makes it possible to concentrate business and work activities while allowing for those who so choose to work away from their offices. Without the telephone, for example, the sky-scraper would not be possible; more space would have been required for elevators to move people from floor to floor and little would be available for offices. At the same time, today the telephone is touted as a means for decentralizing business activities and for reducing travel.

Satellite broadcasting is seen as a means for providing vast coverage and immediacy and very low cost per listener or viewer, but it also can select a small target audience unreached by any other means for very high costs per message communicated.

The semiconductor chip made possible the design and construction of very large, extremely powerful computers, enabling the centralization of dispersed activities. Yet today, the chip is perceived as a means for personalizing computing and communications and for returning computing activities to a human scale.

NEW COMMUNICATIONS TECHNOLOGY, NEW MEDIA

The new media that will develop out of this communications explosion will have dual powers; they will enable messages to reach around the world instantaneously, and they will make possible the targeting of special audiences, equally instantaneously. They will, if allowed, make possible interactive communication from periphery to center, but they also will have the ability to concentrate more power to the center. In Indonesia, the Palapa satellite has made viewers citizens of the world, but it has not yet reduced the cost of relevant information to a level that has significantly closed information gaps.

The new telecommunications networks will be multimedia networks. They will have sufficient band width or capacity to carry voice, data, image, text, and video messages as easily as today's telephone call. They will carry all of this information power on a single channel to be accessed by a single terminal under the care of a single operator. The more you fill this channel with information, the more you use all of its capacity, and the lower the cost for each message transmitted; such is the economics of networks.

The language flexibility that this can provide offers enormous power to the information provider. Research has shown that a message enhanced by visuals has an entirely different impact than one provided merely by text or even by a television "talking head." With the reductions underway in the cost of video production, almost every message can be accompanied by images that can shape understanding and influence behavior. The context of a story, if illustrated by video, can alter meaning. An experienced reporter, using the multimedia power offered by the new communications technology, can tailor a message for the audience in the most appropriate way, almost approaching a sort of one-to-one intimacy that is so effective for shaping opinions.

Both Abel (Chapter 6) and Arno (Chapter 1) say that the news media are storytellers. It is essential to consider how much more powerfully a story can be told with the new and more readily available media forms offered by the new communications technologies. New media power brings to light again certain basic questions that existed before the revolution in communications technology, the answers to which will determine the course of the technology's impact on society in the end. These questions, which were addressed in the preceding chapters by Mowlana (Chapter 3) and Coser (Chapter 2), concern the storytellers' moral and ethical standards, which must be based on their—and our—understanding of the social situations in which their actions can exacerbate conflict or manage it in a beneficial way.

REFERENCES

Berting, J., S. C. Mells, and H. Wintersberger, editors. 1980. *The Socio-Economic Impact of Microelectronics*. New York: Pergamon Press.

Carey, James W. 1983. High speed communication in an unstable world. *Chronicle of Higher Education*, July 27, 48.

Cherry, Colin. 1971. *World Communications: Threat or Promise?* New York: Wiley-Interscience.

Pool, Ithiel de Sola, editor. 1977. *The Social Impact of the Telephone*. Cambridge: MIT Press.

Rada, J. 1980. *The Impact of Microelectronics*. Geneva: International Labour Office.

CHAPTER 5

EVENTS, PSEUDO-EVENTS, MEDIA EVENTS: IMAGE POLITICS AND THE FUTURE OF INTERNATIONAL DIPLOMACY

Majid Tehranian

In a brilliant polemic, *The Image: A Guide to Pseudo-Events in America*, Daniel Boorstin (1975) has identified and diagnosed a new malady of modern civilization: Mediacracy.* Boorstin argues, powerfully and disturbingly, that the new, complex apparatus of image-making in America (and by now, throughout the world) is systematically creating not only serious distortions about life, but also a distinct cultural preference for lively illusions over dull facts, colorful celebrities over honest citizens, actors over presidents, commercialized tourism over inquisitive traveling, shortcuts to salvation over long spiritual journeys, and glittering images over challenging ideals.

The arguments against "hidden persuaders," "mind managers," "captains of consciousness," "electronic colonialists," and "media imperialists" have become so familiar by now that even the media themselves have begun adopting the arguments. In a thoughtful essay, however, Elihu Katz (1981) has proposed a counterargument. In an article entitled "In Defense of Media Events," Katz focuses on the positive and integrative role that certain historic events, dramatized by the media, play in the lives of viewers and nations. The media coverage of President John F. Kennedy's assassination, man's landing on the moon, Anwar Sadat's journey to Jerusalem, and Pope John Paul II's trip to Poland all seem to have brought home great moments in history to their millions of viewers around the world and produced, at least in some, a catharsis of the tensions and conflicts that divide humankind. Whether or not these momentary sentiments and revelations on the common destiny of humans and their planet Earth can result in lasting consequences remains to be seen.

The Iranian hostage crisis presented yet another dramatic illustration of both the triumphs and tragedies of the "new electronic age" upon which

---

* I am grateful to my good friend, Marion Just, for first introducing this term to me. See her forthcoming *Mediacracy: Mass Media and American Democracy*.

the world seems to have embarked. The crisis showed: (1) how image politics centering on the uses of new telecommunications facilities can supersede traditional power politics in some situations of international conflict; (2) how old cultural stereotypes and new political fears blown up by the international mass media can sometimes impede progress in negotiations; and (3) how increased awareness by the public of the complexities of an international issue can also serve to limit excessive reactions to redress legitimate grievances. In other words, on balance, the ultimate outcome of the hostage crisis leaves some room for hope on the positive contributions of telecommunications to international relations. Neither Iran (which felt aggrieved by past U.S. interferences) nor the United States (which felt unjustly treated by terroristic tactics) used its ultimate weapons. The hostages came home safely, no serious military actions were taken, and Iranian assets were returned. However, in the meantime simplistic explanations of a complex political and human drama have left lasting images and stereotypes in the minds of the two nations over the conduct of the other, and this may prove to be an impediment to future relations for some time to come.

This chapter will show how the emergence of image politics in international affairs has affected the traditional pursuits of power and peace, will demonstrate that emergence through the example of the Iranian hostage crisis, and finally will sound some warnings on the increasing reliance of international diplomacy on images and image politics.

THE EMERGENCE OF IMAGE POLITICS

There is a baffling paradox in contemporary international relations that can hardly escape the attention of discerning observers. Technological abundance in the availability and use of telecommunication facilities, media, and channels is coupled increasingly with dramatic events and processes (such as the Vietnam War, the hostage crisis, and to a lesser degree perhaps, the north-south dialogue leading to the Brandt et al. [1980] and MacBride et al. [1980] reports) in which rational discourse is often drowned in a flood of abusive words, images, and noise that limits the possibilities for meaningful negotiation of international conflicts. The mass media and their practitioners are held by some at least partially responsible for this state of affairs, while others point to the constructive role that the media can and have played in direct and unadulterated reportage of international events and in providing channels of international communication hitherto unknown and unexplored.

What is the real role of telecommunications services in international conflict? Traditional realist theories of international relations consider the national interest struggle for power as the dominant factor in national conduct (Morgenthau 1978). The international political system is considered an excellent example of a primitive political community still largely devoid of the essential properties of sovereignty. A weak world moral and political consensus and the low level of methods development for rule making, rule adjudication, and rule enforcement characterize the international community. The system is thus considered far more prone to the rule of violence than its domestic constituent parts. The realist theorists have maintained that pursuing a policy of naked national interest to achieve a balance-of-power system is a far more effective guarantee of peace than idealist pursuits of human rights, social justice, national self-determination, and world disarmament. In such views, the media as well as all the paraphernalia of an idealist foreign policy (e.g., public opinion, diplomacy, ideology and propaganda, morality) are subordinate to the considerations of power politics.

In the meantime, however, the realist school itself has undergone some changes. In the words of one eminent theorist of the school:

> It is perhaps no exaggeration to say that today half of power politics consists of "image making." With the rising importance of publics in foreign affairs, image making has steadily increased. Today, hardly anything remains in the open conduct of foreign policy that does not have a propaganda or public relations aspect, aiming at presenting a favorable image to allies, opponents, neutrals, and, last but not least, one's own domestic audiences (Hertz 1981, 187).

Perhaps a vivid and timely illustration of this point is President Ronald Reagan's refusal at the Ottawa Summit of July 1981 to sit next to either Prime Minister Margaret Thatcher of Great Britain or President Francois Mitterand of France in the official photograph. For the media-conscious U.S. president, it was considered undesirable to be compared or contrasted with the other two leaders whose domestic policies represented different ideological views.

In the past twenty-five years, at least three major technological, socioeconomic, and political forces have altered the structure of international politics to such a degree that even a "realistic" view would have to consider the vital role that the apparatuses of image making are playing in international relations.

Technological Forces

First, the accelerating technological explosion in the field of communications, with revolutions in satellite communication and microprocessing techniques representing the most dramatic illustrations, have both universalized and personalized world communication (Dordick et al. 1981). The convergence of six somewhat separately developed technologies (i.e., printing, broadcasting, point-to-point telecommunications, computers, satellites, and microprocessors) into a single technological revolution has been characterized by some as a second industrial revolution. The accelerating processes of miniaturization and mass production and consumption of information and communication goods (from transistor radio-tape-video to pocket calculators and home-office word processors) have led others to hail the phenomenon as the coming of the "postindustrial society" and the "age of information" (Bell 1973, Porat 1977, Kumar 1978, Dordick et al. 1981, Gerbner et al. 1981).

Without necessarily accepting such claims, we may readily recognize that the traditional notions of national sovereignty are undermined seriously by the ability of the superpowers and transnational corporations to conduct constant surveillance of national resources (both subterranean and suboceanic), military personnel movements, changing patterns in weather and crops, and transborder information data flows. The domination of world news gathering and dissemination systems as well as of the cultural industries (e.g., printing, movies, audio-video hardware and software) by a few countries and companies also has created anxieties about preservation of cultural autonomy and national identity in smaller countries (Nordenstreng and Schiller 1979). Thanks to extraordinary achievements in telecommunications, however, it is now technically possible for one person to speak directly and simultaneously to untold millions of people all over the world, and it is also becoming increasingly possible for millions of individuals to reach millions of others personally and instantaneously. The new communications technologies thus exhibit both centralizing (the global village) as well as fragmenting (the global chaos) potential. If their centralizing effects have served as a primary force, it is because the world system is still organized around nation-states and transnational corporations that are primarily interested in control rather than dissemination of information. There is also the problem of a cultural lag; the international political system has not yet fully developed the authentic supranational channels and institutions that the new communication technologies make possible.

Socioeconomic Forces

A second set of forces has been set in motion by the democratizing pressures of a worldwide revolutionary process that owes its origins in no small measure to the introduction of the mass media from printing onward. Ex-

posure to mass media through print and audiovisual means has created
rising levels of expectation, envy, and frustration. While the big media (national newspapers, broadcasting networks, satellites, central data processing) have provided channels for communication, decision making, dissemination, and legitimation of elite views and interests, the small media (small
and underground press, xeroxing, mimeographing, transistor radio, tape)
have facilitated the channels of communication among diverse disenfran-
chised groups. Thanks to the power of the new media, such groups as the
Islamic revolutionaries in Iran, the Irish Republican Army, the Kurds, and
the Palestinians can attract the attention of the world to their own cause for
sustained periods (Tehranian 1979a and b, 1980). The polarization of
world politics into superpower rivalries is thus countered by its fragmenta-
tion into a series of essentially local conflicts that nevertheless manage to
attract and sometimes divide world public opinion.

Political Forces

In the meantime, however, a third set of forces has been at work to provide
some measure of the integration of the world community. While the media
have served as channels for occurrence of world ideological conflict as well
as of consensus generation, crises of worldwide dimension have also contributed to the emergence of a "new tribe" of world citizens and world organizations that transcend national loyalties and boundaries. The possibility of an accidental or intentional nuclear war causing total annihilation,
the changing balance between world population and world resources, and
the increasing north-south cleavage all threaten to unleash untold suffering and human conflict in the coming decades. International communication, broadly conceived to include not only the mass media but also the
elite, prestige, trade and scientific media and channels such as the U.N.
system, international commissions, scientific and professional associations, world conferences, tourism, and world travel, as well as traveling
journalists, seems to have contributed its share to the emergence of a new
"world consciousness."
    Telecommunications seem to have contributed to the conduct of inter-
national relations in three basic ways: (1) by providing expanding channels
of communication; (2) by mobilizing support for opposition to certain issues of international significance; and (3) by creating new international
interest groups to bring pressure upon the existing machineries of nation-
states, transnational corporations, and intergovernmental organizations.

HOSTAGES TO IMAGES: SOME HISTORICAL EVIDENCE

The confluence of "image politics" and "power politics" in international relations is perhaps best illustrated in the Iranian hostage crisis of November 4, 1979, through January 20, 1981. This crisis is not alone, however, in contemporary affairs in suggesting the increasing role of image and image making in international politics. Egyptian President Anwar Sadat's trip to Jerusalem was not only a symbolic gesture of his peaceful intentions but also a powerful bid for U.S. and European public opinion support. Maintaining credibility was the chief U.S. aim in later Vietnam policy in spite of the bankruptcy of the war effort. The wish not to seem untrustworthy to allies has been, in fact, a continuing theme in most great power politics. This was true of American support of the shah of Iran almost to the end, and also in regard to the Portuguese, as NATO allies, until their end in Africa. Or, as Hertz puts it,

> . . . consider the incursion of Vietnam by China. There was no real substantive conflict there. But China felt it had to preserve its image as a power through a show of force meant to wipe out any adverse reflection on its power that might have been created by the Vietnamese overthrow of the China-backed Pol Pot regime in Cambodia. Suppose the Soviets, to wipe out the adverse image of *their* power, created by the Chinese invasion of their Vietnam ally, in turn found it necessary to "incurse" into China, whereupon the Americans, to preserve their image as a reliable friend of Deng's China, had taken measures against the Soviet Union (1981, 187).

In image politics, the media play a central and sometimes autonomous role. However, as media-projected images (of "strong and unwavering allies," "determined and relentless revolutionaries," "reasonable and peace-loving states") become larger-than-life mental pictures, media manipulation becomes far more difficult. Every image, so to speak, creates its own reality. Certain postures that were perhaps valuable at certain stages of a conflict become impediments at other stages. Therefore, frozen images can prove as serious an obstacle to negotiations as real conflicts of interest. Conversely, when the media manage to break through the barriers of control and censorship and show the real state of affairs as one of confusion of facts and ambivalence of minds—as in the Vietnam War or the Iranian hostage crisis—international conflict assumes a fluidity of form and complexity of substance beyond the relatively simpler calculations of power and rational interest. The many domestic and international audiences, each with its own claims and interests, blur the traditional boundaries between domestic and international politics.

Following Jurgen Habermas (1971), John Hertz (1981), and Richard Ashley (1981), we may argue that the media serve three basically different and often contradictory cognitive interests in international conflict situations: national solidarity interests, national or subnational instrumental interests, and global community interests.*

National Solidarity Interests

This corresponds to Habermas's "practical cognitive interest," and interest in knowledge as a basis for furthering mutual intersubjective understanding. The mass media have provided powerful means for governments to further national integration and national solidarity on issues of international conflict. The media in this role concentrate mostly on myths, symbols, and rituals that have emerged out of a particular historical and cultural tradition. They provide, therefore, a way for people to understand an issue, interpret developments, and decide to act within common traditions. In this sense, the uses of the media in international conflict are primarily directed toward domestic audiences.

National or Subnational Instrumental Interests

This corresponds to Habermas's category of "technical cognitive interest, an interest in knowledge as a basis for extending control over objects in the subject's environment (possibly including strategic dominance over other human beings)" (Ashley 1981, 208). The media in this role concentrate on the legitimation of material or strategic interests (e.g., the price and security of oil supplies, the missile gaps) and employ images of power rivalries among nations and corporate groupings that are inherently in conflict over the ownership, control, and manipulation of world resources.

Global Community Interests

This corresponds to Habermas's "emancipatory cognitive interest, an interest in securing freedom from 'hypothesized forces' and conditions of distorted communication (e.g., ideology)" (Ashley 1981, 208). The function of the media in this role is rooted in the human capacities for the communicative exercise of reflective reason in light of needs, knowledge, and rules. In the international arena, the media have to break through the

---

* My choice of terminology here, different from those of Habermas and Ashley, is more with a view to intelligibility of concepts than any philosophical justifications. The three layers of interest discussed here may correspond to the philosophical distinctions between the three types of reason — *practical, instrumental, and reflective.*

overpowering needs of national solidarity and instrumental manipulation in conflict situations and focus on the long-term strategic interests of a global community that is increasingly threatened by what Waltz aptly calls the four p's of global self-destruction—pollution, poverty, population, and (nuclear) proliferation (1979, 139).

THE IRANIAN HOSTAGE CRISIS

The Iranian hostage crisis, so significant and multifaceted in its global implications, lends itself particularly well to an analysis within the forego-ing theoretical framework. At every major point in the decision-making process, the media managed to reveal the underlying interests of the par-ties involved in the conflict and thereby played an important role in the evolution and resolution of the drama. On the other hand, the crisis be-came a "media event" in Iran as well as the United States, with its own autonomous political and commercial "ratings" playing a crucial role in the domestic politics of both nations as well as in intermedia rivalries.* The "image" of the hostages rather than their reality came thus to serve the threefold interests of both nations. The hostage crisis mobilized national solidarity at critical junctures in the two nations' histories, catered to the instrumental control of the other's behavior, and in the end acknowledged their common and global strategic interests within the sanctity of diplo-matic immunity, preservation of innocent human lives, and deescalation of a local conflict that threatened to turn into a larger, more damaging con-flict. Let us examine the drama in greater detail and at the major points in its unfolding†(see Table 1).

Background

The overthrow of the shah's regime in Iran should be considered in the light of the struggle of that nation of 35 million people for some 180 years to assert its independence against considerable geopolitical odds in a stra-tegically and economically important region of the world. American in-volvement in Iran was, on the other hand, motivated partly by strategic and economic interests and partly by a postwar ideology of liberal interna-tionalism-interventionism. The role of the United States in Iran, however, underwent a major shift when, in the CIA-sponsored coup d'etat of 1953,

---

* The rivalry of the American television networks for access, for instance, provided the Ira-nian authorities not only with some political leverage but also some commercial revenues.

† For an excellent review of the case, see *The New York Times Magazine's* Special Issue, Spring 1981.

Dr. Mohammad Mosaddegh's liberal democratic government was replaced by the shah's authoritarian regime. The United States became increasingly identified with the shah's regime, while the shah came to look to the United States as his main ally and benefactor. The Iranian Revolution in 1978 fundamentally altered this set of relationships between the two countries, but the images of continued U.S. domination and Iranian dependency lingered on. The hostage crisis took place in the context of these historical circumstances. It revived the memories of August 1953, when the shah had fled the country only to be returned to power in four days by what seemed to be outside forces. Under President Jimmy Carter's administration, however, the United States was still emerging from a post-Vietnam War period of withdrawal and retrenchment. The crisis thus lent itself to profound misperceptions and symbolic uses on both sides, and it provided the media with an insuperable human drama endowed with a beginning, a middle, and an end.

Enter the Shah

Following the overthrow of the shah in February 1979, the debate on U.S. policy in Iran centered on whether or not to give refuge to the fallen and wandering monarch. Loyalty to an old and faithful ally clearly called not only for his admission to the United States, but also assistance to regain his throne. This was considered an "American tradition" upon which national solidarity interests rested, but U.S. instrumental interests dictated otherwise. The revolution in Iran was by all accounts considered a popular uprising. It manifested strong religious and anticommunist tendencies; therefore, it could be manipulated to the advantage of U.S. strategic interests. A refuge for the shah would have thoroughly undermined the U.S. position with the new regime; therefore, U.S. diplomatic dispatches from Tehran as well as policy analysis in Washington recommended against his admission. But the medical diagnosis of his terminal cancer changed the picture totally. United States global interests in human rights, considered as a cornerstone of President Carter's foreign policy, were combined with pressures of the "old boy" network of Henry Kissinger, David Rockefeller, and John J. McCloy to gain the shah's admission into the United States for medical treatment. This decision was made against the explicit warnings by the U.S. embassy in Tehran, which had been occupied on February 14, 1979, by revolutionary militants for a few hours. President Carter's fateful decision seems to have served three different symbolic functions at the time: (1) to soothe the guilt feelings of having let down an ally; (2) to placate those who were posing a question of "who lost Iran"; and (3) to project

Table 1. The Hostage Crisis: A Schematic View of Symbolic Uses in International Politics

Points of Decision	Cognitive Interests		
	National Solidarity	National/Subnational Instrumental	Global Community
Admission of the Shah into U.S., October 22, 1979.	**USA** To alleviate guilt feelings about letting down an ally	**USA** To placate "old boy" network of interests posing the question of "who lost Iran"	**USA** To fulfill human rights claims in providing medical treatment to a dying man
Seizure of the U.S. Embassy in Tehran, November 4, 1979	**Iran** To mobilize sagging public enthusiasm for the revolutionary cause	**Iran** To embarrass and unseat Prime Minister Bazargan's government and his liberal-secular, moderate faction from power	**Iran** To dramatize Iranian grievances against the Shah and U.S. imperialism and appeal for world public opinion support
Abortive Negotiations, November 4, 1979–April 11, 1980	**Iran** To resolve an embarrassing issue (for the secular faction); to continue using the issue for national solidarity (the clerical faction) **USA** To release the hostages without resort to military means	**Iran** To reverse its own decline (the secular faction); to undermine the credibility of the secular faction (clerical faction) **USA** To regain influence in a vital area without losing face	**Iran** To appear to be standard bearer of a just cause (bringing justice to a tyrant) without damage to innocent lives **USA** To defend the basic rules of international conduct

Event			
The Rescue Attempt, April 24, 1980	**USA** To assert its military power without endangering innocent lives or world conflict	**USA** To improve the image of a weak president in an election year	**USA** To project an image of a strong yet restrained superpower
Resumption of Negotiations, September 9, 1980–January 20, 1981	**Iran** To dispose of an issue that had substantially lost its unifying value after the Iraqi invasion **USA** To resume efforts for a peaceful settlement of a national humiliation	**Iran** To relieve the clerical faction of accusations of irresponsibility leveled by the secular faction and to prove who the real power is in Iran **USA** To achieve a settlement acceptable to national as well as parochial financial interests before the end of Carter's term	**Iran** To prove Iranian goodwill and expose U.S. financial interests **USA** To achieve world approval in a just cause
Final Settlement and Catharsis, January 20, 1981	**USA** Joy of homecoming of captive sons and daughters and release from a national ordeal symbolic of America's declining powers **Iran** Shift from an increasingly costly and divisive issue to another unifying issue for national solidarity, i.e., the war against Iraq	**USA** The continuity of U.S. foreign policy despite the change of administrations with two different outlooks and approaches — Reagan's tough words actually helping Carter's conciliatory approach **Iran** Projection of the new, clerically controlled government as the real center of power in Iran	**USA** The honoring of U.S. commitments by the new administration and refusal to engage in reprisals **Iran** Projection of the revolutionary government as responsible and responsive to global Third World community interests and sentiments

an image of a president who is sensitive to human rights while tough on issues of national interest.

The Siege of the Embassy

On November 4, 1979, the U.S. embassy in Tehran was seized by a group of so-called Islamic student revolutionaries in a sit-in protest against the shah's admission into the United States. In retrospect, the seizure of the embassy also seems to have served three different symbolic functions in Iran's postrevolutionary politics. First, revolutionary enthusiasm was beginning to ebb in the face of mounting economic and political difficulties when protests against the shah's admission into the United States and demands for his immediate return to Iran for a trial presented themselves. There is evidence that both the student militants and their mentors were surprised by the degree of spontaneous national support they received for the seizure of the embassy. The sit-in thus turned into a siege to galvanize further support and serve revolutionary solidarity interests. Second, however, the seizure of the embassy came at a time when the conflict between the liberal moderates led by Prime Minister Mehdi Bazatrgan and the revolutionary radicals led by Ayatollah Beheshti as well as a myriad of leftist political parties and groups had reached a breaking point. A week earlier, Bazatrgan and Foreign Minister Ibrahim Yazdi had met U.S. National Security Adviser Zbigniew Brzezinski in Algiers to discuss an improvement in U.S.-Iranian relations. The seizure of the embassy therefore served as a virtual coup d'etat against Bazatrgan's government, which had to resign under the circumstances. Thus, for a while at least, opposition to the clerical leadership was successfully silenced by a national frenzy of emotions against the crimes of the shah and U.S. imperialism. The seizure of the embassy provided both the excuse and the "evidence" in the shredded files to intimidate and eliminate whoever was regarded as liberal, moderate, or Westernized. Finally, the siege of the embassy contained elements of enormous international symbolic significance for the revolutionaries. It served to dramatize the cause of Iran in international forums as well as to "emancipate" the oppressed everywhere from the fear of U.S. omnipotence. The release of thirteen women and blacks from among the hostages, the organization of an international conference in Tehran to unmask the crimes of the shah and U.S. imperialism, the advertising of Ayatollah Khomeini's letter to the Pope in some major Western newspapers, and the friendly reception given to Third World journalists and mediators, all symbolized efforts to mobilize world public opinion on Iran's behalf. Although this was somewhat successful among those nations that had suffered colonial domination and were gleeful in a vicarious satisfaction over the humiliation of the United States, the international state system as a whole could not accept the violation of its most essential rules of conduct, that is, the protection and immunity of diplomats.

Abortive Negotiations

In the first round of negotiations for the release of the hostages, three factors worked against real progress: (1) U.S. misperceptions of the locus of power in Iran; (2) Iranian misperceptions of the response of U.S. public opinion to the fate of the hostages; and (3) the intense symbolic uses made of the issue in the domestic politics of the two countries. Throughout this first round, the United States continued to deal primarily with the wrong faction, i.e., the liberal secular moderates (Mehdi Bazatrgan, Ibrahim Yazdi, Abholhassan Bani-Sadr, Sadeq Ghotbzadeh) who were neither for hostage-taking nor had the power to release them. In fact, U.S. admission of the shah into the United States had been partly encouraged by assurances by Prime Minister Bazatrgan and his Foreign Minister Ibrahim Yazdi that American embassy personnel would be protected. While Bani-Sadr and Ghotbzadeh were also against hostage-taking as detrimental to the good name of Islam and the revolution, they could not afford to be perceived as siding with the "U.S. imperialists" in the domestic power struggle. Once the leftist and clerical factions had realized the enormous symbolic uses of the hostages in unmasking and destroying the liberal "appeasers and lackeys of imperialism," however, the negotiations for their release were continually and effectively undermined. This was aided in part by the issue of the hostages becoming an important symbolic factor in the U.S. presidential elections and receiving unprecedented media attention. In retrospect, President Carter acknowledged that some benign neglect regarding the hostages issue might have actually helped to hasten their release (New York Times Magazine editors 1981).

The series of bizarre encounters and plans that were engaged in by a variety of world personalities (Kurt Waldheim, Amadou-Mahtar M'Bow, Sean MacBride, Yasir Arafat) as well as by actual negotiators (Jody Powell, Sadeq Ghotbzadeh, and their go-betweens, Christian Bourguet and Hector Villalon) all came to naught with one significant exception. In a personal intervention with the Ayatollah, PLO leader Yasir Arafat is credited with having obtained the release of the first thirteen black and women hostages only sixteen days after their capture. Neither the source nor the symbolic significance of this act of "clemency" should have been lost on the negotiators.

The Rescue Attempt

Having reached what appeared to be a negotiating impasse, President Carter on April 11, 1980, decided to embark on a plan to rescue the hostages. The mission was actually undertaken on April 24; it was, however, canceled on April 25 in a grim scene of death and destruction at an airstrip code-named Desert One in a remote section of Iran. "The full story of the aborted mission may not be known for years, or even decades," according to *The New York Times* military analyst Drew Middleton (*New York Times Magazine* 1981, 103). The rescue mission again served three basic symbolic functions. First, it came when the crisis had become an American obsession that the media and the president had managed to make a centerpiece of national attention and a series of fruitless attempts at a negotiated settlement had left the public fully frustrated at U.S. impotence. The rescue attempt, half-hearted as it seems in retrospect, may be interpreted, therefore, as an effort by President Carter to assert the national will and to regain national solidarity behind his leadership. Second, the mission came at a time when President Carter's popularity and campaign efforts were facing serious setbacks. While earlier in the crisis his presidential posture in defense of the hostages' lives had served him well against Senator Edward Kennedy and others in depoliticizing the issue, his inability to solve it was becoming a symbol of his weaknesses in foreign policy. Although the mission cost him the services of a respected secretary of state, Cyrus Vance, he emerged from this crisis as a president willing to use force when necessary. Finally, the strict limitations he had imposed on the use of this force served to symbolize his intentions to contain the conflict, while possibly ensuring the failure of the mission right from the start.

Resumption of Negotiations

Negotiations were resumed for a second time only at the initiation of the newly constituted Iranian Majlis (parliament) and government, which were both controlled by the radical clerics. For the clerics, the hostages had by now served their threefold symbolic function of whipping up sagging national enthusiasm, undermining the position of the secular liberals, and mobilizing world public opinion in support of the Iranian cause. In fact, the Iraqi invasion of September 22, 1980, dwarfed the hostage issue as a rallying cry, while it brought home to the clerical faction the liberals' claims that the issue was increasingly isolating Iran and making it vulnerable. In the negotiations that followed, the positions of the two sides shifted from symbolic to substantive issues—the release of the hostages as a quid pro quo for the return of Iranian assets frozen in the American and European banks. The complex settlement that was reached through the mediation efforts of Algeria had to reconcile Western banking interests with Iran's desire to receive the full return of its assets. Iran's decision to pay off the entire $3.67 billion in outstanding low-interest loans with Western banks, while setting aside another $5.1 billion against American and European claims, contributed to the financial settlement. The financial loss to Iran in this transaction was substantial. Iran thus gained little and paid heavily in political and economic terms, while the United States suffered in prestige and mental anguish.

The Catharsis

The tumultuous welcome the hostages received upon their return home symbolized in no uncertain terms the extraordinary significance of this affair in recent U.S. history. It also underlined the symbiotic power of the media in combination with the presidency to focus on a single issue for 444 days to the detriment of most other domestic and international issues. After the humiliations of Vietnam and Watergate, the hostage crisis symbolized to some yet another facet of a weakening America. A nation yearning to believe in itself seized upon the hostage crisis and its victims/heroes as symbols of traditional American virtues of quiet strength under stress. The crisis also presented a test case for the Carter presidency. As Steven Weisman put it,

> . . . a president who had risen to office because of his mastery of symbolism, achieving its height in his walk down Pennsylvania Avenue on Inauguration Day, met his fate in large measure because Iran had become a symbol of what Americans had come to dislike about their country—its seeming inability to get control of events and serve as the master of its fate (New York Times Magazine editors 1981, 120).

For this symbolism, President Carter has to share some of the responsibility along with the U.S. media, which often act in consonance rather than dissonance with the presidency. In 1968, for instance, when thirty-eight U.S. crewmembers aboard the intelligence ship Pueblo were seized by North Korea, the hostages were not made into a media event. 'It is true," George Ball pointed out, "they were naval personnel, but they were in much worse shape, because they were tortured, and they were kept for nearly a year (New York Times Magazine, 1981, 117). Subsequent to their release, the media once again responded to the presidency when it relegated the hostages to its back pages. As in the case of Vietnam, the nation wished to forget and opted for a collective amnesia. The symbiotic relation between the presidency and the media, particularly on issues of foreign policy, was well brought out by the comments of Jeff Gralnick, executive producer of ABC's "World News Tonight":

> If the government had nothing to say, except that it would run things as if no crisis existed and we will negotiate quietly until they are released, the media would not have been able to do anything with the Iran story (New York Times Magazine editors 1981, 117).

CONCLUSION

This chapter does not argue for a mediacentric view of contemporary international relations. It suggests, however, that a combination of three circumstances has created an extraordinary role for the media and the "image politics" they generate. The rapid and worldwide expansion of telecommunication facilities leading to the universalization and personalization of international communication, the mobilization of untold millions into the position of actors on the stage of history, and the gradual creation of transnational channels of communication (e.g., international news agencies, professional and scientific associations, international forums) have created multiple crossnational actors and audiences and have thus blurred the traditional boundaries between domestic and international politics. Thus, for every public act a statesman undertakes today, he or she must calculate its substantive as well as its symbolic significance in relation to a great number of interests and audiences.

"For international or world public opinion to develop as a political force," W. Phillips Davison has proposed, "three requirements must be fulfilled: People in several countries must give their attention to a given issue; they must have sufficient means of interacting so that common and mutually reinforcing attitudes can form; and there must be some mechanism through which shared attitudes can be translated into action . . ." (Davison 1973, 874). If we accept Davison's three criteria, the hostage crisis illustrates how under certain circumstances and with respect to certain emotionally charged issues (threats of nuclear war, revolutions, acts of terrorism), image politics can become a factor of autonomous importance. The hostage crisis received relentless international attention, particularly in the two countries involved; the worldwide networks of travel, the press, and electronic media provided sufficient means of interaction among elements of the two nations (Iranian students and exiles in the United States, U.S. clergymen, journalists, congressmen in Iran) so that a dislike for the support of the shah's dictatorship and disfavor for hostage-taking tactics gradually evolved in the two countries; and, finally, these sentiments were translated into a settlement that resolved the crisis. The settlement did not come, however, until the two sides had exhausted the symbolic uses of the issue in their own domestic politics.

For the United States, as a superpower, the hostage crisis also marked a turning point in its climate of opinion—from aversion to war and foreign entanglements born out of Korean and Vietnam experiences to one of support for assertiveness and military preparedness. As Yankelovich and Kaagan argue on the basis of their 1980 public opinion polls,

> Americans have become surprisingly explicit about how the United States should seek to regain control of its destiny, and in the context of the disquieting realities of the 1980s, these ideas create a new, different and complex foreign policy mandate for the Reagan presidency. The national pride has been deeply wounded; Americans are fiercely determined to restore our honor and respect abroad. This outlook makes it easy for the Reagan Administration to win support for bold, assertive initiative, but much more difficult to shape consensus behind policies that involve compromise, subtlety, patience, restrained gestures, prior consultation with allies, and the deft geopolitical maneuvering that is required when one is no longer the world's preeminent locus of military and economic power" (Yankelovich and Kaagan 1981, 696–97).

One consequence of this has been the dramatic rise in the defense budget; another will be renewed efforts by the Reagan administration toward what one author has called "public diplomacy"—the dissemination of America's message abroad—expected to "become Washington's major growth industry over the coming four years" (Adelman 1981, 913).

For Iran, as a small power in the grip of a revolutionary upheaval, the hostage crisis suggested once again its weaknesses and vulnerability to international political, economic, and public opinion pressures. Despite its doggedness, the clerical leadership in Iran failed in the end to achieve any of its original objectives: the return of the shah and his wealth, a public apology from the United States for its past interferences in Iran, and world sympathy for its cause. Despite its seeming resilience to outside opinion, the Iranian leadership also had to bow to the pressures exerted from foes as well as friends for the freedom of the hostages. World public opinion in favor of diplomatic immunity in the meantime had undermined the initial domestic support in Iran for hostage-taking.

Beyond these considerations, this chapter suggests the threats as well as the promises that the new telecommunication facilities offer for the conduct of international relations. The threats are very real: the menace of unreality. What Daniel J. Boorstin (1975) has said of America is now perhaps true for an increasingly "Americanized" world:

We risk being the first people in history to have been able to make their illusions so vivid, so persuasive, so "realistic," that they can live in them. We are the most illusioned people on earth. Yet we dare not become disillusioned, because our illusions are the very house in which we live; they are our news, our heroes, our adventure, our forms of art, our very existence.

The Iranian people were no less victimized by this particular pathology than the Americans during the hostage crisis.

On the other hand, the new telecommunications provide unprecedented facilities for the construction of those channels of genuine transnational communication that could give global interests and the world community an extraordinary opportunity for development. For this task, professional communicators (politicians, artists, scientists, journalists, publicists, teachers, clergy) have both a special training and a special obligation.

ACKNOWLEDGMENTS

This work was prepared for presentation at the Fourth General Assembly of World Future Society, July 18– 22, 1982, Washington, D.C. A different version, under the title of "International Communication: A Dialogue of the Deaf?" appeared in *Political Communication and Persuasion*, 2:2, 1982. The author is deeply grateful to the East-West Communication Institute and its former director, Dr. Jack Lyle, for their generous and continuing support of his work. Thanks are due also to Cherylene Hidano for her kind and efficient secretarial help.

REFERENCES

Adelman, Kenneth L. 1981. Speaking of America: Public diplomacy in our time. *Foreign Affairs* 59:4, 913– 36.

Ashley, Richard K. 1981. Political realism and human interests. *International Studies Quarterly* 25:2, 204– 36.

Bell, Daniel, 1973. *The Coming of Post Industrial Society: A Venture in Social Forecasting*. New York: Basic Books.

Boorstin, Daniel J. 1975. *The Image: A Guide to Pseudo-Events in America*. New York: Atheneum.

Brandt, Willy, et al. 1980. *North-South: A Programme for Survival*. London: Pan Books.

Davison, W. Phillips. 1973. International and world public opinion. In *Handbook of Communication*, edited by Ithiel de Sola Pool et al. Chicago: Rand McNally College Publishing Co.

Dordick, Herbert S., Helen G. Bradley, and Burt Nanaus. 1981. *The Emerging Network Marketplace*. Norwood, New Jersey: Ablex Publishing Corp.

Gerbner, George, et al. 1981. The information society. *Journal of Communication*, 31:1, winter, 131– 94.

Habermas, Jurgen. 1971. *Knowledge and Human Interests*, trans. by J. Shapiro. London: Heinemann.

Hertz, John H. 1981. Political realism revisited. *International Studies Quarterly* 25:2, June, 182– 97.

Katz, Elihu. 1981. In defense of media events. Chapter 4 in *Communications in the Twenty-First Century*, edited by Robert W. Haigh, George Gerbner, and Richard B. Byrne. New York: John Wiley and Sons.

Kumar, Krishan. 1978. *Prophecy and Progress: The Sociology of Industrial and Post-Industrial Society*. New York: Penguin.

MacBride, Sean, et al. 1980. *Many Voices, One World*. Paris: UNESCO.

Morgenthau, Hans J. 1978. *Politics Among Nations: The Struggle for Power and Peace*, 5th ed. New York: Knopf.

New York Times Magazine Editors. 1981. America in captivity: Points of decision in the hostage crisis. *The New York Times Magazine*, Special Issue, spring.

Nordenstreng, Kaarle, and Herbert I. Schiller. 1979. *National Sovereignty and International Communication*. Norwood, New Jersey: Ablex Publishing Corp.

Porat, Mark. 1977. *The Information Economy*. Washington: U.S. Department of Commerce, Office of Telecommunication Policy.

Tehranian, Majid. 1979a. Iran: Communication, alienation, revolution. *Intermedia* 7:2.

Tehranian, Majid, 1979b. Communication and international development: Some theoretical considerations. *Cultures* 6:3.

Tehranian, Majid. 1980. The curse of modernity: The dialectics of modernization and communication. *International Social Science Journal* 32:2.

Waltz, Kenneth N. 1979. *Theory of International Politics*. Reading, Mass.: Addison-Wesley.

Yankelovich, Daniel, and Larry Kaagan. 1981. Assertive America. *Foreign Affairs* 59:3, 696– 713.

THE NEWS MEDIA IN
INTERNATIONAL CONFLICT

CHAPTER 6

TELEVISION IN
INTERNATIONAL CONFLICT
Elie Abel

Although this chapter focuses primarily upon television in international conflict situations, the reason for singling out television has nothing to do with the intrinsic merits of the medium. Print, or even radio, does a better job of handling complexity, and complexity is characteristic of most international conflicts. We are bound to look closely at television's performance for one reason—the vast multitudes it reaches and influences in ways never fully charted by students of the medium.

LIMITATIONS OF TELEVISION NEWS COVERAGE

Telling the news on television is perhaps the least natural, certainly the least spontaneous, of communication processes. Here I speak from personal experience over a nine-year period in the sixties. The late Edward R. Murrow, that giant among broadcast journalists, confessed that he had never felt at ease before the camera. "Whenever that red light went on," he said, "I felt as if there were a mass of molten lead in my stomach. I never got over it. You won't either." Murrow was using the past tense because, for him, the ordeal had ended. Mine was just beginning.

What prompted Murrow's confession was the fact that I had started doing television news and commentary and he had observed that I tended to look nervous—or in pain—on the tube. He was being compassionate, the grizzled veteran offering cold comfort to a novice. Murrow was, of course, a founding father of broadcast news. He had been at the job almost daily since the Munich crisis of 1938. Yet even after all those years on the air— the early years in radio and, by my reckoning, a full decade after that on television—he did not feel comfortable on camera. I found it somewhat reassuring to learn that Murrow, the most admired professional of his time, found it as difficult as I did to address his carefully scripted lines to the cold glassy eye of the camera as if he were talking to live people.

Working in a medium that assigns major priority to physical appearances — how the newscaster looks and sounds — is an element of strain. Details of dress, lighting, voice quality, and even makeup tend, I suggest, to count for a great deal in American television, rather more than understanding of the issues, experience, clarity of thinking, and presentation. Any number of successful broadcasters have acknowledged that television imposes certain cosmetic requirements. According to one experienced practitioner, the image a broadcaster projects necessarily includes "a whole bunch of intangibles . . . magnetism, style, tilt of the head, animalism, a whole bunch of things that can't be bottled" (Jensen 1978). These are among the qualities that President Ronald Reagan brought to the presidency, the qualities that make him a more effective communicator than his recent predecessors.

Journalistic excellence is, I suggest, far from being the chief determinant of success in American television. I take a shred of comfort from the recent rise to prominence on CBS of Charles Kuralt, who appears to defy many of the conventions that television networks live by. He is rather stout, mostly bald, and stubbornly nontheatrical. Kuralt, moreover, is well informed, a good writer, and a perceptive reporter. He remains, however, the shining exception in an industry dedicated above all to mass entertainment. The news and public affairs departments of our commercial networks can be compared to a caboose, rattling along at the end of a long string of railroad cars. It is mass entertainment that supplies the motive power, building audience and advertiser appeal. The fact that the industry as a whole lives by show business values dictates its episodic attention to public affairs. Substantial ignorance of issues and events has not, to my fairly certain knowledge, severely handicapped the advancement of many anchorpersons. As long as the competitive ratings hold up, these men — and they are still chiefly men even in this enlightened age of sexual equality — continue to prosper.

What I have said till now may strike some as a diversion from the topic of this book. I would argue, to the contrary, that it bears directly upon the discussion of international conflicts and the role played by the media, at least in the United States. It is not, I believe, a gross exaggeration to suggest that certain characteristics of television news are inherent in a value system that can be traced back to the show business origins of our commercial networks, and that its shortcomings as a medium of information, above all in crisis situations, have something to do with that value system. One has only to sit through an evening of prime time television in Britain or France or the Federal Republic of Germany to understand that other countries live by other values.

It may be useful to begin this assessment with a short checklist of certain salient features associated with news on television. There is:

- The tyranny of the clock;
- The powerful pull of spectacle;
- The concentration upon events, which are visual, as against ideas or trends, which may not be; and
- Above all, the search for dramatic unity as if the television journalist were writing a three-act play with a beginning, a middle, and an end, when in fact he is dealing with fragments of reality as they come to light day by day.

The imperious clock, not unique to American television, is the most obvious of these salient features. The time allotted to news programs varies from country to country, but whether the system schedules ten or twenty or even thirty minutes for news (mostly in the early evening), each fleeting moment is treated as pure gold. There can be no dallying or digression. Each item of news that can be slotted into the program must be concise, uncomplicated, and swiftly paced. The inescapable effect of this forced compression is frequently a loss of nuance, qualification, or perspective. Nothing is gained by reproaching the reporter or anchorperson for superficiality or distortion. Walter Cronkite has made the point that a newspaper can make room for lengthy, complicated items on its inside pages but that television news is all front page.

Only when the camera is eavesdropping on an historic happening (Anwar Sadat in Jerusalem, the recent royal wedding in London, a World Cup soccer final, the funeral of a fallen leader) does television free itself from the tyranny of time. It is not, perhaps, accidental that on such great occasions television seems to be at its best, its most memorable. It becomes the great unifier, creating a community of shared feeling and excitement across a nation and, in some cases, around the world. Many of these events are, of course, carefully staged, not, however, by television producers. The Prince of Wales did not in fact marry his princess for the sake of that vast international television audience, even though the camera shots inside St. Paul's Cathedral made magnificent television images. The absence of commercial interruptions helps mightily to sustain the mood of the occasion. But there are other hazards. A contemporary critic noted that the network commentators seemed intent not only on convincing the audience that the event was "historic" but also on emphasizing their own roles in it.

A shrewd judgment, I believe. The intrusive babble added little to this viewer's experience of the event. I recall learning that lesson from a viewer in California back in 1963 as President Kennedy's funeral cortege, led by a riderless horse, was making its way along Pennsylvania Avenue in Washington. The caller pleaded for less talk from my colleagues stationed along the line of march. "We can scarcely hear the drums," she complained. "The beat is so very moving. Please tell them to talk less." My caller had it right, I felt at the time. Those muffled drums needed no explication. They spoke directly to a grieving woman as they did to millions of others.

TV COVERAGE OF PSEUDO-EVENTS

We are all familiar with Boorstin's (1971) distinction between events, real events, and what he has called pseudo- or nonevents. Television is not fastidious about such distinctions. It feasts on wars, insurrections, hostage-takings—all of these legitimate events by Boorstin's definition. But television is equally hospitable to pseudo-events: press conferences, hearings, so-called photo opportunities, contrived confrontations designed to catch the camera's eye to dramatize a cause or issue, and gimmicks devised for commercial exploitation. Let me suggest that Boorstin's distinction is difficult to apply in all circumstances. There is a quality of ambiguity about certain happenings that defies resolution. Consider, for example, the scene that was reenacted day after day on our home television screens in front of the United States Embassy in Tehran in 1980.

That first day and for a day or two thereafter we were, I suppose, observing a real event. A group of Iranians calling themselves students had violated the extraterritorial rights of the United States Embassy, seized the compound, and taken hostage all staff members who were not occupied elsewhere at the time. Here was an overt expression of the depth of feeling among a group of Iranians against the departed shah and his American allies. No one will argue, I suspect, that the embassy takeover was not real news. The difficult question was to decide how long it would be treated as real news: Two days longer? A week? A month? At what point did these carefully stage-managed demonstrations become a pseudo-event? You will recall how day after day, for many wearying weeks, we were shown the same dismal scene: downy-cheeked boys and grizzled elders shouting "Death to Carter!" and "Death to the shah!" in raucous unison, burning both in effigy, hurling imprecations against "The Great Satan" and shaking their fists on cue. Day after day we winced at the sight. But what did we learn, what could we have learned, from all that shouting and fist-shaking? Had a whole nation gone berserk? Did other Iranians approve of the hostage-taking? Was nothing else happening in Tehran? Were the peasants outside the capital still working their land? What was going on in the oil-fields and refineries? There were so many questions, so few answers. And there was no direct contact between the two governments. From time to time Iran's foreign minister or President Abholhassan Bani-Sadr would appear to be sending a message to Washington through the camera crews, in the absence of official channels. But it was all too clear that these gentlemen were not in charge of events inside Iran.

We cannot in fairness charge the network crews with lack of enterprise; I am sure they tried to do more than they were allowed to do. Suppose they had attempted to roam elsewhere in the city and indeed to other regions of the country. Even if the authorities, such as they were, had allowed them free movement, their home offices expected daily coverage of the noisy charade outside the embassy. Thus day after day, until the crews were finally expelled from Iran, that was what we saw and heard. The deeper problem was that most of the correspondents, through no fault of their own, were poorly equipped to understand and explain the convulsion Iran was experiencing. They were transients, flown into Tehran at the first hint of trouble in all but total ignorance of Iran's language, history, politics, or culture. These were not specialists with the benefit of long years of residence in the country such as Eric Rouleau, the correspondent of *Le Monde*, whose dispatches offered a depth of perspective other correspondents could not match.

The technological revolution we are living through has, by my observation, decimated the ranks of resident network correspondents. The jet plane, the satellite, and electronic newsgathering techniques have seen to that. Why keep a highly paid and presumably competent correspondent in one post long enough to understand the play of social and political forces in his assigned country or region when he may not get air time for weeks on end? The networks today shuttle correspondents and crews around the world as if they were chessmen; they seem to concede that expertise and seasoned judgment belong in newspapers and magazines, but not on the tube. The few overseas bureaus the networks still maintain (in London, for example) are essentially forward bases from which they can dispatch reporters, cameramen, and equipment on a moment's notice to Iran, Pakistan, or Nigeria. They rush in, alerted by the news agencies to the possibility of action, do a piece or two, and then they are off again, like firemen, to the next hot spot. Most know little about the country when they arrive, and they don't stay long enough to learn a great deal more before they are reassigned. The product we see on the evening news is marvelously fresh, almost instantaneous. It is also marvelously superficial.

An event, however defined, is easier to report than a trend or an idea. It takes less time, meets the definition of hard news more squarely, and is, of course, inherently visual. Hence the preoccupation with the hostage story and the angry scene outside the Tehran embassy. To have explored the nature of the Islamic movement, the sources of the ayatollah's power, and at least the *recent* history of the shah's regime that led to his downfall would have made for more understanding on the part of the public; but that task clearly would have strained the resources of the TV crews and, I concede, produced less vivid imagery on the home tube.

Finally, the dramatic element. Reality does not come neatly packaged in two- or three-minute lengths; raw history is filled with perversities, contradictions, ragged edges; it is not in fact history until the event has been weighed, measured, compared, and assayed by a person trained to make judgments of this sort. There is no time for that laborious process in the news business, nor are reporters equipped to hand down definitive judgments about the long-term significance of events they have witnessed. TV is a storytelling medium. It abhors ragged edges, ambiguities, and unresolved issues. One of our younger critics makes this point:

> Camera techniques and editing styles aside, news is shaped fundamentally like any other TV drama. News reporters feel compelled to find individual people to symbolize each story. Sometimes they are "spokesmen," sometimes "experts," sometimes random representatives of some beleaguered group. Always they are personally, passionately, involved.
>
> A news story works better if the antagonists are physically different—a man and a woman, a black and a white, a young person and an old one, someone obviously rich and educated and someone else obviously ignorant or poor. . . . The differences may be purely incidental but dramaturgically useful in getting an audience to identify with one side or the other (Henry 1981, 146).

The effect all too frequently is to impose upon an event or situation a preconceived form that alters reality, heightening one aspect at the expense of another for the sake of a more compelling story, blocking out complications that get in the way of the narrative. We have seen this process of story-shaping at work in TV reports on any number of international conflict situations—the Middle East, El Salvador and Nicaragua, the Indian Subcontinent—as well as in purely domestic conflicts.

TELEVISION'S RESPONSIBILITY

My purpose here is not to condemn or criticize TV as a news medium so much as to understand its characteristics and its limitations. Its salient role as the prime source of information for millions of people in many parts of the world can scarcely be overstated. TV's unique quality is that it makes ordinary people (regardless of class, race, or degree of literacy) feel that they are witnessing, indeed that they are part of, a distant event. It is the most accessible of media because it makes so few intellectual demands upon the viewer. Its power to engage the emotions more completely than radio or newspapers do, however, raises a question of responsibility. It can be used to amuse, to stupefy, to whip up nationalist feelings; it can also be used (less effectively, I suspect) to educate and uplift, to counter superstition and xenophobia, to teach that strangers are not necessarily enemies.

Because television everywhere operates by permission of the state and in most countries is directed and controlled more or less directly by government, it also can serve as an instrument of national mobilization. It is a medium whose patriotism can seldom be challenged. Even in the United States, former Vice President Spiro Agnew notwithstanding, TV is an infrequent critic of the status quo. That was true, I believe, even at the height of the Vietnam fighting when a few prominent broadcasters were moved to depart from their traditional detachment and call for an end to the killing and dying. This was dissent in the name of a higher patriotism, as they would have defined it. But the larger number of broadcasters did not distinguish themselves by publicly questioning the wisdom of presidential policy. They did, of course, turn their cameras on antiwar demonstrations, making the public aware of the movement's rising strength, but that was done for the most part without taking a position on the war itself. The day-to-day erosion of public support for the war owed more to the cumulative effect of filmed reports from Vietnam by network reporters than to any show of advocacy by the big-name commentators. These were necessarily reports from one side of the battle line. But large numbers of Americans came away from watching them with the depressing thought that the war was not being won, in spite of all the upbeat communiques from Saigon, and that in all probability it could not be won. In living color, those pictures from the front were anything but upbeat.

We may, in short, be asking more of television than it can reasonably be expected to deliver. There is room for improvement, admittedly; cosmetic requirements can be played down, time constraints eased. But TV, as it is structured and controlled today, is likely to remain a medium that cannot—or dare not—be too far out of step with the national consensus. In most countries, where TV operates as an arm of the state or ruling party, it cannot do otherwise. In the comparatively few countries, including the United States, where government does not control TV content, competitive business pressures tend to ensure that its programming will not alienate significant portions of the audience or the advertisers.

It has been said that the mass media in the United States today have become an independent power center. I suggest that their actual power has been overestimated, because their independence or autonomy has been overstated. In situations of international conflict to which the United States is a party, TV in particular only seldom feels free to play the role of third party, sufficiently autonomous, that is, to take positions that diverge markedly from the national consensus. For a decently skeptical view of government claims and contentions, cutting through the propaganda and the righteous posturings we can expect from any government caught up in a major conflict, we must continue to look to the print media, at least in those countries where newspapers and magazines are more or less free of state control.

REFERENCES

Boorstin, Daniel J. 1971. *The Image, A Guide to Pseudo-Events in America.* New York: Atheneum.

Jensen, Jim. 1978. As quoted in *Broadcasting*, August 28, 1978, p. 42.

Henry, William A., III. 1981. "News as Entertainment: The Search for Dramatic Unity." In *What's News: The Media in American Society*, edited by Elie Abel. San Francisco: Institute for Contemporary Studies.

CHAPTER 7

THE ROLE OF THE MEDIA IN THE U.S.-IRANIAN CONFLICT
Hamid Mowlana

STRUCTURAL CONSTRAINTS ON THE MEDIA

The crucial question in the analysis of the media in international conflict is not so much what the media *can* or *should* do, but rather how the media *do* operate under certain structural conditions and in response to particular environmental factors. In other words, what constraints inherent to the structures of the media ultimately govern the media and, at times, prevent them from performing optimally?

Despite the fact that the media not only reflect but also have functional relationships to public controversies both within and among nations, their role in conflict management is, at best, a tenuous one. Conflict management, or as Arno defines it in his introduction to this volume, "the social process of allowing conflict to run its course and perform its beneficial functions in society without becoming destructive to basic structural relationships," implies an awareness of a responsibility for defusing tension in a reasoned, empathetic, and comprehensive way, mindful of short- and long-term consequences for all parties involved. It also suggests that the managers are knowledgeable about, and have at their disposal, a variety of resources to reduce conflict.

This idealized picture of a conflict manager rarely applies to those pervasive yet too often culture bound and parochial products of our modern, large-scale societies—the mass media. Blinded by their adherence to the false concept of "objectivity," the media perceive themselves as somehow operating outside society, eschewing all responsibility for what takes place within it.

The media are more appropriately viewed as unwilling and unwitting participants in the social process as opposed to enlightened managers of or neutral third parties to it. Moreover, their participatory roles vary with

71

the circumstances in which they find themselves. And this role differentiation is exacerbated by the refusal of the media to place themselves in social
contexts and view events in terms of structural considerations and historical patterns.

Given the volatility and unpredictability of conflict situations and the
media's reluctance to provide either context or overview, the normative
question of what media *can* do to reduce enmity is less important than what
media actually *do* to either increase or diminish conflicts. This more realistic perspective encompasses the activities of both the media and the larger
sociopolitical structures of which they are a part (Mowlana 1975). In this
sense it reveals not only the cultural, structural, financial, and time-bound
aspects of the media, but also other competing channels of information
that either hinder or facilitate mass media messages (Mowlana 1976).

Since the case study approach is one of the most applicable to this type of
in-depth analysis, it might prove useful to investigate a relatively recent
conflict situation that received an inordinate amount of media attention
and was characterized by cultural misunderstandings and political confusion—the Iranian Revolution and the U.S.-Iranian conflict.

A keystone of stability for, and a vital advocate of, the U.S. interests in the
volatile and strategic Middle East for more than two decades, Iran was also
on the feeder end of a global umbilical cord through which passed the
industrial world's sustenance—oil. Thus, it is not difficult to understand
why the world in general, and the United States in particular, began to look
more closely at the unrest that threatened the monarchy of Mohammad
Reza Pahlavi in early 1978. But, as is the case with most modern events of
international significance, this increased scrutiny was largely performed
by, and therefore interpreted through the eyes of, the media.

REPORTING OF IRAN BEFORE THE REVOLUTION

Sporadic but consistently supportive coverage of the Iranian royal regime
by the media with their almost total neglect of the social fabric and poten-
tially revolutionary forces in Iran during the last two decades played a crucial role in the eventual U.S.-Iranian conflict as it manifested itself in the
late 1970s. It is difficult to alter significantly the views of Americans who
have formulated attitudes on world affairs, particularly through mass media alone, and most media reinforce the original views of individuals more
frequently than they alter them. But regardless of the extent to which attitudes can be influenced, the media are often capable of affecting the mood
of individuals or larger groups. Therefore, it is plausible to assume that the
media at worst created radically biased stereotypes detrimental to the
emerging government of Iran, or, in a more objective but culturally limited
spirit, created a mood of uncertainty in the United States regarding the

Confessions of a Storyteller

During the preparation of this chapter, I was encouraged by my friends and colleagues to include some personal anecdotes about my own experiences with the U.S. media since the onset of the Iranian Revolution, anecdotes that up until now I had only shared with a few through the oral tradition of storytelling. The suggestion greatly appealed to me for several reasons.

First, I feel the concept of storytelling provides a very interesting framework for the study of the act of reporting, no matter how "sophisticated" the form.

Second, my academic interest in the subject of this piece naturally stems from both my heritage as an Iranian and my professional background as a working journalist in both the United States and in Iran and now as a professor and observer/analyst of trends in communication, the media, and politics. In short, it is difficult to separate one's personal experience from what one studies.

Third, although they are not sufficient to corroborate hypotheses empirically (in the strict sense of the word), the array of personal encounters that we all experience, either as experts or laypersons, tends to give us a certain grounding in the ideas we espouse.

Finally, but most important, I find the act of storytelling, something we probably associate most with our childhood but engage in daily as adults, to be a very effective and human form of communication, one that creates the kind of experiential linkages that ultimately enrich our analyses of ourselves and outside phenomena.

legitimacy of the new Islamic state. This point not only illustrates a precedent for the media's reporting of Iran, but it implies that the media had already played a participatory role in creating feelings and distinct cultural misperceptions in the United States vis-à-vis Iran. Indeed, for more than two decades, an iron triangle of media-government-academe, through reports, policies, and research, had created a mood or a frame of mind about the shah, Iran, and its people. This suggests that foundations of hardening public opinion about Iran had been laid down prior to the 1978–79 Iranian Revolution and continued to exist through the next three years of Iran's postrevolutionary history, including the period of the so-called hostage crisis.

The success of the CIA operation in 1953 that overthrew the popular and nationalistic government of Dr. Mohammad Mossadegh and brought Mohammad Reza Shah Pahlavi back to power, paradoxically, was the failure of U.S. diplomacy in Iran. The cost of this venture, we were told by the then-in-charge CIA operative, Kermit Roosevelt, was less than a million dollars. But it is now clear that it was a multibillion dollar misunderstanding.

From the Iranian point of view, the consequence of the 1953 coup was two-fold: The shah and the monarchy in Iran lost legitimacy and the

United States lost prestige. Until the 1950s, the tendency was to believe that the American government was genuinely sympathetic to Iranian yearnings for national independence.

How did the United States manage to do so little to counter this tarnishing of its image? What was the extent of the so-called knowledge gap in regard to Iran? The answers lie in examining more closely the unified institutionalized thinking of government, academe, and media in the years the shah was in power.

The most telling example of U.S. governmental myopia was that less than ten days before the shah was forced to flee Iran in 1979, the Carter administration was still confident of the Iranian army's ability to control the situation indefinitely. Both President Carter and his National Security Adviser Zbigniew Brzezinski assured America's West European allies, which were meeting in Guadaloupe, of the Iranian armed forces' superb quality, high discipline, and loyalty to the monarch. Washington not only overestimated the ability of the Iranian army to assume political control (as later evidenced by the short-lived government of General Azhari), but the United States dangerously misread the meaning of the Iranian revolutionary ferment.

The United States comprehended neither the depth of the revolt then underway nor its political, cultural, sociological, and religious ingredients. The problem in the Iranian situation was not so much a lack of information as it was the tendency of the government bureaucrats to limit themselves to information that reinforced their own misperceptions.

It is true that the shah used his own secret intelligence network, SAVAK, to suppress dissent and maintain tight censorship, thus depriving himself of information sources in assessing the domestic undercurrent. But, as is now clear, the United States made virtually no effort to seek information from such sources as British and French intelligence, which unlike our own maintained open access to the opposition forces. Nor did it heed the warnings of numerous observers outside the bureaucracy who had long predicted the ultimate uprising.

It is hardly surprising that the Iranian Revolution caught everyone in Washington by surprise, blindfolded as they were. Commenting on ABC's "Issues and Answers," CIA Director Admiral Stansfield Turner said, "What we didn't forecast was that a seventy-eight-year-old cleric who had been in exile for fourteen years would be the catalyst that would bring these forces together, and that we would have one huge volcano . . . a truly national revolution."

A second factor was the inability of a large segment of the academic community to foresee the spontaneous events of the year and the fall of the regime. A few Iranian and American scholars predicted the surfacing instability and the ultimate downfall of the shah, but their predictions were largely ignored.

Daniel Lerner, a long-time student of modernization and a professor of sociology at the Massachusetts Institute of Technology who had spent four months in Iran working with a national research institute, reported upon his return from Tehran in September 1978: "Let us note that a substantial majority of the Iranians interviewed last May support their regime, believe that it has done a good job in the recent past and expect that it will do even better in the years ahead" (1978).

Not only in 1978 but also during the earlier years, any indication of approval by the population could have been deceptive. Traditional survey research on public opinion always had more problems in Iran than elsewhere, and Western scholars had not found a way of dealing with the Iranian tradition of *taqieh* or crypticism under a repressive regime. *Taqieh* is a technique, rooted in the Shia branch of Islam, to escape the danger of death from those who oppose one's belief, and its utility has been reinforced in Iran by historical realities. From the point of unobtrusive measures, the fall of the shah could more easily have been predicted by analyzing the "palace jokes" circulating in Tehran than by monitoring the reports of the government officials and the media. Similar misperceptions about the Iranian political climate stemmed from a number of otherwise credible sources in the academic field.

Too Many Commercials

In November 1978, the government of Sharif Emami had collapsed, followed by General Azhari's takeover and the declaration of martial law. Already sensitized by the overthrow of the shah, the U.S. news media, particularly network television, tended to cover events, especially acts of violence and protest, as they occurred rather than devote their considerable energies to a careful analysis of what might happen under certain circumstances.

On one occasion, when the political situation had entered an advanced state of deterioration, I was called by the news producer of a Washington network affiliate to appear live on the station's six o'clock news broadcast to comment on the developments in Iran. After cancelling the class I was scheduled to teach that evening and encouraging my students to watch the broadcast, I rushed to the station to be on time for the interview, only to find that my efforts had been to no avail. I waited in the station lobby until 6:30 p.m., when I was finally informed by one of the coproducers that I had been bumped by "too many commercials, but, perhaps, you could come back at another time"!

A classic example is a 492-page area handbook series entitled, *Iran: A Country Study*, published by the Foreign Area Studies, an organization af-

filiated with the American University in Washington, D.C., and funded by
the U.S. government. The third edition (1978), released on the heels of
large demonstrations against the shah in Iran, is intended to give governmental and nongovernmental agencies and individuals dealing with Iran
"basic insights" into the traditions and dominant values of Iranian society,
"their community of interests and the issues on which they are divided, the
nature and extent of their involvement with national institutions, and their
attitudes toward one another and toward the social system and political
order within which they live."

Instead, the book focuses less on Iran's people and more on the shah. His
army, his police force, his judiciary system, his foreign relations, his "White
Revolution," the structure of his government, and his road to modernization appear to obsess the "multi-disciplinary team of social scientists" contributing to the book.

Although, according to its editor, the research for this study was com-
pleted in January 1978, not even a single mention is made of Ayatollah
Ruhollah Khomeini, or such political opposition leaders to the shah as
Mehdi Bazatrgan or Dr. Karim Sanjabi. "Terrorist" groups are referred to
as a "persistent nuisance and embarrassment to the monarch." No mention
is made of the eight years of activities by the Marxist-oriented Fedayeen
Khalgh, and only brief reference is made to the Islamic Mujahedeen, who
at the time formed a rival front in the political activities in Iran. Threats to
the security of the Peacock Throne center instead on the pro-Moscow Tu-
deh (Communist) Party.

The shah's one-party system, created in 1975, is viewed in the country
study as "a political instrument designed to animate the proverbially apathetic citizenry and mobilize them into the government-controlled mainstream of political life." Stated otherwise, Iranians are not yet ready for
participatory democracy.

No mention is made of the reduction in legitimacy of monarchy for Iranians and the corresponding rise of popularity of religious leaders and secular opposition. On the contrary, we are told that "the symbolism of continuity associated with the monarchy is an undeniably important historic
source of strength for the Shah." Thus, in a review of the 1977 political
situation, the reader is given the following evaluation:

> It appeared unlikely . . . that the Shah would be troubled by political destabi-
> lization of any major proportions. Opposition was scattered, ephemeral and
> ineffective; and the organizational outlets were virtually non-existent (For-
> eign Area Studies, 1978, 202).

This perception, coupled with near total disregard for the informal
operations of traditional channels of communication such as *bazaar* and

doreh (Iranian circle of friends), lead the book to assert that the shah's position in Iran was relatively stable. This domestic stability, according to the book, "made for continuity in the direction and structure of Iran's foreign relations."

It appears that the authors carried out their study of Iran through a lens shaped solely by official perspective—a lens whose contours were so ingrained in their minds that the distortion effect went virtually unnoticed.

In a study at the American University, we reviewed all issues of the *Middle East Journal, Foreign Affairs,* and *Foreign Policy* between 1970 and the summer of 1978 to ascertain just what was written on Iran and the shah's regime that might have shown clear indications of gross internal instability and revolutionary portent caused by the Pahlavi dynasty. The review covered approximately 100 issues of these journals combined. Thirty-three articles, twenty from the *Middle East Journal,* seven from *Foreign Affairs* and six from *Foreign Policy* were found that dealt with or contained a significant amount of information on Iran.

Our analysis more than adequately supported our original hypothesis that few of the experts on Iran detected or predicted the revolution that occurred in Iran, at least none of those who wrote for the three journals analyzed. It is acknowledged that many articles did describe problems, some minor and some major. Even these articles, however, missed the mark as far as reporting the grass roots anti-shah sentiment or detecting a popular revolution boiling right beneath the surface.

But the most serious misunderstandings of the Iranian situation in terms of their effect on public opinion were promulgated by the media. The communication media rarely strayed from the administration's official line, in either their perceptions or coverage of the Iranian political upheaval. The images created by the press and broadcasting industries failed to shed any new light on the existing darkness surrounding the American public's search for a better understanding of the facts and implications of Iran's unique political process (Dorman and Omeed 1979, Said 1980).

By limiting themselves to official information sources, the media failed in many instances to live up to their social responsibility of ensuring a free and balanced flow of information to their audience. Consequently, the following myths were created:

- The myth of underlying causes—the media, mistaking superficial appearances for social forces, described the Iranian revolt as a religious reaction against economic change and social modernization. In fact, it was a mass movement to rectify deep-seated economic and social inequalities with the more antiregime religious authorities acting as public spokesmen.

- The myth of the opposition—the Western press, at least initially, failed to present the full spectrum characterizing the "opposition." By depicting all students as "Marxists" and all the religious leaders as "reactionaries" or "radical fanatics," the media not only attached inaccurate labels to these groups but fell short of presenting the comprehensive nature of the opposition.
- The myth of civil war—the movement to oust the shah was frequently referred to as a "civil war." Yet the grass roots revolt was aimed exclusively at one individual and the institution he embodied—the monarchy. A unified, mass revolt against a central authority denoted a revolutionary situation and not a civil war.
- The myth of liberalization—the media continually used the terms "liberalization" to describe the shah's "modernization" programs. These two hardly developed hand in hand in Iran. Suppression of criticism and dissent, press censorship, and the outlawing of political opposition parties did not conjure up an image of liberalization in most minds.
- The myth of concession—the media promulgated the notion that the shah made a great concession by promising free elections to his people. Yet this could hardly be considered a concession, for it was a right guaranteed the Iranian people by their own constitution. Similarly, division of power of the three branches of government, press coverage of parliamentary proceedings, and the inclusion of a group of Moslem clergy as members of the National Consultative Assembly to review legislation were all constitutional rights, and thus could not be construed as concessions unless it was assumed that the government until then had functioned in an unconstitutional manner, which was not an unlikely conclusion.

CULTURAL VALUES AND IDEOLOGICAL FACTORS

Cultural values and ideological frames of reference reduce the media's ability to serve as independent sources of information, particularly in times of international conflict. Given this historical background, it is little wonder that content analysis of the American media during the prerevolutionary as well as revolutionary years found in nearly all the accounts a theme of "leftist-backed," "religious," "reactionary forces" pitted against a shah determined to drag his "stubborn," "backward" people into the present century. The inability of the American media to question the shah's modernization plan and their failure to understand the history and motives of Iranians were important factors in their overall inability to explain the dynamics of the Iranian Revolution. The cultural nearsightedness reflected in the U.S. national interest and the characteristics of both the policyma-

New, Dramatic Developments

From the beginning of the Iranian Revolution, the major U.S. television networks not only realized their lack of knowledge of Iranian culture, history, and religion but also were in search of area experts to add commentary and color to their reporting.

At the request of a Washington producer for one of the major networks, I agreed to participate in a series of special broadcasts on Iran. The same producer bombarded me with telephone calls over the next few months, constantly advising me to remain ready for supposedly imminent production sessions. I continued to be most cooperative, leaving numbers where I could be reached whenever I traveled.

As it turns out, production was either delayed to await "new, dramatic developments," or, in the one instance when a tape was made, it was never broadcast.

In that one set of interviews, my commentary tended to be rather analytical, focusing on the cultural and historical nature of the revolution. But, without exception, the reporters were more interested in crisis and conflict behavior and outcomes, not ideas. Questions on how potential conflicts among ayatollahs might lead to civil war were typical. When I explained that enmity of that nature would not be manifested in the ways we were familiar with, I evoked not interest or a new line of questioning but puzzlement and discomfort on the part of the reporters. My taped interview was never broadcast on that national network.

kers and the media, particularly in viewing religious beliefs and the relationship of religion and society, and the ideological estrangements such as the portrayal of Iranian dissidents as opportunistic religious reactionaries as opposed to the moral, heroic dissidents of the Soviet Union—all presented psychological barriers for Americans covering Iran. As a result of these alienating factors, the media during the last two decades of the shah's regime and the following months of revolution planted stereotypes in the public mind.

It is not surprising, then, that inherent in the demands for the deposed shah's extradition and the return of his wealth was an always explicit assumption that the world, and particularly the United States, needed to be reeducated about the true nature of the shah's regime and about U.S. foreign policy toward the shah. Iran progressed toward this goal through many channels. By whetting the voracious American news appetite and by supporting the United Nations Commission, Iranians succeeded in revealing previously unseen information on the shah's assets and his torture of dissidents. Additionally, nongovernmental organizations, church groups, and individuals played important roles as channels for this reeducation. The purpose of the campaign was a veritable rewrite of U.S.-Iranian history.

In short, once again, the Iranian Revolution proved that ideological and symbolized conflicts are more important than economic or political conflicts in straining international relations (Mowlana 1979a, 1979b).

CRISIS VS CONFLICT

The treatment of the U.S.-Iranian conflict by the United States media as a "crisis" rather than a "conflict" created a fragmentary, ahistorical, and unidimensional picture of the events as they unfolded. The Iranian seizure of the embassy was referred to repeatedly as a "crisis" situation by the media. A definition of crisis accepted by many scholars identifies it as a situation that threatens high-priority goals of a decision-making unit, restricts the amount of time available for response before the decision is transformed, and surprises the members of the decision-making unit by its occurrence. Thus, threat, time, and surprise all have been cited as necessary traits of a crisis (Hermann 1968, 1969). Underlying this definition is the hypothesis that if all these traits are present, the decision-making process will be substantially different than if only one or two of the characteristics appear.

It must be noted that in operationalizing this definition of crisis for research purposes, international relations analysts have used the *New York Times Index* as an indicator of salience and potential threat. The first requirement is a minimum of three *New York Times Index* entries per day, and a minimum of ten additional entries for any event to be considered a high threat. Inherent in this operational definition is the implication that the number of times the press reports an event adds to its salience and, in effect, can create a crisis. In the case of the U.S. embassy seizure in Iran, the *New York Times Index* listed an average of fifteen daily entries from November 4 to December 4, 1980, and an additional five separate but related entries.

The last element, surprise, was a major factor in the taking of the hostages, as was the threat to the high-priority goals of U.S. interests in Iran. But the time element in decision-making precluded the use of this definition of "crisis" in the Iranian situation. The time allotted for a crisis is usually one month for a perceptible change in the situation. The hostages were in Iran for more than a year, and, while there was much dialogue, there had been no perceivable change during this period. Thus it would appear that the term crisis as applied by the media to the hostage situation was in fact a misnomer.

Perhaps a more appropriate characterization would have been that of a conflict situation. Conflict exists when two or more groups make mutually exclusive claims to the same resources or positions. This definition does not impose time constraints or the element of surprise, but it does imply existing threat of loss or gain with respect to a claim. Conflict, unlike crisis, does not necessarily involve a short time period, and therefore it allows for different handling of the decision process and lends itself to the use of various techniques for conflict resolution. In addition, conflict as a characterization connotes real discrepancies in power relationships between nations that demand redress and systemic change as opposed to fleeting aberrations on the international scene that do not affect the political order.

THE MEDIA AND DIPLOMACY

Because the reporting role of the media is in many ways contradictory to that of the traditional pattern of diplomacy, the media in many instances acted as an alternative source of information for diplomats when governmental channels were closed off during the U.S.-Iranian conflict. Diplomacy, the traditional means for conflict resolution, became one of the roles ascribed to the media in the U.S.-Iranian standoff. The classical definition of diplomacy is the application of intelligence and fact to the conduct of official relations between governments' negotiation, reporting, and representation. Diplomatic relations can only be established subsequent to the mutual consent of both parties, and such relations endow the diplomat with certain privileges and immunities from the host's civil and criminal jurisdictions. An examination of performance of diplomatic functions, in the context of these definitions, may shed some light on the media's actual role in the Iranian conflict.

The function of negotiating involves mostly the transmission of messages between two parties, and, regardless of the nature of a message, much depends on the manner and style in which it is delivered. One difficulty for U.S. officials in the situation was the inability to establish contact with the high leadership in Iran, and there was much uncertainty about how much control the various elements in the leadership actually had over the students. All the traditional channels and approaches toward direct diplomatic communication had been closed by both sides.

Thus, with the total breakdown of U.S.-Iranian official communication, the media were burdened with a crucial and delicate role in the confrontation. They had become conduits for semiofficial exchanges, reluctant publicists for the actors, and a valuable source of information for the governments. In addition, the atrophy of diplomatic and trade relations increased both the traffic and significance of messages carried by the mass media and private citizens.

In the early stages of the situation, and in spite of the difficulties that already existed, the Carter administration had apparently favored the traditional approach toward secret negotiations and frowned upon any attempts at "public" diplomacy. Assistant Secretary of State C. William Maynes met with former United Nations Ambassador Andrew Young to discourage him from going to Iran with a group of Iranian experts to seek the hostages' release, and Young agreed not to go (*New York Times*, November 21, 1979). Idaho Congressman George Hansen (who flew to Tehran to see the hostages) was labeled a "crisismonger" by the press and "out of bounds" by House Speaker Thomas O'Neill (*Newsweek*, February 18, 1980b). District of Columbia school board member Frank Shaffer-Corona also met with strong criticism for his appeals to Iranian officials (*Washington Post*, December 19, 1979, p. A18). The State Department ordered telephone companies to refuse all calls from private citizens in the United States to the embassy in order to discourage meddling, and, one correspondent noted after U.N. Secretary General Kurt Waldheim's mission to Tehran that "the effort to free the hostages through diplomatic means seemed to be at a dead end" (*Newsweek*, February 18, 1980a).

THE ROLE OF THE ELECTRONIC MEDIA

Electronic communication, especially live television coverage, created an atmosphere where every action and reaction of the U.S. and Iranian governments, as well as those of other actors, were subjected to instant scrutiny. As the absence of direct diplomatic contact continued, communication through the news media became the quickest channel for the exchange of messages. The result was a series of polemics carried through the news print and the air waves. The following is typical: Tehran—

> Iran's foreign minister today expressed doubts that any of the 50 American hostages here will be freed before Christmas. . . . He (Foreign Minister Sadegh Ghotbzadeh) reported twice that he was using this interview to signal Washington on ways to end the impasse that has dragged on for more than six weeks.

> The State Department took pains yesterday to knock down the latest journalistically conveyed message from Tehran. . . . The latest Washington initiative in the public exchange was a White House statement . . . reinforced by official hints conveyed to reporters as not-for-attribution guidance, that certain types of US military action could be triggered by such a provocation (*Washington Post*, December 19, 1979).

With a daily outpouring of such information, particularly from what appeared to be competing and often conflicting centers of power in Iran, the outcome was often a sense of confusion rather than clarity. For this reason mass communication was widely regarded as an obstacle to the negotiation, mediation, arbitration, or adjudication processes of conflict resolution.

Electronic communication also has increased the accessibility of the leaders to the masses. This immediate contact with their constituencies has a direct impact on daily decision-making. In the United States, of course, government leaders have easy access to national networks of millions of listeners and viewers. When necessary, the entire U.S. population can be mobilized in a few hours.

In U.S. television history, Iran more than any other country became a stock element in the morning and nightly news, often despite the absence of any tangible development. Only the war in Vietnam could compare to the amount of coverage given to the Iranian Revolution and the U.S.-Iranian conflict over the hostage issue. One study reported that during the first six months of the hostage story, nightly coverage of Iran surpassed average nightly coverage given to Vietnam (Adams and Heyl 1981). At the beginning of 1972 more than 150,000 American troops were in Vietnam, and that year the CBS television network devoted a total of 1,092 minutes to events in Vietnam, whereas the amount of the CBS coverage of Iran during the first twelve months of the hostage story amounted to a total of 1,026 minutes. Yet, unlike Vietnam where a substantial number of the media were critical of U.S. policy, the actions and "justness" of the U.S. role with regard to Iran was clearly endorsed by the networks.

In the case of Iran, this instant accessibility to the masses through electronic communication had the same effect both in the United States and Iran. It created a condition of instantaneous demand for and supply of information. It forced plans and courses of action to be evaluated and appraised daily. Even small changes in policy were magnified to the point where government policies and action became susceptible to the immediate reaction of the masses. The triangular relationship of politicians, media, and the public created a plebiscite atmosphere in which every action and reaction was subject to instant scrutiny.

The repercussions of revolution, battles, and terrorist actions on live television, reducing decision time and creating soap-opera-like consumer fare, can be enormously important for the role of the media in international conflict. Would the American government, for example, in a future Iran-type incident, feel compelled to make its military or economic response before the networks have time to turn the hostages and their families into a television drama? To what extent do American television's news reports at home and presence on the scene affect the conduct of governments and outcome of events? Is it possible for the media to maintain a clear distinction between covering an event and participating in it? In the New York Times, James Reston observed the following:

Oddly, but seriously, one of the innocent villains in motivating Carter to want to "do something" was my old buddy, the Ayatollah Walter Cronkite. It seems slightly mad, but it happened to be true, that these characters in the White House really felt some pressure from Uncle Walter's announcing every night the number of days of captivity of the hostages. Nobody really knows why Carter ordered the mission into Iran at this particular time—what combination of political and psychological puzzles made him do it—but we know the results (April 27, 1980).

This observation was shared by many analysts in Washington and elsewhere, including the *Washington Post* columnist Henry Failie (May 11, 1980) who wrote:

It is not right to put the blame on President Carter alone and to exempt, for example, the melodramatic way in which CBS ends its nightly news with the incantation, "And that's the way it is in this, the 185th day of captivity for the Americans in Tehran." That is inflammatory. It is also stupid.

THE ROLE OF INTERNATIONAL TELECOMMUNICATIONS

The growth and concomitant centralization of international telecommunications hardware, combined with the expanding role of transnational media, have increased the motivation for and the possibility of using these developments as tools of foreign policy. As part of his sanctions package against Iran, President Carter on April 17, 1980, proposed an interruption in the Iranian use of communication satellites. Nearly 70 percent of Iran's international telecommunication needs are served by ten communication satellites of Intelsat—an international organization responsible for the smooth operation of this kind of technology. "If a constructive response is not forthcoming soon," said Carter in a prepared statement in reference to Iran's action, "the United States should and will proceed with other measures. We will legally forbid shipment of food and medicine, and the United Nations Charter, as you know, stipulates interruption of communications as a legitimate sanction. Accordingly, I am prepared to initiate consultations with the member nations of Intelsat to bar Iran's use of international communications facilities" (Broad 1980). Later Carter strengthened his position on Iran by saying that "Unless there is immediate action on the part of Iran, these items and the interruption of communications are still available to us. . . ."

The president's proposal to cut off Iran's access to the satellites of Intelsat was quietly shelved, however, partially due to the feelings in Washington and in Intelsat that such an action would set a bad precedent, one with unforeseeable outcomes. Once the use of commercial satellite networks for political purposes began, it would prove difficult to stop. But consideration of such a scenario, coupled with the development of new generation of sophisticated satellites, would open up unseemly visions of space wars and national or regional communication blackouts.

In fact, the role of telecommunications technology, especially satellite communications, proved to be an important one—both during the hostage negotiations and the release of the Americans from Iran. Atlantic basin satellites became so saturated during the release of American hostages that some video transmissions from Europe had to be brought in the back door—double-hopped via Indian and Pacific ocean spacecraft for delivery at Comsat's west coast Earth stations. Comsat was so delighted with its role that it rushed an "instant" TV commercial on the air in Washington, heralding the role of satellite communications during negotiations leading to the hostage release, and for news coverage of hostage arrivals in Algiers, Frankfurt, and Shannon. Video traffic on a normal day amounts to ten to fifteen transmissions totaling eight to ten hours, but according to Comsat, from 4 a.m. on January 20 to 4 a.m. January 21, 1981, there were fifty-three transmissions. During January 15–21, Comsat handled a total of nearly 177 hours of video transmission.

Closely related to this aspect of international communication is the role played in situations such as the U.S.-Iranian conflict and the Iranian Revolution in general by the transnational media such as *Time*, *Newsweek*, the BBC, Voice of America, major international news agencies, and certain nongovernmental but international organizations. The worldwide distribution facilities of these organizations make them authoritative, legitimate, and often the only source of information for the general public as well as policymakers in so-called Third World countries. Their daily reporting of international and national events sets the climate for action and creates reality for those deprived of other sources of information. This was certainly true during the Iranian Revolution of 1978–79 when the people in Iran were deprived of their own media systems. If the exiled press played an important role in the 1906 Iranian constitutional revolution, the international media made the difference in the way the 1978–79 revolution in Iran was reported. It is no surprise, therefore, that exiled groups of Iranians now opposing the Islamic Republic of Iran can do so little with their many newspapers and pamphlets published outside the country. They need to gain legitimacy within the traditional communication systems, such as the ones used by Ayatollah Khomeini during the struggle against the shah, and gain some systematic access to the international network of newsgathering and dissemination.

NATIONAL INTEREST AND LOYALTY

In international conflict, as was illustrated in the U.S.-Iranian case, the media often side with the perceived national interests of the system of which they are a part, making it difficult to maintain journalistic independence and neutrality in the face of patriotism and national loyalty. One function of diplomacy—representation—contradicts the traditional spirit of "objectivity" inherent in the classical role of a journalist; to represent one view over another is to forsake a position of neutrality. It implies the use (voluntary or otherwise) of the media as a tool to be manipulated, a recurring accusation about the media in the U.S.-Iranian conflict. Correspondent Walter Cronkite commented on a television interview with one of the hostages: "(Monday) night's interview with Corp. Gallegos . . . goes to the heart of a classic journalistic conflict. It's the clash between a reporter's duty to learn whatever he can about a story and tell it, and the danger of being used as a propaganda tool. . . ." (*Washington Post*, December 13, 1979).

The first indication of Iran's ability to "use" the media came when word was leaked that Ayatollah Khomeini had granted PBS's Robert MacNeil an exclusive interview. This set all the commercial networks battling for equal access. When the choice was between CBS' 60 Minutes' 50 million viewers and public television's much smaller audience, MacNeil went away empty handed. Mike Wallace received a sixty-minute interview with Khomeini, and ABC and NBC got fifteen minutes each. All three networks had to submit their questions in advance and agree not to broadcast until 6:30 p.m., prime time in New York. The networks faced charges of lending themselves to Iran's propaganda:

I would make the arrangements with anybody who would give a good story, explained Don Hewitt, executive producer of CBS' "60 Minutes" program, and so would the *Washington Post* or anybody else, as long as you level with your audience and tell them how the thing was set up.

So what? asked Stan Opotowsky, ABC's director of television news, . . . The questions are obvious. (Peter) Jennings asked the right ones, the ones you would ask or I would ask.

Here's a guy (the Ayatollah) who's suddenly become a very important figure in this whole thing, and we have to find out what makes him tick, said Ed Plumer, NBC vice president for news.

What it comes down to, said Robert Chandler, director of public affairs for CBS-TV, was do we get an interview with the Ayatollah or don't we? (Bagdikian 1980).

But the item that led to major polemics charging the media with overkill, lack of ethics, and lack of patriotism, was the December 10 NBC interview with one of the hostages. All three networks had negotiated for the interview and all had turned down Iran's restrictions. Only NBC made a counteroffer. The resulting agreement permitted NBC to use its own camera crew and correspondents asking uncleared questions. NBC had the right to reject the whole program if unacceptable and retained full control of the editing. The Iranians would pick the hostage and would get prime-time exposure of the interview, along with an unedited five minute statement.

Reactions to the interview were mixed; approvals were supportive, but critics were sharp and numerous. Ford Rowan, NBC's own correspondent, resigned because he considered the broadcast a "violation of journalistic ethics." The rival networks were the first to accuse NBC of being a propaganda tool. Roone Arledge, president of ABC news and sports said, "It's a setback for those of us trying to operate responsibly in sensitive tension" (*New York Times*, December 12, 1979). The CBS spokesman said "As long as they were dictating the spokesman, the cameras, the hostages, and when we could televise it, they were asking us to be a conduit rather than a journalistic organization" (Bagdikian 1980). Ironically, ABC and CBS each later aired their own interviews with the same hostage, except theirs were produced entirely by the Iranians. "As long as we identified it as a handout . . . and as long as we were free to use it or not . . . it does not breach editorial integrity. We didn't have to pay for it with a five minute vehicle of propaganda" (*The Quill*, January 1980).

Congress and the White House added their remarks. National Security Adviser Zbigniew Brzezinski called the program a "propaganda spectacle." President Carter was reported to be so angry that he turned his TV set off in mid-program and House Speaker Thomas "Tip" O'Neill said it was "regrettable and dangerous" (*Washington Post*, December 12, 1979).

The print media were equally audible. The *Chicago Sun Times* critic called it "obscure" for NBC to give prime time to "a bunch of international hoodlums" (*The Quill*, January 1980). *TV Guide* took out a full-page ad in the *Wall Street Journal*, saying that ratings were being put ahead of national welfare.

On the other hand, CBS Correspondent Walter Cronkite said, "Questions by the NBC reporters did seem vigorous enough and we did learn something, no matter how heavily screened or influenced, of one hostage's views of captivity" (*The Quill*, January 1980). The *Washington Post*'s Haynes Johnson wrote, "The resulting interview was solid, informative, revealing. The NBC questioners and most especially the corporal handled themselves with distinction. Mary's (the reader of the five-minute statement) remarks were seen for what they were, heavy-handed propaganda, only further infuriating Americans who watched" (*Washington Post*, December 13, 1980).

COMMERCIAL AND POLITICAL FACTORS

As opportunism of politicians and the commercial considerations of news media hope fanned the feelings of a significant segment of the American population, the media became the instruments through which individuals, organizations, and government officials could manipulate public opinion and stir mass emotion. It is difficult for the commercial media to avoid playing a part in creating a crisis atmosphere. This is an innate difficulty in the media's function of reporting, and it is a function shared by both professional diplomats and journalists. Diplomatic reporting involves observing the political, economic, military, and social conditions of the host country and accurately transmitting the findings to the home office. Journalistic reporting entails the same duties, with the added responsibilities of meeting standards of so-called "objectivity" (to the audience) and newsworthiness (for the editorial office). Several factors have been identified as contributing to the latter:

1. Brevity of time period involved;
2. Loudness or prominence;
3. Unambiguity as to what occurred;
4. Meaningfulness to the audience;
5. Consistency with the audience's existing ideas;
6. Unexpectedness;
7. Continuity;
8. Balance, relative to available space on air time;
9. Reference to large or powerful nations;
10. Reference to prominent persons;
11. Reference to the "human" dimension rather than only to inanimate objects; and
12. Reference to something negative, such as dishonest officials, a destructive fire, or a war.

Another factor, with which students of television production are familiar, is the availability of film footage. A visual story will usually take precedence over a written one on television news.

If these criteria are used to determine the newsworthiness of a situation, then conflict and crisis stories will receive a great deal of attention. An analysis of several categories of foreign news stories from 1961 to 1963 did, in fact, find that the stronger the element of conflict, crisis, unpleasantness, or inhumanity in a story, the greater the probability it would be reported and given prominence (Galtung and Ruge 1965). Seizure of a U.S. embassy and fifty hostages by student-militants seeking the return of the shah and backed by an ayatollah described as "fanatic," "tyrannic," and "enigmatic" all point to an extremely newsworthy story, and the media were quick to recognize it.

If the first two and a half months of the hostage story, a period in which the American media were allowed to cover Tehran freely, were not an unqualified success for the Iranian revolutionary government or the media, they certainly created new personalities on both media and political scenes and revived the political fortunes of President Carter. Such names as Sadeq Ghotbzadeh (though network newsmen never learned to pronounce his name correctly), Abholhassan Bani-Sadr, Hodding Carter, and even Ted Kopple, became household words in the United States. Meanwhile, the conflict, as it continued, catapulted the president back into favor in every political poll, and the nationalist atmosphere created by the conflict did not help the future of Ted Kennedy, who had dared to criticize the shah.

THE USES AND MISUSES OF THE MEDIA

To the extent that the media did act as a third party in the U.S.-Iranian conflict, they were used, on the one hand, by Iran to reeducate the world about U.S. interventionist foreign policy as well as to legitimize the Islamic revolution and, on the other, by the U.S. to reinforce its position on and perception of the Iranian revolutionary regime. It is difficult to clarify many issues of the continually evolving American-Iranian epic. But with the involvement of the media, there surfaced several salient questions:

1. Did the media, through greed, incompetence, or even ignorance, allow themselves to be manipulated by the Iranians?
2. Did the rush for exclusives lead to excessive exposure of "evil" forces at the expense of "good"?
3. Did television compromise to improve ratings?
4. Did the media create news and heighten the feeling of "crisis," thereby exacerbating the conflict?

Since most actions and information originate with the holders of power who divulge or suppress information in ways most beneficial to themselves, journalists are subject to excessive manipulation by these authority figures. Armed with an abundance of the world's supply of oil and fifty American hostages, Iranians were convinced that justice was on their side. As one reporter stationed in Tehran explained, "they (the Iranian government) believed that if we could be made aware of their grievances—if the public could be told the horrors of the Shah's regime—public opinion, in the U.S. and elsewhere, could force the Shah back to Iran" (*TV Guide*, April 5, 1980).

Since there was from the beginning of this conflict a paucity of information among the participants, and since there existed a very real problem of identifying the ultimate decision-making voice in Iran, the media repeated the statements of all the major characters at the risk of their being repudiated later by counterstatements from members of the same government. By putting the media between the proverbial rock and hard place, the Iranian government was guaranteed news coverage. But the American government also manipulated the media, with equally uncertain results. In the early days of the conflict, the White House requested self-restraint from television and the press for fear of angering the students in Tehran. The resulting news coverage was a poorly balanced, one-sided account of events.

Another point of discussion has been television ethics in compromising the news to improve ratings. Network correspondents reportedly complained that they were being pressured to come up with better "action" than their competitors; and ratings for all three networks rose 18 percent in the six weeks after the embassy takeover. A net of 2 percent above the normal ratings for that period can equal $60 million a year in revenues. A primary component of "news" is its relevance and interest for the public. Ratings are a measure of interest. According to these ratings, the conflict over the hostages in Tehran was of great interest and future consequence. Add to this the networks' other criteria for newsworthiness stated previously, and it became important news. But this raises a new question: Did the media sacrifice quality for quantity in order to satiate this appetite for news?

THE AUTONOMY OF THE MEDIA

By treating the United States and Iran as large, ambiguous entities (i.e., "America Held Hostage"), the media reduced their own autonomy as an independent third party in the conflict. With the exception of a few articles by Harvard University Professor Roger Fisher published in the *New York Times* and by Brown University Professor William Beeman in the *Christian Science Monitor*, no serious attempts were made by the media to see the Iranian side of the story in its cultural and sociopolitical context. Much of the information available at the time to the media, such as mounting pressure from the "old boy network" of the shah's powerful friends to admit him to the United States and *Science* magazine's reporting (Broad 1979) that it was not medically necessary to treat the shah in the United States, were not publicized or reported in the major newspapers and on the television networks.

It was not until the release of the hostages that the *New York Times* editors made an effort to put the hostage negotiations into some accurate historical perspective. In fact the *New York Times* (May 13, 1981) reported that

"Jimmy Carter's decision that ignited the 444-day hostage crisis was based in significant ways on misinformation and misinterpretation of the nature and urgency of the Shah's medical problems." This new perception of that key decision was one of a series that received emphasis in a 40,000-word report of the *New York Times* inquiry entitled "America in Captivity: Points of Decision in the Hostage Crisis" (*New York Times Magazine*, May 17, 1981) by Terence Smith and others. Most of the information contained in the report was available earlier but was not put together and legitimized by the media and the networks that had the greatest audiences.

No Need for Alternative Analyses

In late December 1978, when the shah had been forced to leave the country and Iran was preparing itself for some type of transition, the prevailing ideas among the American press and public about Iran's future can be summarized in the following scenarios:

- There would be a coup d'etat by the shah's army, instituting a military dictatorship not unlike those found in Latin America or the Qaddafi regime.
- Civil war between the royalists and the revolutionaries would ensue (the most prevalent prediction).
- There would be a leftist, Communist takeover.

At that time, I wrote a piece in which I argued that not only would there not be a civil war, but there was also little chance that a coup d'etat would succeed if attempted. My argument was based upon a number of historical and political factors indicating that any efforts by political elites to regain control would fail. Further, I predicted that the Islamic revolutionaries would ultimately take over.

My article was rejected by both of the major Washington dailies (existing at the time) either without explanation or on the grounds that my argument was both implausible and unnecessary given the number of reporters they had on the scene each day.

During the last week of December, when I was vacationing in Florida, on sheer impulse I contacted the managing editor of the *Miami Herald* and offered him the piece that had been rejected by the Washington dailies. The *Miami Herald*, not subject to the same pressures and meglomania of nationally known newspapers, published the article on January 5, 1979. One month later, the situation had so deteriorated that the army was rendered powerless to deal with the revolutionaries. And, of course, by the third week of February 1979, the shah's army had collapsed. The *Miami Herald* was the only U.S. news outlet that presented the possibility of this eventuality.

On the contrary, throughout the hostage story, there was a tendency to see the other side in a simplistic way as a monolithic and largely ambiguous entity. This psychological mechanism takes over when a crisis situation arises between nations whose relations are already distorted by misperception. The crisis pushes the actors, already insecure due to lack of understanding, to retreat into defensive positions. They take refuge in familiar perspectives of the situation, however unrealistic they may be. They tend to define the crisis or conflict in whatever way best confirms their most firmly established perception of the events that led to it.

Most salient in our study of both the *New York Times* and *Kayhan*, the leading newspaper in Iran, during the period of hostage story, was the amount of coverage given to statements concerning moral absolutism (e.g., extremism, fanaticism, irrationality, dictatorialism, martyrdom, religious fervor, zealotry, exaggeration, and radicalism) in the United States as compared with the Iranian paper, especially reflecting what could be interpreted as absolutist positions on the part of the Iranians. Thus American readers were getting a perspective of Iranians as unreasonable extremists and their own leaders as morally absolute, and that perspective was practically absent in *Kayhan*'s treatment of either side's position. The data show, however, that selective inattention was at play in the United States and Iranian papers' treatment of each other's view of the situation. Both sides gave disproportionate attention to the other's leader, not recognizing the weight of public feeling toward the situation. This lack of attention to popular feeling in the opposing nation also illustrates autistic hostility, or expressing hostility by cutting off communication with the other party and thereby eliminating the possibility of achieving empathy.

Through the selective perception of the media, the general American audiences were exposed to "the mad Ayatollah Khomeini" so out of touch with the modern world that he could neither speak English nor identify Mike Wallace of CBS. At one point during Edwin Newman's interview with the Italian journalist Oriana Fallaci on NBC, he asked the Italian writer, who had had an audience with Ayatollah Khomeini, if the Iranian revolutionary leader had ever heard of Blake or Shakespeare. Fallaci's answer was to ask if Newman could name a Persian poet, painter, or philosopher. It was easier to allow the television audience to feel superior to the Ayatollah than to analyze the complex relations existing between the United States and Iran.

Psychodramatic analysis of the revolutionary leaders and the characterization of the Iranian nation in simplistic terms were not confined to media personnel who, although they had little knowledge of Iranian history and culture, were in a position of influence and commentary. It also found its way into the diplomatic cables of the American Embassy in Tehran that were later printed in the media. In one of the excerpts from a confidential cable sent on August 13, 1979, to Secretary of State Cyrus R. Vance and signed by L. Bruce Laingen, charge d'affaires at the embassy in Tehran, the American diplomat went into great length in describing the Iranian psychology:

> Perhaps the single dominant aspect of the Persian psyche is an overriding egoism. Its antecedents lie in the long Iranian history of instability and insecurity which put a premium on self preservation. The practical effect of it is an almost total Persian preoccupation with self and leaves little room for understanding other points of view other than one's own. . . ." (*New York Times*, January 27, 1981).

Laingen did not stop there. After discussing the "bazaar mentality" of the Persian, he concludes that "coupled with these psychological limitations is a general incomprehension of causality." To him "Islam, with its emphasis on the omnipotence of God, appears to account at least in major part for this phenomenon." Otherwise stated, "he (the Persian) is going to resist the very concept of a rational (from the Western point of view) negotiating process." This instant psychoreligious analysis of the Persian character by a diplomat whose training has been in politics and diplomacy reinforced those perceptions already held by the media during the Iranian Revolution. Imagine the impact of these lines, published in the prestigious *New York Times*, on an Iranian policymaker who remembers vividly the assertion of columnist Joseph Kraft in the *Washington Post* during the hostage negotiation that "this country's best interest would be served by the overthrow of the present Iranian government and the establishment of a pro-Western regime in Tehran" (Kraft 1980). Kraft was even more explicit:

> Anwar Sadat has been practically advertising willingness to lead the way. France has important Iraqi connections, a long tradition of influence in Iran and a have-gun-will-travel approach to foreign policy. The Saudis would find occasion to resume their favorite role as paymaster of Arab consensus. Indeed, it is hard to think of any country—Russia and its clients excepted—that would not like a piece of the action.

For all these reasons, many of the positive functions the media may have served in the conflict were overlooked by those involved. These factors, however, suggest not only drawbacks but also potential successes for the media in their role as participants in the U.S.-Iranian conflict.

WHAT COULD THE MEDIA DO?

In conclusion, let us return to a question often raised in discussions of this nature, in which the structure of the media must be kept in mind: What *could* the media do in a conflict situation such as the one just described?

A major function of the media in activating one of the mechanisms for peaceful solutions is to issue reminders that such mechanisms are available. In the case of the hostages, this might have been done through a greater vote of confidence for the U.N. commission's investigation (a fact-finding rather than rescue mission), which was labeled a dismal failure in press reports.

The mass media could contribute to the success of negotiations by helping to ensure that each side is truly familiar with the other's position. This employs the concept of empathy to reduce misunderstandings and distortions through factual reporting of opposing points of view. This perhaps was the single greatest factor leading to accusations of media manipulation in the U.S.-Iranian conflict.

Agreement would also be facilitated if each party were willing to acknowledge publicly and in its own media that it understands the position of the other side, a point suggested by many analysts of the U.S.-Iranian conflict. The mass media also could have called new alternatives to the attention of negotiators and their governments. Since studies indicate that leaders often fail to explore alternatives and may subsequently distort information contrary to their policies, the media might have served as a powerful reminder that alternatives do exist.

In situations of mediation, mass communication can make the mediator's task somewhat easier through media's ability to confer prestige on the mediators. This prestige will depend on treatment accorded mediators by the international press. It is also possible for public channels to inform mediators when it would be impolitic for them to seek out their own information sources. Public coverage of a negotiation (and emphasis of mediatory values) may also facilitate agreement among negotiators if public opinion generally favors it. This is what President Carter tried to achieve by seeking the support of the world public in isolating Iran as a global delinquent. But the values that were emphasized were often Western values of conduct and behavior. Their failure suggests that perhaps more universal concepts of religious, ideological, or traditional values should be used to bridge the existing cultural communication gap. The common aspects of life that unite rather than divide the two cultures could be emphasized.

Perhaps the greatest potential contribution of mass communication to peaceful conflict resolution is in the media's ability to influence the *moods* of government, elites, and the public. It is ironic that the trait of the media that perhaps has done the greatest damage also has the potential for doing the greatest good. The "mood" of the hostage conflict might be characterized, depending on one's perspective, as fanatic, religious intransigence from Iran leading to national frustration in the United States, or as cultural domination of Iran with material and tacit support of oppression by the United States, culminating in the taking of the hostages as a gesture of rebellion against the United States and an international plea for justice for Iran.

The media's capacity to create new attitudes is greatest during periods when international tension is relatively low. Internal struggles during the Iranian Revolution provided fertile soil for sowing receptive, or at least neutral, attitudes regarding the new government's legitimacy and possible grievances, but this apparently did not occur. Once the hostage conflict was underway, the attitudes of both sides became more difficult to alter, and the previously mentioned "hardening" of perception began to crystallize. The power of the mass media to alter such attitudes now rested not so much with creation of a mood, but with avoidance of a "crisis" mood.

As noted previously, the hostage situation was not a crisis by social scientific definition, but it had been repeatedly referred to as a crisis by the media. A perceived crisis hampers the ability to utilize information.

Information utilization occurs most effectively at a moderate stress level where the seriousness of a situation is apparent but it is not perceived as a crisis. A sense of crisis also tends to make people look for more information to justify their fears, and it promotes polarization of attitudes.

RESEARCH DIRECTION

The foregoing analysis of the U.S.-Iranian conflict suggests a number of areas in which research on the role of media in international conflict might be directed. It is now obvious that analysis of the structure and political economy of the media in an integrated fashion is a must for understanding the functions and roles played by news organizations and their personnel in any conflict situation. However, certain specific areas might shed further light on the hypotheses developed in this chapter. Some of the most salient points for investigation might include:

- The role played by a particular communication technology in international conflict;
- The role of transnational media in "agenda setting" and legitimizing events and personalities;
- The role of international broadcasting as both the only and an alternative source of news and information;

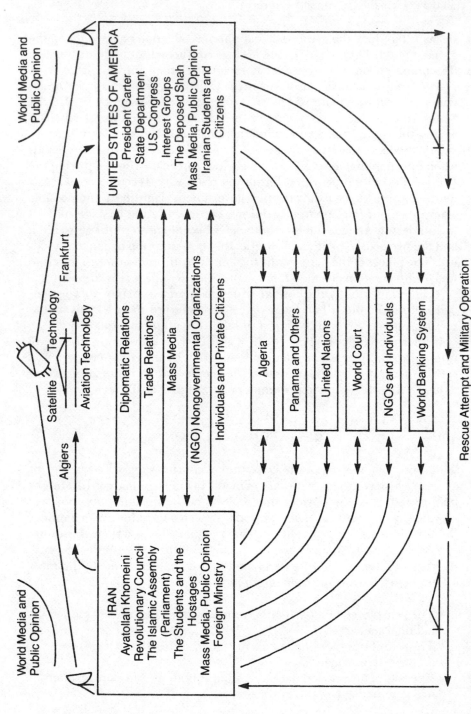

Figure 1. Communication pattern in the hostage crises.

TV Guide. April 5, 1980, 11.

Washington Post. December 12, 1979, A1. NBC is criticized for broadcast on American hostage.

Washington Post. December 13, 1979, A18. "For the record" from commentary by Walter Cronkite on CBS radio network (December 11, 1979).

Washington Post. December 19, 1979, A1. Ghotbzadeh says U.S. probe of shah could resolve crisis.

Washington Post. May 11, 1980, C2. Henry Failie.

CHAPTER 8

TREATING THE INDO-PAKISTAN CONFLICT: THE ROLE OF INDIAN NEWSPAPERS AND MAGAZINES

Sripada K. S. Raju
S. K. Jagadeswari
Wimal Dissanayake

International political conflicts directly involve the governments of the day as the main actors. Public opinion and other group pressures—national and international—influence the course of events, although their efficacy in molding national and international policy varies according to political institutions and structures and the openness of the people's participation in national government. A national government's sensitivity to international influence on policy goals and strategies during a conflict is very much conditioned by historical and contemporary structures of political and economic alignments, but transnational networks in business, industry, finance, education, religion, and human rights could influence decisions of national-level government actors involved in international conflicts. The roles of the mass media and their styles of management during international conflicts need to be understood as a subsystemic or infrastructural activity affecting the political psychology of the national and international actors and structures. The expected and actual role sets and performances of mass media, their autonomy, their entrepreneurial structure, and the control over news management and editorial policies are, to a large extent, a function of the political, economic, and sociocultural institutions of a given country. These observations are set forth here because there are perceptible differences in the national media systems of India and Pakistan, and the media system linkages with the international communication system are also different. In each country, there are different types of constraints on the media in gaining access to political information and participation by the public.

INDO-PAKISTAN CONFLICT BACKGROUND

The history of international relations between India and Pakistan has been one of political dissension and conflict, much of it based on religion and its role in making a nation-state. The beneficial influences of the cultural and economic bonds between the two countries, though obvious, have become irrelevant and inconsequential in forging any sense of cordiality and harmony that could bring about lasting political collaboration and economic cooperation. Historically, in the nineteenth and the first half of the twentieth centuries India and Pakistan have shared struggles, sacrifices, and commitments in gaining freedom from the British colonial bondage. But the two-nation theory based on separate identities of the Hindus and the Muslims, after prolonged negotiations, deadlocks, and political struggles gave birth to two sovereign countries. India committed herself to secularism, socialism, and democracy; Pakistan dedicated herself to Islamic ideology for realizing political, economic, and cultural aspirations.

Since 1947 when complex political, legal, and procedural formulas for dividing the territory of the Indian subcontinent into two countries were adopted and implemented, there have been four armed conflicts between India and Pakistan. Among many issues, two prominent ones that brought India and Pakistan to war were claims over the State of Kashmir and the movement for autonomy in East Pakistan. The latter led to the separatist movement which gave birth to Bangladesh in 1971. There were other unresolved issues such as the boundary dispute over the territory in the Rann of Kutch, sharing of river waters, and settlement of refugee property. Subsequently, some of these issues have been resolved through bilateral agreements, and others have been referred to international tribunals and organizations for arbitration and mediation, but the major issue still outstanding relates to Kashmir.

Figure 2 shows the armed conflict situations and indicates their durations. For example, the conflict that arose in 1947–48 went on for fourteen months and ended in a cease-fire. The issue was taken to the United Nations, but the conflict is still unresolved. The second war, fought for the Rann of Kutch in 1965–66, also ended in a cease-fire. It was mediated by an international tribunal, and the award was accepted. The third war in the same year took place again in Kashmir and also ended in a cease-fire. A further outcome was the Tashkent Agreement mediated by the Soviet Union, which became the basis for ending the war between the two countries.

The biggest armed conflict between India and Pakistan took place in the area that is now Bangladesh during December 1971. It was a fourteen-day war that resulted in the creation of Bangladesh. Later, in June 1972, Indian Prime Minister Indira Gandhi and Pakistan President Zulfikar Ali Bhutto met at Simla and drew up an agreement known as the Simla Agreement.

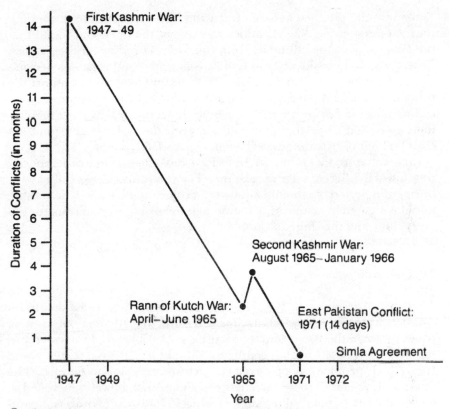

Continuing Unresolved Issues: Kashmir, traditional enmity.
Emerging Issues: Nuclear weapons development, high-tech weapons buildup.

Figure 2.   History of Indo-Pakistan conflicts.

This has become one of the basic documents and a watershed in providing
a bilateral framework within which India and Pakistan are still trying to
resolve some of the outstanding issues and conflicts.

As shown in Figure 2, the duration of conflicts has grown shorter and
shorter over the period of 1947–71, but the intensity of conflicts has become more and more severe. The international and intranational responses to the conflicts have contributed to the unstable political structure
in the Indian subcontinent.

MASS MEDIA AND THE INDO-PAKISTAN CONFLICT

Among the few relevant studies in Indo-Pakistan mass communication,
the work of N. Bhaskara Rao (1971) focuses on Indo-Pakistan conflict.

Looking at the 1965 war between India and Pakistan from a mass communication perspective, Rao examined the role of the press and found that the frequency of the editorials from the *Times of India* and the *Pakistan Times* increased considerably as tensions mounted and relations became strained between the two countries. This finding led him to support the thinking of James W. Markham, who observed that "as the volume of direct communication between the parties fell, the countries involved increasingly used their respective mass media systems through which to pour out their feelings of frustration and hostility" (Rao 1971, 168).

In this chapter we look at the Indo-Pakistan situation in a different setting and at a different stage of relations. The two countries were not at war during the period of our study but were exploring the ways to defuse the tensions created by actions and interactions involving Afghanistan, the Soviet Union, and the United States.

The Present Situation

The Simla Agreement of 1972 laid out that Pakistan and India should resolve the Kashmir issue without using force and that all other outstanding issues between the two countries must be settled bilaterally. This accord has become a base for both countries to build a structure of peace and from which people-to-people free contact was expected to develop. The internal problems of these two countries since 1972, however, have led to different types of political regimes. During 1975 to 1977, India came under national emergency. Later in Pakistan under Zia Ue-haq's military regime Former President Bhutto was tried and executed. From 1975 to 1981, both countries were engaged in managing their internal political problems, seeking stability but using different political methods. One noticeable thing is that neither country has interfered in any way in the other's internal problems, sticking to the spirit of the Simla Agreement and respecting each other's national integrity. In Pakistan after Bhutto's execution, the people's voice and political participation by elected representatives in the formation of the government have receded increasingly to the background, and a militaristic regime committed to Islamic ideology has characterized the political ethos. The press in Pakistan has been controlled by the government.

In India, the national emergency of 1975 led to a series of events that resulted in the general election of 1977 when Indira Gandhi's Congress government was defeated, and the Janatha government, with Murarji Desai as prime minister, was installed.

Thus, when both countries were undergoing political adjustments, there was no visible tension between them. But concerns, strains, and tensions began to be felt actively when the Soviet Union moved into Afghanistan in 1979. International events external to both India and Pakistan began creating new strains in their relationship. Pakistan perceived her security as being threatened by the Soviet military activities in Afghanistan as well as by the internal discontent and separatist tendencies erupting in the Pakistan territory of Baluchistan with possible interference by the Soviet Union in supporting the Baluchi rebels. In addition, as a result of the Soviet operations the refugees from Afghanistan began entering Pakistan. The Afghans were organizing themselves to fight against the Soviet-supported government of Afghanistan, and the base for their operation was in and around the border of Afghanistan and Pakistan. These developments involving the Soviet Union, Afghanistan, and Pakistan created a new international situation for Pakistan. There is a lurking fear that further dismemberment of Pakistan may occur and that India may conspire with the Soviet Union. These security concerns have led Pakistan to seek support and assistance from as many outside sources as possible, especially from the United States, China, Saudi Arabia, and other Arab countries.

The emerging conflict situation between India and Pakistan is thus being precipitated by the Soviet presence in Afghanistan. In addition, the role and the perceived security interests of the United States in western Asia have added another international dimension to the situation involving India and Pakistan. As interpreted under the administration of President Reagan, the security interests of the United States both in terms of energy politics and international political power politics have made it imperative to build military bases around the Indian Ocean and western Asia to keep the growing influence and power of the Soviet Union in check. In effect, perceptions of the U.S. security interests have harmonized with the needs and security perceptions of Pakistan. This has led to talks, dealings, and agreements for arms shipment and support from the United States to Pakistan.

Still another factor that has added to the conflict situation is the military nuclear development program leading to nuclear weapons development by Pakistan. Observers of the Pakistan nuclear development program have indicated that Pakistan has enough expertise and materials to develop nuclear weapons.

The increased foreign military supplies to Pakistan and the expectation of nuclear weapons development by Pakistan created obvious concerns for security in India. We see here how the chain of concerns for national and regional security interests on the part of several countries have been influencing each nation's perception of itself and the others. Pakistan became more concerned with her national security when the Soviets came into Afghanistan. India, however, was not concerned at that point, as evidenced by its mild and sometimes ambiguous stands on the Soviet presence in Afghanistan. When the U.S. administration saw the developments in Iran and western Asia after the fall of the shah, it felt U.S. national energy security was very much in jeopardy. The United States began to devise steps to strengthen her security interests, leading to the establishment of the bases at the Indian Ocean (Diego Garcia) and western Asia where Pakistan has become pivotally important. When these developments began to take shape, India felt its national security interests were being threatened. Hence, this chain effect of security concerns for each country in terms of its own sphere of influence and interest has created a situation in which India and Pakistan view each other in a new context. As a result, the relationship between India and Pakistan now has gone beyond the circumstances and conditions that produced the Simla Agreement in 1972. The question now asked is: To what extent would the Simla Agreement again become a viable framework for developing a harmonious and peaceful relationship between these two countries? When we look at the interactions and interlocking friendships of the superpowers in the perspective of historical animosities, and the competition for power between India and Pakistan on the one hand and Indian subcontinental countries on the other, we begin to understand the rising tensions and conflicts between India and Pakistan. It is in this context that we look at the role of newspapers and newsmagazines in managing the Indo-Pakistan relationship.

The Function and Role of the Mass Media

Communication textbooks assert that the function of the mass media is to inform the people about public affairs. The media create awareness and reinforce the opinions and attitudes of the readers, listeners, and viewers. They present alternative views and approaches to the problems and issues and interpret the events in a given arena, constructing a coherent framework, taking a position, and bringing to bear on the issues the strength of evidence and values. They open their forums to the public for discussion of the implications of a given event or policy. The media mobilize historical and contemporary evidence to support a particular position or oppose it. They provide information and insights to the public so that they will be able to make informed judgments on given issues in given situations. In playing such roles, the media have to operate within the context of laws and traditions that reflect the values of equity, justice, and fairness.

Of course not all societies conform to this ideal. Some critical differences among countries concern the structure of governmental organization; the communication participation and styles of the governmental and nongovernmental actors playing different roles in the policy arena; the resources, quality, capacity, and expertise available for media; the laws and regulations that promote and maintain certain journalistic traditions and freedom of information; and the culture of restraint and self-policing rules in the media profession.

Given this broad understanding of the media and the institutional context in which the media have to function, India provides an example of a press that has faced challenges both from within its own profession and from the government in several ways—control and influence on editorial policies by the owners of the mass media, censorship regulations, newsprint supply regulations, advertisement, patronage, and supply restrictions on industrial and communication hardware. The national emergency situation in 1975 was a trying and testing period for the press in India. Some newspapers, like the *Statesman* and the *Indian Express*, in the opinion of free press advocates, did live up to the expectations of upholding the cause of citizens' rights and freedom of the press. Other newspapers could not stand up to the stresses of the press crackdown. After all these national convulsions and assertions, however, the press has strengthened its autonomous role in India. It has grown in its professional influence as an institutional mechanism to influence public opinion and attitudes. There is in India a special situation where broadcast media are completely under governmental control while the print media enjoy freedom from such control. This media mix has open access to information from within the country and outside as well. It is important to understand these mass media channels and the roles the media play in managing Indo-Pakistan relationships in peace, conflict, and war.

Pakistan news and information gets reported in the Indian press regularly. For example, in the case of the *Hindustan Times*, there is a weekly corner every Friday in which a summary of events and news in Pakistan is presented. This feature provides the Indian public with information on what is happening in Pakistan, not only in the political arena, but also in economic and cultural fields.

Given the kind of role that the Indian press has played in providing freedom and access to national and international information resources, the questions raised here are: How do these media handle news and information? What kinds of perspectives do they bring to bear on a situation that is developing in the Indo-Pakistan relationship during a period when a new definition of the situation is emerging? How is the press trying to present the situation where the national actors, the international observers, the media personnel, and the public are trying to define the situation as it is developing? Guided by these questions, we have chosen some representative newspapers and a selection of newsmagazines to examine the role those news media played in managing, handling, collecting, and interpreting information relating to India and Pakistan during a specific period when formal visits and talks were taking place between the national leaders.

Hypotheses and Rationale

In order to explore the role and the ways Indian news media have managed the information on the Indo-Pakistan situation during June 1981, we formulated the following propositions:

1. The Indian news media tend to play up the news and information relating to Pakistan military development/agreement/assistance.
2. The Indian news media adopt a positive stance towards the Indian government positions and carry information that is not critical of India's stand for developing cordial relations with Pakistan.
3. The Indian news media are very critical of Pakistan and are hostile toward the military regime of Pakistan.
4. The Indian news media play the role of informing the public on the views and comments expressed in Pakistan, the United States, the Soviet Union, and other foreign countries insofar as they have a bearing on Indo-Pakistan relations.
5. The media take the initiative for in-depth and in-person interviews with government leaders, policymakers, and opposition leaders relating to issues involving Indo-Pakistan relations.
6. The kinds of coverage and treatment of Indo-Pakistan relations in the English-language papers are more in-depth and detailed than those presented in Tamil- and Kannada-language dailies.

These hypotheses are not theoretically derived. The literature on international relations and communication, especially that concerning the developing nations, deals with the large issues, including the factors that influence bilateral and multilateral international relations in bringing about ideological realignment; the role of ethnic, linguistic, and religious factors; economic and larger collective security interests; the need to maintain a balance of power; and the need for military determent and containment. There is a need, however, for low-level general propositions to aid us in observing, analyzing, and understanding a particular situation. In many cases, common sense propositions have the most direct approach and pragmatic applicability. For example, in the logic underlying the many statements made by public figures and political leaders in India regarding the issue of U.S. military aid to Pakistan, we see a "theory" or hypothetical scenario with an argument somewhat like the following:

- Whenever Pakistan gets military aid from the United States, Pakistan uses it against India.
- Pakistan has repeatedly done so during previous conflicts.
- From 1981 through 1986, Pakistan is getting military aid in the form of sophisticated weapons.
- During the coming years Pakistan will develop her military nuclear capability.
- Therefore, Pakistan will use her military power against India to realize her goal of liberating Kashmir from India.

Based on this scenario, the policy recommendation for India is: India should develop its military capability and use nuclear technology for making nuclear bombs as a deterrent and for self-defense.

Consider another such theory from the Pakistan side:

- The Soviet Union and India have been friends all along. When India fought with Pakistan in 1971 it dismembered Pakistan and helped create Bangladesh.
- The Soviet Union is now militarily active in Afghanistan. Indo-Soviet friendship continues.
- India, together with the Soviet Union, will further dismember Pakistan, taking advantage of the discontent among the Baluchis and others in Pakistan.
- Therefore, Pakistan should strengthen its security and military strength to maintain territorial integrity and national identity.

These are the kinds of arguments underlying Indo-Pakistan conflict theory. The political actors and defense analysts have to contend with them in making their foreign policy moves and plans for defense strategies.

In an international situation such as the Indo-Pakistan one that is built upon mutual perceptions and images based on conflicting theories, what is the role of news media? Assuming that the newspapers' function is to keep the people informed of national and international situations and provide them with well-argued positions, perspectives, and analyses of situations, the contribution of the newspapers to the management of conflict situations can be inferred from the content and sources of information, and also from the way they present conflict related issues in their columns. An analysis of news content and information presentation, therefore, would produce evidence to support or refute the hypotheses presented earlier.

Table 2. Profile of the Newspaper and Newsmagazine Samples from India (June 1 – 30, 1981)

Newspapers[a]

	Hindu	Hindustan Times	Times of India	Dinamani	Kannada Prabha
Language[a]	English	English	English	Tamil	Kannada
Circulation[a]	289,356	222,033	423,497	160,544	41,049
Place of publication[a]	Madras and four other towns	New Delhi	Bombay Delhi Ahmedabad	Madras Madurai	Bangalore
No. of pages (daily)	16	16	16	8	8
No. of columns (2-inch)	8	8	8	8	8

Newsmagazines

	India Today[b]	The Sunday[b]	Link[b]	Mainstream[c]	Economic and Political Weekly[c]
Language	English	English	English	English	English
Circulation	160,000	194,003	11,730	11,500	6,000
Place of publication	New Delhi	Calcutta	New Delhi	New Delhi	Bombay
Periodicity	fortnightly	weekly	weekly	weekly	weekly

Sources: [a]The 1979–80 Asian Press and Media Directory, World Trade Centre.
[b]The Far East and Australasia, 1981 – 82. Europa Publications, London 1981.
[c]Ulrich's International Periodicals Directory, 19th Edition, R. R. Bowker Co, New York, 1980.

STUDY SAMPLING AND MEASUREMENT

Selection of Newspapers

Table 2 gives some characteristics of the newspapers selected for the study. We selected five newspapers—three English-language national newspapers, and one newspaper each from the Tamil and Kannada languages. The English-language papers we analyzed included the *Hindu* published in Madras and four other cities in South India, the *Hindustan Times* published in New Delhi, and the *Times of India* published in Bombay and two other cities in northern India. The *Dinamani* and the *Kannada Prabha* are published in Madurai and Madras of Tamil Nadu, and Bangalore of Karnataka, respectively. The English-language newspapers represent the north, south, and western areas of the country. In addition to representing two other Indian languages, namely, the *Dinamani* for Tamil and *Kannada Prabha* for Kannada, the latter two newspapers belong to the *Indian Express* (English-language daily) chain of newspapers.

All the English papers publish sixteen pages daily with additional pages on Sundays and other special occasions. The *Dinamani* and the *Kannada Prabha* have eight pages daily, with additional pages on Sundays and special occasions.

The *Times of India* has the largest circulation, 423,497, the *Hindu* is next with 289,356, the *Hindustan Times* has 222,033, the *Dinamani* has 160,544, and the *Kannada Prabha* has 41,049.

Additional considerations for choosing these newspapers were the availability of newspapers and the language skills needed to study the Tamil and Kannada newspapers.

Selection of Magazines

We considered two types of English-language magazines in India, namely, newsmagazines and quasi-academic magazines. They carry regular periodical analyses and commentaries on national and international political and economic affairs. The newsmagazines we examined were *India Today* (fortnightly), *The Sunday* (weekly), and *Link* (weekly). The quasi-academic magazines we looked at were *Mainstream* (weekly) and *The Economic and Political Weekly*. Again, the reason for selecting these magazines was their ready availability within the time constraint of our study and the wide use of these magazines among English-language readers in India.

India Today is a fortnightly newsmagazine published from New Delhi. It carries features of pictorial, cartoon, and diagram presentations with writings from noted journalists and columnists such as V. G. Verghese, Babhani Sen Gupta, and Rajendra Puri in addition to the stories reported from its own special correspondents. The general features of *India Today* are cover pictures and cover stories, letters to the editor, special reports and investigations, international events, global and neighboring country developments, and trade, economic, and business trends—all both national and international. Other features, such as reviews and comments on the developments in religion, environment, medicine, science, athletics, arts, cinema, and books, are also presented.

The Sunday, a weekly newsmagazine operated by Ananda Bazaar Publication from Calcutta presents its main features under sections such as comments and opinions, letters to the editor, cover story, Sunday special, special report, conversation, news, science, cinema, and comics. It is illustrated with photographs. On an average, it is about sixty pages.

Link is a weekly newsmagazine that presents cover stories with pictures, letters to the editor, newslets, editorials, signed articles, regular commentaries from columnist Chalapathi Rau, *Link*'s own correspondents' reports from various states in India and international regions, and comments and reviews on arts, music, cinema, sports, and books.

Mainstream is a quasi-academic weekly from New Delhi. It has regular features such as an editor's notebook, commentary, communication, discussions, extracts from other journals and periodicals, and articles on theoretical and empirical problems of a political, economic, and sociological nature.

The *Economic and Political Weekly* is also a quasi-academic weekly with features such as editorials, letters to the editor, business, Capital View, a regular column with commentary by Romesh Thapar, commentary and discussion on international affairs, its own correspondents' reports from different states in India, book reviews, and special articles with empirical and theoretical reports, discussions, and perspectives.

Selection of the Study Period

We selected the month of June 1981 to look at the management of news and information by the newspapers on the topics relating to Indo-Pakistan relations. There were several reasons for selecting the month of June. First, between June 6 and 10, P. Narasimha Rao, minister for external affairs, visited Pakistan to initiate talks for improving relations between Pakistan and India. Second, there was a series of visits by the Chinese leaders (prime minister and foreign minister) to Pakistan, India, and other South Asian countries; and third, there were visits from the United States by state department officials for talks and agreement on military hardware supplies to Pakistan. All three events converged on issues that have a bear-

Table 3. Number of Items about Indo-Pakistan Relations in Five Indian Newspapers (June 1981)

Newspaper	Information Items
Hindu	55
Hindustan Times	78
Times of India	65
Dinamani	51
Kannada Prabha	32

ing on developments in the Indo-Pakistan relationship. They had the potential for either increasing the tension or helping India and Pakistan to initiate amicable and friendly relations.

Method of Analysis

A content analysis procedure was adopted for examining the five newspapers. For the magazines, a systematic study of all features devoted to the Indo-Pakistan theme was undertaken.

In surveying the five newspapers for June 1981, we looked for news stories and information about Indo-Pakistan relations by reading headlines and skimming newspaper columns to identify the key words and expressions relating to Indo-Pakistan relations and note the information items that explicitly dealt with Pakistan. These information items were listed on a coding sheet. In the scanning process, we found many items about Indo-Pakistan relations, as shown in Table 3. The next step was to read through each item more than once and indicate the attributes of each for the following variables:

- Volume of information—length of the 2-inch column.
- Source—whether the information item was from wire services, newspaper correspondents, columnists, analysts, author of articles, or other sources.
- Place—the city or town where the information originated.
- Display mode—whether the news story or information was presented on the front page, editorial or central page, or other pages or blocks.
- Type of information—whether the news story or information was a news report, news analysis, editorial, commentary, backgrounder, in-depth treatment in a feature article, or carried a correspondent's by-line.

- Actors—the main participants in the situation covered by the news story, analysis, or other presentation.
- Context—a brief description of the setting of the news or information situation.
- Theme—broad classifications of the central meanings of the items were made about whether the story tended toward peace, including harmony, need for understanding, need for cooperation, amity, friendship, and working together toward a common goal. If the story tended toward feelings and situations of military preparedness, national insecurity, distrust, hatred, dislike, threats, disagreements, hesitation, and unpreparedness to work together for a common goal, we considered the message to be one of conflict.
- Posture of the message—after reading an item, a judgment was made regarding the implications of the message to India and Pakistan, that is, whether the reader would consider the message favorable to India or Pakistan, or whether the message was unfavorably disposed toward India or Pakistan. We rated these subjective judgments on a scale of +5 to −5. If the message was extremely favorable, it was rated +5; if the message was extremely unfavorable, it was rated −5. If the message was neutral, or not relevant for judgmental rating, then we assigned the score of 0. Other scores between +5 and −5 represented the range of message disposition.

Reliability of Measures

We do not claim complete intercoder objectivity, especially regarding the posture of the messages. But we believe that by our repeated reconsideration of the ratings, we provided a reliable element of subjectivity. Nationality biases among the coders were overcome to some extent because one of the coders was from Sri Lanka and two others were from India.

FINDINGS

Newspaper Treatment of Indo-Pakistan Relations

During June 1981, all five newspapers played up the news stories relating to Indo-Pakistan relations. In addition to reporting the news events, they treated the issue in feature articles, news analyses, and editorials. Table 4 indicates this very clearly. The stories and analyses of Indo-Pakistan relations appear on the front page and the editorial, center, and special pages.

Table 4. Display of News Items (Stories, Feature Articles, Comments, and Editorials) Relating to Indo-Pakistan Relations in Indian Newspapers (June 1981)

Display Mode	Hindu				Hindustan Times				Times of India				Dinamani				Kannada Prabha			
	P	C	O	Total	P	C	O	Total	P	C	O	Total	P	C	O	Total	P	C	O	Total
Front, editorial, center pages																				
Number of information items	23 (76.7%)	19 (79.1%)	1 (100%)	43 (78.2%)	22 (71.0%)	16 (55.2%)	7 (38.9%)	45 (57.7%)	16 (72.7%)	19 (59.3%)	3 (27.3%)	38 (58.5%)	18 (82.1%)	18 (81.8%)	0	36 (70.6%)	8 (57.0%)	6 (60.0%)	7 (87.5%)	21 (65.6%)
Volume (in 2-inch column)	399 (83.2%)	308 (89.0%)	6 (100%)	713 (85.7%)	373 (83.8%)	200 (63.9%)	65 (32.2%)	639 (66.6%)	228 (81.7%)	271 (66.6%)	36 (48.6%)	535 (70.4%)	381 (77.1%)	335 (87.9%)	0	716 (81.8%)	84 (61.6%)	48 (69.6%)	59 (90.7%)	191 (72.3%)
Other pages																				
Number of information items	7 (23.3%)	5 (20.8%)	0	12 (21.8%)	9 (29.0%)	13 (44.8%)	11 (61.1%)	33 (42.5%)	6 (27.3%)	13 (40.7%)	8 (72.7%)	27 (41.5%)	11 (37.9%)	4 (18.2%)	0	15 (29.4%)	6 (43.0%)	4 (40.0%)	1 (12.5%)	11 (34.4%)
Volume (in 2-inch column)	81 (16.9%)	38 (11.0%)	0	119 (14.3%)	72 (16.2%)	112 (35.8%)	136 (67.2%)	321 (33.4%)	51 (18.3%)	136 (33.4%)	38 (51.4%)	225 (29.6%)	113 (22.9%)	46 (12.1%)	0	159 (18.2%)	46 (35.4%)	21 (30.4%)	6 (9.2%)	73 (27.7%)
Total																				
Number of information items	30 (54.6%)	24 (43.6%)	1 (1.8%)	55 (100%)	31 (39.7%)	29 (37.2%)	18 (63.1%)	78 (100%)	22 (33.8%)	32 (49.2%)	11 (17%)	65 (100%)	29 (56.9%)	22 (43.1%)	0	51 (100%)	14 (44.0%)	10 (31.25%)	8 (25%)	32 (100%)
Volume (in 2-inch column)	480 (57.7%)	346 (41.6%)	6 (0.7%)	832 (100%)	415 (46.3%)	313 (32.6%)	202 (51.1%)	960 (100%)	279 (36.7%)	407 (53.5%)	74 (9.8%)	760 (100%)	494 (56.4%)	381 (43.6%)	0	875 (100%)	130 (49.2%)	69 (26.1%)	65 (25.0%)	264 (100%)

P = Information items whose contents were oriented to peace or neutral posture.

C = Information items whose contents were oriented to conflict, hostility, or security threats.

O = Others.

The *Hindustan Times'* last page also was used for displaying important stories, but in our coding scheme we did not include the last page of the *Hindustan Times* as a mode of presenting the story prominently. The *Times of India* regularly devoted a block on the inside page for displaying foreign news where news events from Pakistan were also reported. When we took these special page presentations into account we saw a consistent pattern across all of the newspapers—the Indo-Pakistan news stories were given prominence both in terms of the number of stories covered (58–78 percent), and the volume of information in 2-inch columns presented (67–83 percent).

Peace-oriented messages received consistent prominence in the *Dinamani*, the *Hindu*, the *Kannada Prabha*, and the *Hindustan Times* both in terms of the number of stories covered (57, 55, 44, and 40 percent, respectively), and the volume of information (56, 58, 49, and 46 percent, respectively). The *Times of India* showed an overall pattern of giving prominence to conflict-related information both in terms of the number of stories (49 percent) and the volume of information (54 percent).

On pages other than the front, editorial, center, and special pages, the *Hindu*, the *Dinamani*, and the *Kannada Prabha* still showed their prominent disposition to present peace-oriented themes. Out of twelve stories on the other pages in the *Hindu* seven stories (58 percent) were peace-oriented. In the *Dinamani*, out of fifteen stories, eleven (73 percent) were peace-oriented. In the *Kannada Prabha*, out of eleven stories, six (54 percent) were peace-oriented. In the *Hindustan Times* and the *Times of India*, stories oriented to the conflict themes received greater treatment on the inside pages and the last page. For example, in the *Hindustan Times*, out of thirty-three stories on other pages, thirteen (39 percent) related to the conflict theme and nine (27 percent) related to the peace theme. In the *Times of India*, out of twenty-seven stories on other pages, thirteen (48 percent) related to conflict themes and six (22 percent) related to peace themes.

On the whole, the *Hindu*, the *Dinamani*, and the *Kannada Prabha* tended toward presenting peace and reconciliation themes. The *Hindustan Times* treated both conflict and peace in a somewhat balanced fashion, managing more peace stories on the front page and more conflict stories on the inside pages. The *Times of India* definitely played up the conflict themes.

The sources of information on Indo-Pakistan relations are shown in Table 5. For all the English newspapers, information on Indo-Pakistan affairs originated from the Indian and foreign wire services and reports and bylines were those of the special correspondents of the respective newspapers.

In the *Hindu*, out of fifty-five news stories and information items, thirty-two (58 percent) were from the wire services, and twenty-seven (49 percent) were analyses and feature articles by the correspondents of the newspaper. There was only one editorial and a few other types of information such as letters to the editor on Indo-Pakistan relations.

**Table 5. Sources of News and Information on Indo-Pakistan Relations
(June 1981)**

Information Sources/Forms	Hindu	Hindustan Times	Times of India	Dinamani[a]	Kannada Prabha[b]
(NUMBER OF NEWS STORIES)					
Editorial	1	4	1	4	—
Special correspondents	6	12	5	—	2
By-lines and feature articles	21	19	26	3	—
Wire services					
Reuters	2	4	4	—	—
AFP	—	2	5	—	—
AP	1	6	—	—	4
UPI	—	1	—	—	—
PTI	9	17	11	—	16
UNI	5	10	12	—	1
Combined wire services (AP-PTI, UNI-PTI, Reuters-PTI, UNI-DPA, PTI-Reuters and UNI)	5	2	1	—	—
Others	5	1	—	—	9
TOTAL	55	78	65	7	32

[a]*Dinamani* does not indicate systematically its source of news stories
and information.
[b]*Kannada Prabha* has its own news services. (Five news stories were reported by
Kannada Prabha Service.)

In the *Hindustan Times*, forty-two (54 percent) out of seventy-eight news
stories were from the wire services; thirty-one (40 percent) were analyses
and feature stories by its correspondents. There were four editorials in the
Hindustan Times.

In the *Times of India*, out of sixty-five items, thirty-three (51 percent)
were news stories from the wire services; and thirty-one (48 percent) were
analyses and writings by its correspondents. There was only one editorial.

The *Dinamani* did not print explicitly the sources of news in its columns.

The sources of news and information on Indo-Pakistan affairs for the
Kannada Prabha were mainly the wire services: twenty-one stories (66 percent) out of thirty-two came from the wire services. The *Kannada Prabha*
has its own news services. There was no editorial on Indo-Pakistan affairs

Table 6. Place of Origin and Flow of News and Information Relating to Indo-Pakistan Relations (June 1981)

Display Mode	Thematic Content	Hindu			Hindustan Times			Times of India			Dinamani			Kannada Prabha		
		Within India	From Outside[a]	Total	Within India	From Outside[b]	Total	Within India	From Outside[c]	Total	Within India	From Outside[d]	Total	Within India	From Outside[e]	Total
Front page and center page	Peace	10	14	24	14	11	25	7	9	16	6	12	18	1	7	8
	Conflict	10	9	19	8	8	16	9	10	19	12	6	18	6	1	7
	Others	—	—	—	—	1	1	1	1	2	—	—	—	2	4	6
Other pages	Peace	2	5	7	1	8	9	4	4	8	7	4	11	4	2	6
	Conflict	2	3	5	8	5	13	2	11	13	1	3	4	1	3	4
	Others	—	—	—	4	7	11	1	—	1	—	—	—	0	1	1
TOTAL		24	31	55	35	40	75	24	35	59	26	25	51	14	18	32

[a] Islamabad, London, Lahore, Karachi, Rawalpindi, Washington, New York, Paris, Bonn, Moscow.
[b] Moscow, New York, Islamabad, Ankara, Karachi, The Hague, Paris, Washington, Rawalpindi.
[c] Islamabad, Lahore, Karachi, Rawalpindi, New York, Washington, Moscow, London.
[d] Washington, Lahore, Rawalpindi, Kathmandu, Karachi, New York, Moscow, Islamabad, London, Peking, New York.
[e] Islamabad, Rawalpindi, Karachi, Washington, New York.

during June. Two dispatches from its special correspondents regarding Indo-Pakistan affairs provided some analytical insights.

It was clear that the main source of information for all three English dailies and the Kannada-language daily was the wire services. The wire service agencies were Press Trust of India (PTI) and United News of India (UNI), both Indian organizations. Transnational news services like Reuters and AFP made minor contributions—less than 8 percent of the news on Indo-Pakistan affairs. The *Hindustan Times* mainly used AP (Associated Press); the *Hindu* used combined wire services: AP-PTI, UI-PTI, Reuters-PTI, and UNI-DPA.

All three English dailies, the *Hindu*, the *Hindustan Times*, and the *Times of India*, and the Kannada-language daily, the *Kannada Prabha*, presented to a large extent news and information originating from sources outside India (Table 6). Evidently this was so because the main scene of the five-day visit of the Indian external affairs minister was Pakistan during June 1981. In the case of the Tamil daily, the *Dinamani*, there was no clear dominance of one or the other source.

The following were the most frequent origins of news and information used by all five newspapers: Islamabad, Lahore, Karachi, Rawalpindi, London, Washington, New York, and Moscow. Paris, Bonn, The Hague, Ankara, Peking, and Kathmandu were some of the other places from which stories or information originated.

In the *Hindu*, peace-oriented information on the front page was more from outside sources, and conflict-oriented information was evenly distributed among sources within and outside of India. In the *Hindustan Times*, the front page depicted more peace-oriented news originating within India, while conflict news was evenly distributed among sources within and outside India. The *Times of India* reported and displayed more peace news from outside of India, and conflict-oriented information was evenly distributed among sources originating within and outside of India. The *Dinamani* displayed on its front page more peace news originating from outside of India, but conflict-oriented information originated mainly within India.

The treatment of peace and conflict-oriented news on other inside pages in the *Hindu* was similar to its treatment on the front and center pages. The *Hindustan Times* reported on inside pages more peace themes originating outside of India and more conflict themes originating within India. The *Times of India* reported on inside pages peace themes that originated evenly within India and outside, while a greater number of stories with conflict themes originated outside India. The *Dinamani* reported more peace themes on inside pages originating from sources within India, while it displayed more conflict themes originating from outside India.

In the case of the *Kannada Prabha*, as in the *Dinamani*, the peace-oriented front-page stories originated from sources outside of India and conflict-oriented stories originated within India. On the inside pages the pattern was reversed.

Results on the posture of the messages in the news stories on Indo-Pakistan relations in terms of the positive and negative dispositions toward India and Pakistan are shown in Table 7. In the *Hindu*, out of fifty-five news items, eleven stories (20 percent) were considered neutral. Twenty-four stories (44 percent) showed a positive posture towards India and twenty stories (36 percent) showed a negative posture towards India. A large number of stories oriented to peace were positively disposed toward India, while the conflict-oriented stories showed a negative posture toward India.

Regarding Pakistan, thirty-four items (52 percent) out of fifty-five were neutral; eighteen stories (33 percent) were definitely positive. All except one were oriented to the peace theme. Two stories out of fifty-five that related to conflict showed a negative posture toward Pakistan. Probably the *Hindu* is more India-oriented in its focus of analysis and concern, although when it comes to peace it takes into account Pakistan's affairs also.

In the *Hindustan Times*, out of seventy-eight news items, forty-seven (60 percent) belonged to the neutral category. Twenty-five news stories (32 percent) had a positive posture towards India and six stories (8 percent) had a negative posture. Twenty-three stories (30 percent) that depicted or described peace themes were positive toward India. Two stories that had conflict themes also had a positive posture. All six that had a negative posture toward India had conflict-oriented themes.

In the case of Pakistan, out of seventy-eight news items, thirty-seven (47 percent) were neutral or did not have any relevance to Pakistan. Thirty-three stories (42 percent) were positive toward Pakistan. Eight stories (10 percent) were negative toward Pakistan. Peace theme stories tended to show a positive posture toward Pakistan. Six stories (8 percent) that were conflict-oriented were also positive toward Pakistan. Similarly, another six stories that were conflict-oriented were negative toward Pakistan.

In the *Times of India*, out of sixty-five news stories, forty-seven (72 percent) were either neutral or not relevant in terms of their disposition toward India. Sixteen items (23 percent) had a positive posture toward India; two had a negative posture. Twelve stories (18 percent) that had peace themes showed a positive posture toward India. Four stories with conflict themes also showed a positive posture toward India. Two stories with conflict themes showed a negative posture toward India.

Twenty news stories (31 percent) out of sixty-five items were either neutral or were not relevant to the attitudinal posture toward Pakistan. Eight stories (12 percent) that were peace-oriented were positive toward Pakistan. Twenty-eight conflict-oriented stories (43 percent) indicated a negative posture toward Pakistan. Four stories that were peace-oriented also were disposed unfavorably toward Pakistan.

In the *Dinamani*, out of fifty-one stories, nine (18 percent) had either a neutral posture or were not relevant to the attitudinal concerns toward India. Fourteen stories (27 percent) that contained peace themes showed a positive posture toward India. Twenty-eight conflict-related stories (55 percent) had a negative posture toward India.

Out of the fifty-one news stories, twenty-two items (43 percent) were positive toward Pakistan. Twenty-two stories (43 percent) were negative and seven were neutral toward Pakistan. Out of the twenty-seven conflict-oriented stories (53 percent), twenty-two showed a negative posture toward Pakistan, and five indicated a positive posture. All seventeen peace-oriented stories were positive toward Pakistan.

In the *Kannada Prabha*, the pattern was similar to that in the *Dinamani*. All peace-oriented themes had a positive disposition toward both India and Pakistan, and conflict-oriented themes had negative dispositions toward both India and Pakistan.

The overall pattern, then, in the treatment of the news stories and their disposition toward India and Pakistan was that the *Times of India* treated conflict-oriented stories showing negative implications for Pakistan while the *Hindu*, the *Hindustan Times*, and the *Kannada Prabha* placed more emphasis on peace-oriented stories showing aspects positive to Pakistan. The *Dinamani* treated the stories in a balanced way indicating conflict stories to be of negative value and peace stories to be positive toward Pakistan.

In the *Hindu* and the *Dinamani*, a comparatively smaller number of stories were neutral, whereas in the *Hindustan Times* and the *Times of India*, neutral postures were relatively frequent. Does this mean that the *Dinamani* and the *Hindu* took clear-cut positions in the treatment of the messages in the peace/conflict context? Or does this mean some bias in coding? On the whole, peace themes tended to show positive aspects to India; conflict themes tended to be negative to India in their implication. However, this was not very clear in the case of the *Times of India*.

Magazine Treatment of Indo-Pakistan Relations

The coverage by *India Today* of Indo-Pakistan affairs during the second fortnight of June 1981 had a volume of 146 square inches. An analytical piece by Babhani Sen Gupta looked at India's nuclear options in the context of international relations developing among Pakistan, the United States, and China. The treatment by columnist Gupta was fairly balanced, outlining the two countries' different perceptions of their geopolitical security.

Table 7. Posture of News Stories and Information Relating to Indo-Pakistan Relations (June 1981)

	Toward India												Toward Pakistan												
	Pos. Total	Positive Scale[a]					0	-1	Negative Scale				Neg. Total	Pos. Total	Positive Scale					0	-1	Negative Scale				Neg. Total
		+5	+4	+3	+2	+1	(Number)		-2	-3	-4	-5			+5	+4	+3	+2	+1	(Number)		-2	-3	-4	-5	
Hindu																										
Peace	20	6	11	0	2	1	6	0	0	0	1	0	1	17	3	10	1	3	0	13	0	0	0	0	0	0
Conflict	4	2	0	2	0	0	5	0	3	7	1	8	19	1	0	0	1	0	0	21	0	0	1	0	1	2
Other	0	0	0	0	0	0	0	0	0	0	0	0	0	0	0	0	0	0	0	0	0	1	0	0	0	1
Total	24						11						20	18						34						3
Hindustan Times																										
Peace	23	0	5	15	3	0	9	0	0	0	0	0	0	23	0	5	15	1	2	9	0	2	0	0	0	2
Conflict	2	0	1	1	0	0	22	0	3	2	0	1	6	6	0	1	3	2	0	16	0	1	5	0	0	6
Other	0	0	0	0	0	0	16	0	0	0	0	0	0	4	0	3	0	1	0	12	0	0	0	0	0	0
Total	25						47						6	33						37						8
Times of India																										
Peace	12	1	0	9	2	0	11	0	0	0	0	0	0	8	0	0	5	3	0	12	1	3	0	0	0	4
Conflict	4	0	0	1	3	0	28	1	1	0	0	0	2	0	0	0	0	0	0	4	2	13	9	3	1	28
Other	0	0	0	0	1	0	8	0	0	0	0	0	0	0	0	0	0	0	0	4	3	1	1	0	0	5
Total	16						47						2	8						20						37

	Total	+5	+4	+3	+2	+1	0	−1	−2	−3	−4	−5
Dinamani												
Peace	14	1	6	4	2	1	0	0	0	0	0	0
Conflict	22	0	0	0	0	0	17	5	4	0	0	0
Other	0	0	0	0	0	0	0	0	0	0	0	0
Total							9	28	22	7	6	22
Kannada Prabha												
Peace	13	0	3	7	3	0	1	0	0	0	0	0
Conflict	0	0	0	0	0	0	3	4	0	2	0	0
Other	1	0	0	1	0	0	0	0	5	0	0	0
TOTAL	14						4	21	6	6	5	5

aThe scoring of the posture of the message is on the scale of +1 to +5 for the ones positively disposed, −1 to −5 for those negatively disposed, 0 for neutral:

+1 = somewhat positive	−1 = somewhat negative
+2 = positive	−2 = negative
+3 = slightly more positive	−3 = slightly more negative
+4 = very positive	−4 = very negative
+5 = extremely positive	−5 = extremely negative

The coverage and treatment of the issues central to Indo-Pakistan conflicts received a systematic treatment during April 16– 30, 1981, and May
16– 31, 1981, prior to the visit of India's external affairs minister to Pakistan. The cover page photo in April 16– 30, 1981, depicted General Zia as
the utmost armed military general. The cover story occupied 585 square
inches interspersed with pictures of General Zia, his political opposition,
Bhutto's family, and issues of military balance between India and Pakistan
illustrated with diagrams and sketches. A detailed account of how General
Zia came to power, his attitude and techniques of handling the movements
within Pakistan for restoring democracy, arms deals and defense links with
the United States, Pakistan's problem of Afghan refugees and rebels as a
result of Soviet presence in Afghanistan, and the diplomatic offensive of
India for improving peaceful relations all were issues vividly portrayed in a
way that indicated their links with the economic and political situation
within Pakistan.

The May 16–31, 1981, issue of *India Today* carried a guest column by
Abdul Sattar, the Pakistan ambassador in New Delhi. The magazine devoted 138 square inches of space to Sattar's column, which stressed the
need for better understanding between India and Pakistan in the context
of the growing concerns of an arms buildup. He stated that Pakistan's military development was no threat for India.

In the same issue, Babhani Sen Gupta presented a perspective in 212
square inches of space discussing Indo-Pakistan relations in the larger context of international relations among the United States, the Soviet Union,
and China. He examined critically the moves made by India in her assertion as a major regional power.

The Sunday devoted 199.5 square inches to the events relating to Indo-
Pakistan affairs during the first week of June, 1981. The coverage was
heavy during the week of June 14 (496.38 square inches) and decreased to
133 square inches in the June 21 issue and to 48.75 square inches on July
19.

During the visit of India's external affairs minister in the second week of
June, the Indo-Pakistan affairs treatment was accompanied by four pictures showing General Zia with different leaders of India—Janatha government leaders and Indira Gandhi—and also Zia's other international allies. The cover story dealt extensively with the theme of India's
pragmatism. One thing most noticeable about *The Sunday* newsmagazine
in dealing with the issues relating to the Indo-Pakistan conflict situation
was the high degree of initiative taken by its correspondents in talking to
leaders in both India and Pakistan about the issues that had important
bearing on the political tensions between the two countries.

Shubhabrata Bhattacharya in *The Sunday* (June 7, 1981) discussed the
conditions under which an Indo-Pakistan war was likely to occur. If Paki-

stan acquired nuclear weapons it would risk another war with India: "Pakistan with nuclear weapons would neutralize India's superiority in conventional warfare. The initiative will certainly pass into the hands of Pakistan."

The Sunday (June 7, 1981) brought out the results of a survey (N=800 persons equally distributed among males and females randomly selected to represent different age groups and educational levels) of the metropolitan cities of Bombay, Calcutta, Delhi, and Madras indicating a general consensus that the promised U.S. military aid to Pakistan would be used against India. Public opinion was divided on the possibilities of war between India and Pakistan. People surveyed felt that in the event of a war, however, the United States would definitely aid Pakistan. Public opinion was divided about the possibilities of Pakistan using nuclear weapons against India. In spite of the misgivings about Pakistan, an overwhelming majority of the Indian people did not want a war with Pakistan (*The Sunday* June 7, 1981).

Rajendra Sareen of *The Sunday* obtained a special interview with General Zia on May 30, 1981 (*The Sunday* June 14, 1981). Again, B. N. Kumar of *The Sunday* reported a conversation with S. S. Pirzade, the attorney general of Pakistan (*The Sunday* June 21, 1981). These and other journalistic reports were important indicators of the roles played by the newsmagazines in informing the public and the policymakers about the developments and different perspectives on Indo-Pakistan relations and conflicts as seen and felt by persons close to the political decision makers. However, the journalists who pursued the sources close to the policymakers, especially in Pakistan, had to face reluctance and sometimes avoidance on the part of the national leaders to communicate their views and stands unambiguously regarding the ways they were approaching the problems and issues in Indo-Pakistan relations. Sareen reported that as he was preparing to seek an interview with General Zia many constraints and rules were laid down with regard to the questions to be submitted to the general. The reporter had to take the answers and the positions given by the Pakistan government officials as the position of General Zia. He could only seek clarification while interviewing General Zia, but he did not have the official answers given to him before his interview with the general. All these constraints and limitations on news magazine reporters made it difficult for them to do their professional jobs with efficiency, specificity, and accountability. For example, the media interviews could not be specific about such issues as what kind of policy might evolve in India to reassure Pakistan that India had no intention of further dismembering Pakistan. Sareen felt that his meeting with General Zia indicated the inhospitable situation for the media. He could do no more than simply note the limitations and do the best he could to inform the national and international public. He wrote,

General Zia-ul Haq's answers to my questions are there, and I would like the readers to form their own opinion. But my own feeling is that he prefers not to answer some of the more substantial questions on relations between the two countries because there is a definite reluctance on his part to face the implications of what is involved in these issues. It is one thing to take a position and make generalized statements expressing goodwill, it is quite another to evolve an acceptable and viable basis after carefully working out the nuts and bolts of a policy framework capable of reassuring the two countries of each other's bona fides (Sareen June 14, 1981).

The Sunday of July 12, 1981, published six letters from its readers, three of which were critical of Zia for his evasiveness in answering questions relating to Indo-Pakistan relations, his military rule in Pakistan, and Pakistan's past military actions whenever it had a strong military linkage with the United States. There was one letter that was critical of the Indian press for joining hands with the government in condemning the military ruler of Pakistan. Another letter positively agreed with General Zia when he said that Mrs. Gandhi must be left alone to create her own image among the people of Pakistan. Still another letter was critical of the press correspondent for not giving comprehensive coverage of the issue of Kashmir and nuclear plans in the interview.

Link devoted 747.5 square inches to Indo-Pakistan relations during the week of June 14, 236.5 square inches during the week of June 28, and 153.75 square inches during the week of July 19. During the second week of June, which coincided with the Indian external affairs minister's visit to Pakistan, the coverage was pictorial, with sketches and photographs on the cover page and cover story pages.

The cover page featured a sketch of Indian External Affairs Minister Rao, pondering over the increasing military and weapons supply to Pakistan. The title read, "Indo-Pak Meet . . . From Here Where?"

The cover story in *Link* from R. K. Mishra in Islamabad with a headline "Big Display of Sweet Intentions" concluded with this note: "The visit has achieved a significant result. It has reactivated the process initiated by the Simla Agreement. Agha Shahi has been invited by Rao to come to Delhi . . . President Zia has also indicated his willingness to visit India for understanding at 'leadership level.'" (June 14, 1981).

The article also discussed the element of surprise in India's peace package with India specifying precise and specific steps that both countries could take to improve their relations. Kalim Bahadur sketched a historical perspective of Indo-Pakistan relations in an article titled: "Indo-Pakistan Relations: A Historic Perspective." There were writings that went deeper into the issues of interactions among culture and thought, and there was also an extended discussion of the context of Pakistan-China relations.

Link of June 18, 1981, published a letter to the editor from an organizer of the Defense Committee for Political Prisoners in Pakistan appealing to the friendly governments, democratic organizations, trade unions, and political parties of the world community to show their solidarity and sympathy with the oppressed people of Pakistan and support for the struggle against General Zia's militaristic regime.

In his commentary, Chalapathi Rau observed the illusion of the lasting Indo-Pakistan relations. He considered that Narasimha Rao's visit accomplished a strengthening of the goodwill between the two countries. But he said the issues of Kashmir and human rights in Pakistan should receive proper solutions by Zia's regime (*Link*, June 18, 1981).

In a special article, "Renewal of Arms Race," Kalim Bahadur (June 18, 1981) examined the issue of a renewed arms race between India and Pakistan. He characterized Pakistan's effusive expressions of friendship and amity toward India during the Indian delegation's visit to Pakistan as a charade intended to extract from India the acquiescence to the so-called parameters of Islamabad's defense requirements. He strongly shared the feeling that Pakistan would use U.S. arms against India: "There is no chance of Pakistan fighting a war against any other country except India." Indian commentators perceived the role of Zia as similar to those of Anwar Sadat, Menachem Begin, and the shah of Iran in furthering U.S. interests. Bahadur was critical of U.S. strategy and foreign policies in the Indian subcontinent. He argued that the U.S. stance had contributed to the building of tension, endangering peace and security in South Asia. O. P. Sabherwal (*Link*, June 28, 1981) had mixed comments on the stresses and strains of the Pakistan economy, indicating that industrial development was weak and commending the agricultural sector as a bright spot.

Mainstream devoted a total of 557 square inches to Indo-Pakistan affairs, 189 square inches on June 13 and 368 square inches in the June 27 issue. On July 11, *Mainstream* devoted 412 square inches.

In the weeks previous to the Islamabad visit by India's external affairs minister, *Mainstream* provided information and viewpoints drawn from sources both in India and Pakistan. For example, *Mainstream* (May 16, 1981) reproduced some articles by journalists such as Mazhar Ali Khan, editor of *View Point*, a weekly published in Lahore (the previous week). These writings made a plea for both Pakistan and Indian governments to give their fullest attention to reversing the arms race and to make a beginning toward an understanding that could pave the way for lasting peace and cooperation.

O. P. Sabherwal in a *Mainstream* commentary (June 20, 1981) felt that P. V. Narasimha Rao's stress on India's commitment to Pakistan's sovereign status and Rao's call for careful vigilance of the external forces keeping India and Pakistan divided had helped a great deal in removing lingering misgivings and suspicions about the Indian approach towards Pakistan. On crucial issues, however, such as the Afghanistan question, the U.S. arms flow into Pakistan, and nuclear development, very little progress was achieved in narrowing the differences of perception and actual position although there was some agreement on the peaceful uses of nuclear technology (June 20, 1981).

Mainstream (June 20, 1981) published a text of External Affairs Minister Narasimha Rao's address to the Pakistan Institute of International Affairs at Karachi on June 11, 1981. The main thrust of the address was a call for a future vision of Indo-Pakistan relations that would go beyond normalization and would undertake a deliberate and conscious transformation of the respective psyches of the Indians and the Pakistanis. His address also stressed the convergence of interests of both countries on north-south economic relations, although there were differences of perceptions on the issues of Afghanistan and Kampuchea.

Kuldip Nayar's views, which were critical of U.S. arms supply to Pakistan, were presented in one *Mainstream* article (July 11, 1981). The editorial comment in *Mainstream* (July 18, 1981) was critical of the Indian government for its "ad hocism" on the crucial question of national security when the United States was arming Pakistan.

The *Economic and Political Weekly* (EPW) devoted its columns to Indo-Pakistan relations under sections such as editorial notes, international affairs, capital view, and discussion features. In issues dated June 13, June 20, and July 4, the EPW devoted 244.02 square inches of space to Indo-Pakistan relations. In the weeks previous to P. V. Narasimha Rao's visit to Islamabad, the *Economic and Political Weekly* covered some issues related to Indo-Pakistan affairs. Three pieces devoted to international affairs and India's defenses were critical of Zia's policies within Pakistan and his policies to strengthen Pakistan's military resources based on U.S. armaments.

One discussion was critical of India's hostile relations and suspicious attitude toward Pakistan and called for positive support for Pakistan as it faced problems created by the Soviet presence in Afghanistan.

Two pieces, while considering India's initiatives for achieving better relations through the visit of the foreign affairs minister a success, indicated that more needed to be done to stop the United States from using the situation on the Indian subcontinent to further U.S. security interests, thereby causing "disastrous problems" for India and Pakistan.

DISCUSSION OF FINDINGS

During June 1981, the period of our study, the newspapers and newsmagazines in India played an active role in seeking information from the political leaders and sources close to them in both countries. The news media presented the information gathered from the wire services and their own special correspondents as straight news, news analysis, special articles, and editorials. Our findings provided evidence to support our hypothesis that Indian news media would play up news and information relating to military, political, and trade relations of Pakistan with India and other countries. Three factors may explain this behavior of the mass media. First, political and military security issues in India that have been part of the historical evolution of India and Pakistan are of great concern to the government and people of India. The mass news media have a natural interest in these government- and people-oriented issues. Second, there is a growing consciousness among the news media that they are the public watchdogs on issues of national and foreign policy of India. The public also has high expectations of the news media to give them proper information on various national and international issues. The public has increasing interest and motivation to participate in public opinion formations through print media. Third, there is a growing trend in journalism toward higher quality investigative and critical reporting. This trend combines with a sense of mission to heal the rifts and contribute towards better relations between India and Pakistan. Such factors explain to a large extent the active role of the news media in "managing" the situation between India and Pakistan. It is important to note also that the topical interest created by the visit of the Indian external affairs minister during the period under study influenced the news media to focus and play up the event for coverage during June 1981.

There was no strong evidence that Indian news media have always supported the government of India's policies toward Pakistan. Hence, our hypothesis that the Indian news media adopt a positive stance toward India government positions and carry information less critical of India is not sustainable. The Indian news media are looking at Indo-Pakistan relations from an increasingly multilateral and global perspective. Consequently, we find evidence of a critical stand of the Indian news media toward India's policies and approaches to Pakistan.

Further, our findings suggest that the Indian news media did not show a hostile attitude toward the military regime in Pakistan. Instead, the approach of the media was aimed at facilitating the understanding between the two countries and stressing the need for cordial relations. There was a general support for the initiatives taken by the Pakistan regime for improving the relations with India.

The use of information from transnational wire services and from the dispatches by the special correspondents stationed in Pakistan, the Soviet Union, the United States, and Western Europe indicated that the news media brought information from different places and political perceptions to provide the readers with different interpretations and perspectives. Evidence from our study supports the hypothesis that the Indian news media play an important role in informing the Indian public of the views and comments expressed in Pakistan, the United States, the Soviet Union, and other foreign countries about Indo-Pakistan relations.

The news media, particularly the newsmagazines, provide in-depth special analyses and reports based on information collected through personal interviews and public opinion polls of metropolitan area populations. Different viewpoints of officials and leaders from India and Pakistan were presented. The participation of readers was apparent from letters to the editor and rejoinders. These findings support our hypothesis that the media take the initiative for in-depth and in-person interviews with the government leaders, policymakers, and opposition leaders relating to issues involving Indo-Pakistan relations.

Finally, our findings indicate the existence of notable differences between news coverage and the treatment pattern found in the regional-language newspapers such as the *Dinamani* (Tamil-language daily) and the *Kannada Prabha* (Kannada-language daily) and those found in the three English-language dailies. The tone and expressions in the regional-language dailies were more oriented to peace and reconciliation in Indo-Pakistan relations compared with the English-language dailies. There was not much variation in the volume of news reported by the wire services, but there were definitely important differences in the quality, the complexity, and the detailed manner of the treatment of news events and their implications for the management of Indo-Pakistan conflict. This is evidenced by the extensive treatment given to Indo-Pakistan affairs in the English-language dailies, using the format of editorials, news analysis, and special articles by the correspondents. This confirms our hypothesis that the kinds of coverage and the treatment of Indo-Pakistan relations in the English-language news media are more in-depth and more detailed than those presented in Tamil- and Kannada-language news media.

RESEARCH IMPLICATIONS

Our sample of news media did not cover other major languages in India. Because of the shared common language and culture and the geographical contiguity between India and Pakistan, a study of the news media in languages such as Panjabi, Urdu, and Hindi would be much more interesting to conduct to test our regional language hypothesis. Our findings, based on two language dailies whose cultures are neither contiguous nor common due to geography and language, are limited and not generalizable. We suggest that further studies should be done taking into account Urdu-, Hindi-, and Panjabi-language news media.

Further, the period we chose to examine the role of the news media was highlighted with the visits of state leaders. It would be interesting to see the pattern of news coverage and the role of the news media during other periods when the international communication environment is less affected by major personal meetings between Indian and Pakistani leaders.

It would be interesting to compare the roles of Pakistani news media in managing the relationships between India and Pakistan.

REFERENCES

Link. June 14, 1981, 9. Big display of sweet intention, by R. K. Mishra.

Link. June 18, 1981, 27. Renewal of arms race, by Kalim Bahadur.

Link. June 18, 1981, 8 (Chalapathi Rau).

Link. June 28, 1981 (O. P. Sabherwal).

Mainstream. May 16, 1981, 33 (Mazhar Ali Khan).

Mainstream. June 20, 1981 (O. P. Sabherwal).

Mainstream. July 11, 1981 (Kuldip Nayar).

Mainstream. July 18, 1981, 3 (editor).

Rao, Bhaskara N. 1971. *Indo-Pak Conflict: Controlled Mass Communication in Inter-State Relations.* New Delhi: S. Chand.

The Sunday. June 7, 1981, 21.

The Sunday. June 14, 1981 (Rajendra Sareen).

The Sunday. June 21, 1981, 16– 17 (B. N. Kumar).

CHAPTER 9

THE *PEOPLE'S DAILY* AND NIXON'S VISIT TO CHINA

Georgette Wang

Journalism students traditionally have been taught that conflict is an important element in "newsworthiness." Conflicts among individuals, social groups, and nations attract readers because they are disruptive to normal daily routine, they bring tension and excitement, and they often have some direct impact on readers' lives. Social conflict and the role of newspapers in community conflict has been an important area of research in the past. As pointed out by Tichenor et al., the press reflects society by reporting events, but it cannot remain an outsider. It is not an isolated social institution. The press is often involved in, rather than merely reporting, conflicts:

> While the press does serve as a mirror, however contorted its reflective curvature, it is part of a reciprocal process, being affected by that system and affecting it in turn. ... Community groups may use the press and journalists as sources of intelligence, as indications of reaction of the public to events, and as a device for creating awareness and defining problems. The performance of the press or other medium typically becomes part of the controversy (1980, 220).

In a similar fashion, the press is involved in conflict resolution and consensus generation. By analyzing the situation, making different viewpoints public, and providing information on the issue, the press offers a basis for negotiation and compromise.

There are, of course, many factors involved in how the press functions in such a process: the nature of the conflict, the size and ownership of the paper, the news freedom allowed in the country, and the structure of the mass communication system, for example. Together, these variables interact with one another and others to determine the role of a newspaper in a specific circumstance.

Studies of the role of the press in conflict situations have generally focused on the United States, where a capitalistic-liberal press system is found. Communist countries have different concepts of the press's function, and their mass communication systems are much different from those of the West. The press in the West is expected to be independent of all social factions. In Communist societies, it is a branch of the government charged with the role of "collective propagandist, collective agitator, collective organizer" as stipulated by Lenin (1927, 4).

Conflict and class struggle is usually a constant theme in the press in Communist societies. Reporting of conflicts, however, is highly selective and very much part of the overall government policy. In China, for example, there are many instances in which conflicts are not allowed to appear in the press, especially conflicts among the leaders. As Pye (1978, 239) pointed out, ". . . the Chinese political process is filled with conflict which cannot be legitimately disclosed." Once a conclusion is reached, however, the media usually carry out large-scale campaigns to solicit acceptance and support from the people. Such a tendency was manifested in various "movements" and in purges of political leaders in the past. As pointed out by Nathan (1979, 11), "Most obviously over the course of time the media have been obliged to publicize changes in policy."

In addition to publicizing policy changes, the press almost always tells readers that the changes are "in line" with the ultimate goals of the nation, and that "erroneous concepts" are to be rejected. The Chinese press, therefore, is not merely involved in conflicts, but it is strategically and purposefully used in issues of conflict or the resolution of conflict.

In view of such a background, the way the *People's Daily*, China's most important paper, presented U.S. President Richard Nixon's visit to China in 1972 became a significant and interesting case for at least two reasons: the nature of the event as a dramatic highlight in the process of conflict resolution, and the nature of the mass medium, the official organ of a Communist government.

THE NATURE OF THE EVENT

Before Nixon's trip to China, the two powers had not had official communication for more than twenty years. This breakdown of communication was the by-product of a long-term adversary relationship. When the Communist Chinese established rule in 1949, the ideological orientation and close association with the Soviet Union immediately put China in a hostile position with the United States. Over the years, however, significant changes took place in China's foreign policy; the pro-Soviet and anti-U.S. stance of the 1950s gradually changed into an antisuperpower (including both the United States and the Soviet Union) position in the 1960s. Signs of better relations with the United States began to emerge with exchanges of ping-pong teams in the early 1970s as both parties perceived strategic benefit in an alliance against the USSR.

Although the Vietnam War was not yet over and tension and hostility still existed, Nixon's visit to China was the first major attempt to resolve conflict issues between the two nations. In the past, the United States had always been portrayed as an aggressive imperialist in Chinese media. As pointed out by Edelstein and Liu (1963, 190), the United States is reported as a country "full of contradictions; automation vs unemployment; surplus vs mass poverty; and poor proletariat vs millionaires." Propaganda against the United States often incorporated distorted information and exaggeration of social conflicts. To Edelstein and Liu, the anti-America propaganda was in fact "deeply woven into the fabric of the ideology itself."

A study of the *Peking Review* by Tretiak (1971) showed a softening of Chinese attacks on the United States after 1968, and the Soviet Union seemed to be replacing the United States as the number one enemy of the country as Sino-Soviet relations steadily worsened. During the Vietnam War, however, the United States was once again criticized bitterly and attacked by the Chinese press for its actions in Indochina. The propaganda apparently reinforced the image of the United States as an exploitative and militant capitalist nation doomed to fail. This hostile attitude did not show signs of relief until "ping-pong diplomacy" began in the spring of 1971. A study by Wang and Starck (1972) reported decreased hostility toward the United States in the news released by the New China News Agency. It was predicted that while the relationship with another nation (the United States) was being redefined, "propaganda campaigns may be deliberately altered in relation to particular, immediate objectives. . . ." It was therefore deemed probable that the Chinese authorities would change their communication policy regarding the United States and turn to a more favorable attitude to cope with the changing policy.

THE ROLE AND FUNCTION OF THE *PEOPLE'S DAILY*

China is known to have a thorough as well as a tightly controlled communication system. As pointed out by Barnett (1978, 1), "one of the most striking characteristics of the communication system in China today is its pervasiveness, penetration, and intensity with *minimum technology*." By "minimum technology," Barnett was referring to the fact that China was still quite behind technologically in modern mass communication media in the late 1970s. But specific integrative use of newspapers, radio, loudspeakers, interpersonal networks, and even folk and popular media have made the system a highly efficient one. With purposes directed on "political penetration, control, and regimentation" (Liu 1971, 4), the system was capable of transmitting messages as well as coercing its audience in an effective and efficient way, although its effectiveness was still questioned by communication scholars.

Throughout the Communist rule in China, perhaps with the exception in recent years of relatively liberal-oriented policy changes, the only period of lessened control of the communication system was probably during the cultural revolution. In the late 1960s, red guards all over the country began to put out one- or two-sheet uncensored newspapers. But by the time of Nixon's visit, central news media such as the *People's Daily*, Radio Peking, and the New China News Agency were again dominating the national communication system (Pool 1973, 494).

The communication system in China functions as a whole, but among the various media and channels, the *People's Daily* is often regarded as the most important. Established with the regime, the *People's Daily* has been serving the function of party mouthpiece. Considering its close supervision, the content of the paper can be viewed as an honest reflection of Party policy direction and stance on various issues.

The *People's Daily* had a circulation of 3.4 million in 1974 (estimated circulation in 1980 was 30 million or more [see Wat 1980]), but its influence reached far beyond this figure through such mechanisms as newspaper reading groups and political study sessions. Although other mass media in China may take slightly different viewpoints in some domestic issues, on important matters, and almost always on foreign affairs, they generally turn to the *People's Daily* for guidance and direction. Quoting reports and editorials from the *People's Daily* has been regarded as common practice for regional newspapers in China. It can be said that the *People's Daily* by itself sets the agenda and reporting style for the rest of the mass media in China. Unlike mass media in non-Communist nations that are competing with each other most of the time, the *People's Daily* has been the single most powerful newspaper in China.

Given these facts, I hypothesized that the *People's Daily* would take the responsibility of redirecting and reformulating people's images about the United States in light of a changing relationship (1) by decreasing the level of hostility in reporting news events about the United States, and (2) by providing large quantities of information about the United States and indepth analyses at the time of Nixon's visit to justify a changing policy. I expected the *People's Daily* to take an active role in the process of resolving conflict between the two nations.

METHODOLOGY

To see if there was gradual change of attitude in the *People's Daily* regarding the United States, a content analysis was conducted for the period before and after Nixon's visit. Nixon left for Peking on February 19 and was back in Washington on March 2, 1972. The content analysis focusing on the Nixon visit was done for the second, fourth, sixth, eighth, tenth, and twelfth weeks, both before and after the visit (see Table 8 for all dates).

For comparison, results from a previous content analysis of the *People's Daily* will also be discussed here. In the previous content analysis, the first two weeks of April (2–15) were chosen randomly for 1970, 1972, 1974, 1976, 1978, and 1980. All items regarding the United States were coded for the twelve weeks.

In this 1970–80 study, an item was counted if it concerned the United States and was thus coded if "U.S." appeared in the headline. A number of items (mostly features) also were coded although "U.S." did not appear in the headline, because the item was apparently dealing heavily with the United States, with such heads as "The Vietnam Frontiers," and "Statement from the Ministry of Foreign Affairs."

Items coded included space in square inches, source of news, nature of the item, content category, favorableness toward the United States, source of information, and whether the item directly concerned the United States, that is, whether it was dealing with something happening within the United States or something indirectly concerning the U.S. The degree of favorableness was measured on a five-point scale, with 1 assigned when an item was extremely unfavorable not only by nature (disaster, military maneuver, riots) but loaded with subjective and colored terms in the headline ("U.S. imperialist," "invasion," "liar," "open plot against the people," "doomed to fail"); 2 assigned when the nature of the item was negative, but no subjective or colored terms were involved ("U.S. fighter plane shot down"); 3 assigned to neutral items that were neither favorable nor unfavorable and had no subjective or colored terms; 4 assigned to items that were favorable but involved no subjective or colored terms ("Premier Chou En-lai gave a welcome party to American visitors"); and 5 assigned to the items that were favorable by nature and loaded with colored descriptions ("Ping-Pong team received unprecedented warm welcome from American people").

FINDINGS

Overview of Nixon Visit Study

There were 325 items regarding the United States during the period coded. Of the items coded, 91.7 percent appeared in the "international section," that is, pages five and six. The total of square inches was 11,541, including eighteen pictures. Ninety-five percent of the items were straight news items with Xinhua News Agency almost the only source of information. But among the Xinhua items, a relatively high percentage was directly or indirectly quoted from reports published in foreign media or statements issued by various authorities or political entities reacting to U.S. military actions or foreign and economic policies (77 percent). Because reactions, as such, are defined as items indirectly rather than directly dealing with the United States, the percentage of items that provided readers with information about events happening in the United States was as low as 10.2 percent. In other words, by reading the news about the United States in the *People's Daily* during the study period, a reader would learn much about how selected nations and political entities such as the "Cambodian Kingdom People's United Government," and the "Laotian Patriotic Front Party," responded to U.S. actions and policies but would not know much about the United States as a nation or a culture.

The content categories reported during the six-month period before and after the Nixon visit were mainly about the Vietnam War and fighting in Cambodia. Other articles focused on unrest between North and South Korea, exchange of visitors between the United States and China such as one item on the visit of the leader of the Black Panthers from the United States, and a number of items on the touring ping-pong team.

Of the total number of items, 83 percent were coded as "extremely unfavorable." Included was an item about the North Vietnamese Communist Party chairman wishing the American people a good New Year while at the same time calling for a united struggle against the U.S. government to force it to stop the "invasion" of Vietnam. Another item of a similar nature concerned the status of women in the United States; the headline described how American women "overcame the stumbling block and advanced in the revolutionary struggle." Most of the other articles concerned the war, in which the United States was invariably described as "imperialist," "weakening," "inhumane" (bombing schools and hospitals), or "aggressive." Next to "extremely unfavorable" was "unfavorable" (5.9 percent), closely followed by "neutral" (4.9 percent), and "favorable" (4.3 percent). The total number of items coded as "extremely favorable" was six (1.9 percent).

Table 8. Items in *People's Daily* about the United States Before and After Nixon Visit

	Number of Items	Square Inches	Extremely Negative Items (%)
December 4 – 10	8	546	100
December 17 – 23	9	379	89
December 30–January 4	36	1503	86
January 11 – 17	33	1303	82
January 24 – 30	35	1676	88
February 6 – 12	23	1100	78
February 19–March 2	13	545	77
March 9 – 15	20	533	75
March 22 – 28	17	846	82
April 4 – 10	26	765	96
April 17 – 23	52	1904	73
April 30–May 6	23	986	60
May 13 – 19	43	1600	95
TOTAL	325[a]	11541	83

[a]This total does not include items printed while Nixon was in China.

almost doubled after the visit (6.9 percent to 12.7 percent). Most of these items concerned the exchange of visitors and ping-pong team activities. The space given to these items was generally small (from 3 inches to 50 inches on the story about Nixon's reception of the Chinese ping-pong team) but favorable. These items, together with one about U.S. TV showing Chinese revolutionary drama and one story about pandas sent to the Washington Zoo, constitute the total of "favorable" items about the United States.

The overall picture presented by the *People's Daily* throughout the six-month period was therefore still largely negative, including the few items that appeared while Nixon was still in China. One editorial was entitled "U.S. Government must stop the invasion of Vietnam"; others included accusations of the "new criminal actions of U.S. imperialists." There did not seem to be any effort on the part of the newspaper to explain or analyze the reasons and implications for Nixon's visit, nor was there any apparent change of tone, at least to an outsider, regarding reports about the United States.

General U.S. Coverage During 1970–80

The change in news coverage about the United States seemed to be slow and gradual during the ten-year span from 1970 to 1980. For the total number of items and space involved, there was an apparent decrease from 1970 to 1976, then a slight rise again after 1976 (Table 9). Favorableness to the United States, the nature of items, and the percentage of items directly dealing with events happening in China showed a much clearer indication of policy change. For example, in 1970, 95.5 percent of the items were coded as "extremely unfavorable," and the "neutral items" were no more than 1.1 percent. For 1972 and 1974, the percentage of "extremely unfavorable" items remained at 75 percent, but the "neutral items" went from 12.2 percent to a double of 25 percent. From 1976 to 1980, one or less than one item was coded as "extremely unfavorable," but the percentage of "neutral items" increased from 57 percent to 92 percent. The number of "favorable" and "extremely favorable" items, however, remained low through the years.

The change in the percentage of items directly dealing with the United States also was impressive; there was a steady increase, from 3.3 percent in 1970 to 95.8 percent in 1978, but there was a slight fall to 80.4 percent in 1980 because of the hostage issue in Iran. As to the nature of items, straight news continued to be the major part of items regarding the United States from 1970 to 1976; in 1978, the percentage dropped from 100 percent to 84 percent and was maintained at that level in 1980.

CONCLUSION

The analysis of the *People's Daily* showed that although over the long run there was a change in reporting about the United States, at the time of Nixon's visit, there was almost no effort made to explain the implications of the event. There was subsequently very little said in other mass media in China regarding the visit simply because they had to follow the model set up by the *People's Daily*. Failure of mass media to provide explanations and justification to the public, however, does not necessarily mean that the public was not informed.

While discussing communication and Chinese political culture, Pye (1978, 223) noted a specific feature of the Chinese communication system—mass media were found at times to be tagging behind the interpersonal communication network during the period of purging. In the case of Lin Piao, for example, cadres all over the country were "instructed in secrecy as to what the crimes were and it may take one or even two years . . . before the media are allowed to explain what the cadres already know."

Table 9. Items in *People's Daily* about the United States during 1970– 80 Study

	Number of Items	Square Inches	Neutral Items (%)	Extremely Negative Items (%)
1970	90	3390	1	95.6
1972	49	1420	12	75.0
1974	12	556	25	75.0
1976	7	153	57	14.0
1978	24	747	87	0.0˙
1980	51	962	92	2.0

The interpersonal network, therefore, may play a role quite different from that of the media. A similar case was found with Nixon's visit.

Information revealed through personal interviews* showed it was the interpersonal communication channels that took the responsibility of "educating the masses" and preparing them for the historical visit. Before Nixon's arrival in Peking, meetings were reportedly held in communities almost everywhere in China, at schools, factories, and institutions. Three major subjects were discussed in these meetings: (1) political implications of the visit, or is there a change of policy; (2) the effect of the visit at the national and the international level; and (3) how the people should react to the visit. It was made clear to the people that the United States accepted China's viewpoint concerning Taiwan, but there was no drastic policy change in China toward the United States: the party would continue to express disagreement with the United States over various issues; and the attitude toward the visit should be kept with "no inferiority, no superiority," and "not cold, not warm." A few details were noted of the visit, such as the absence of a red carpet for Nixon as he stepped down from the plane, and that Nixon was the one who initiated the handshake with Chou En-lai. People's reactions toward the visit were said to have been gathered through channels other than the mass media, therefore no letters to the editor concerning the visit appeared in the *People's Daily*.

The communication system in China is in many ways unique. China's domestic communication policy regarding Nixon's visit also seemed to be unique. While it was expected that the *People's Daily* would play an important role in educating the masses, and preparing them for the historical visit, there was a distinct division of labor within the communication system.

The *People's Daily*, while often regarded as the party mouthpiece, kept its role strictly to that of a party spokesman to the outside world before, during, and after Nixon's visit. The newspaper content, although appearing

---

* Personal interviews were conducted with Zheng Bei-wei and Yu Jin-lu of Fudan University in Shanghai by the author on August 20, 1981, at the EWCI.

contradictory by reporting an important "friendly visit," while at the same time viciously attacking the United States, was, in fact, an honest reflection of the party's attitude on the issues. The picture it presented was exactly what was told about government policy in the public meetings: China would continue to disagree with the United States over various issues such as the Vietnam War without seriously offending or damaging future relations. Without being burdened with the responsibility of making the people understand, the messages sent out by the *People's Daily* to the outside world were therefore clear and multifunctional. Background information and the explanations necessary to prepare people for such a dramatic turn in foreign policy were supplied through interpersonal networks. With two-way communication available in group meetings, such a choice of communication channels may be more effective for persuasion purposes. In a way, interpersonal networks were used as supplementary channels that helped the audience to comprehend and interpret media content in a fashion desired by the authorities.

It should also be noted that, although the total number of items favoring a better U.S.-China relationship was rather insignificant to an outsider, for an audience that has acquired the habit of reading between the lines in monotonous propaganda (Pool 1973, 463), the message might be sufficiently clear that a major change was in the offing.

This study showed that in a Communist communication system, each communication channel may be charged with a specific function in time of conflict or conflict resolution. In the case of Nixon's visit to China, the *People's Daily* acted as a party spokesman to the international community, while internal communication took place through interpersonal networks. It is therefore suggested that in future studies, in order to better understand media's role in the outbreak of conflict or conflict resolution, other channels in the communication system should be examined carefully.

REFERENCES

Barnett, A. Doak. 1978. The communication system in China. In *Communication in China—Perspectives and Hypotheses*, edited by A. Doak Barnett and Godwin C. Chu. Honolulu: East-West Communication Institute Papers.

Edelstein, Alex S., and Alan Ping-lin Liu. 1963. Anti-Americanism in Red China's People's Daily: A functional analysis. *Journalism Quarterly* 40(1):187–94.

Lenin, Vladimir Ilyich. 1927. *Collected Works*. New York: International Publishers.

Liu, P. L. Alan. 1971. *Communication and National Integration in Communist China*. Berkeley, Ca.: University of California Press.

Nathan, Andrew J. 1970. Mass mobilization and political participation in China: Do people believe the media? Paper for East-West Center Conference on Communication and Social Integration in China, January 1979. Resource Materials Collection, East-West Communication Institute, East-West Center, Honolulu, Hawaii.

Pool, Ithiel de Sola. 1973. Communication in totalitarian societies. In *Handbook of Communication*, edited by Ithiel de Sola Pool et al. Chicago: Rand McNally College Publishing Co.

Pye, Lucian. 1978. Communications and Chinese political culture. *Asian Survey* 18(3):221–46.

Tichenor, Phillip J., George A. Donohue, and Clarice N. Olien. 1980. *Community Conflict and the Press*. Beverly Hills: Sage.

Tretiak, Daniel. 1971. Is China preparing to 'turn out'?: Changes in Chinese levels of attention to the international environment. *Asian Survey* 11:219–37.

Wang, Kai, and Kenneth Starck. 1972. Red China's external propaganda during Sino-U.S. rapprochement. *Journalism Quarterly* 49(4):674–78.

Wat, Kit-Bing Teresa. 1980. Similarity and diversity in the news: A study of three national media and five regional broadcasting stations in China. M.A. Thesis, University of Hawaii, Honolulu.

NATIONAL LEVEL CONFLICT
AND THE MEDIA

CHAPTER 10

THE CULTURAL ROLE OF THE MEDIA IN IRAN: THE REVOLUTION OF 1978–79 AND AFTER

William O. Beeman

Discussions of mass media often seem to make an assumption of cultural neutrality. Newspapers, television, and radio are thought somehow to be essentially the same phenomena no matter where they are observed. Where cross-cultural differences are noted, the difference is seen to lie in the ways these neutral objects are utilized, rather than in the essential conception of the phenomena.

From an anthropological standpoint, however, this assumption of neutrality is untenable when we consider the differences in the ways media are dealt with culturally in different societies. A mass medium fills a cultural space in the given society and thereby acquires a distinct and unique cultural definition. This cultural space may have been occupied by other institutions at an earlier time, in which case newly developing mass media can be seen as supplanting or becoming merged with what existed before. In some areas of the world, radio and television have led to the death of traditional information and entertainment channels. In other places, however, new media have become vehicles for the support of traditional cultural activities.

At times newly introduced mass media have produced revolutionary effects in the societal management of time and energy as they forged new spaces for themselves. Thus the media are cultural forces as well as cultural objects. In operation, they produce specific concrete effects that cannot be easily predicted. Each case requires close analysis of the web of cultural meanings operative at the given moment in the society under study. In India and the United States, for example, newspapers have traditionally played an important investigative role in government, and they can be credited on occasion with the rise and fall of political regimes. In other nations, newspapers are considered an adjunct of official politics and serve primarily to support official policy rather than as its adversary. In many nations the media have become adjunct to the overall commercial activity of the nation and are potent vehicles for advertising—so much so that they may depend on advertising revenues to keep their operations going. In other nations, the media are thought of primarily as educational or cultural resources, and as such they eschew commercial ties. In each case one can see clearly that the medium has become imbued with a whole range of meanings and potentialities for action within one culture that it will not possess in another.

There is another way the media play a cultural role in today's world that has not been at all well documented. Media can now be seen to be truly international in scope, and because of this they often *overlap* cultural space. Media generated at one place may be received at other places where the effects are not calculated in advance by the originators. The oldest historical example of this kind of overlapping is shortwave radio broadcasts. Such broadcasts have long been used for propaganda purposes, but their unintended effects on political and social developments within receiving nations are not easily seen in advance.

Another example of this kind of unintended effect is seen in the worldwide syndication of television programs. Although the United States is the leader in this area, European nations, Mexico, and Egypt also provide television comedies and dramas for a wide audience outside their country of origin. In all cases, the effects of these television productions over a long period of time have come to be questioned by social critics in the nations importing them. Indeed, if the exporting nations only realized how often these exported programs result in negative views of the country of export, they might look harder at the desirability of allowing this activity to continue unrestricted.*

On the other hand, some areas of media are designed to be international in scope. International newspapers and newsmagazines, as well as shortwave radio broadcasts, are important forces in international political relations. In this case the danger of unintended effects lies in assuming that these areas of publication and broadcasting are somehow above the concerns of national cultural and political relations because they are targeted for an international audience.

The Iranian Revolution offered an unprecedented opportunity to study the functions of the media institutions of a non-Western society during a

---

* Hendricus Johannes Prakke quotes Dutch author Jef Last talking about the impression American "westerns" make on Indonesian film viewers: "From such films the Indonesian forms his image of the American: a guy who drinks, kisses, shoots and thereby pockets the whole world. No American propaganda, however many millions are invested, can ever counterbalance the Indonesian contempt for the white man that the American film induces. . . . they believe that everything they see must correspond with the facts because it was photographed. Historical films, fictional films, documentary films—all have the same reality value, especially for the villager" (Last 1955,167–68, quoted in Prakke 1979).

period of rapid change. During the Iranian Revolution, the press, radio, and television all seemed to undergo a radical transformation. Yet, once the revolution had taken place, within six months the media returned to its familiar well-established cultural role in Iranian society. Remarkably, the same can be said of the role of international media in Iranian society. The one important innovation in Iranian public communication—the cassette tape—continued to play its new-found role as a tool in the media communication of the opposition to the revolutionary government. Studying this phenomenon may help students of the media understand some of the social dynamics that preserve the cultural shape of media institutions in a given setting.

THE IRANIAN MEDIA BEFORE THE REVOLUTION

The Iranian media during the reign of both Mohammad Reza Pahlavi and his father, Reza Shah, were largely kept in check by the central government. They were compelled to reflect views that were approved by central authorities. Only during the period of the prime ministership of Mohammad Mossadeq (1951–53) was there any relaxation of this pattern of rigid censorship. Radio and television, which began as private commercial operations, were taken over by the government in the 1960s and, like the print media, were used to promote officially accepted views.

Newspapers, it was claimed by the government, were not heavily censored. But in fact if anything untoward appeared in the morning papers, the editor would receive a call from the Ministry of Information before breakfast. If the offense was great, all copies of the paper would be confiscated by the government before they went on sale.

The principal control over privately owned newspapers and magazines, however, lay in government licensing procedures. If a publication did not publish for a specific period of time, its license would automatically lapse. If the government found a publication to be continually offensive, it would force suspension of publication through various coercive means, such as electrical inspections, building code violations, restriction on purchase of newsprint, and so on, until the license lapsed. In this way the government could get rid of those magazines and newspapers it didn't like and still claim not to have directly ordered them to close.

Print publications tried to survive as best they could. They downplayed local news, gave prominent coverage to the royal family and their activities, and provided strong coverage of international affairs. It was often frustrating for Iranians to be confronted with a newspaper that contained hundreds of lines of print on government scandals in Europe and America, but nothing of the corruption that all knew to exist at home, but which they could learn about only through the rumor mill. The Ministry of Information often boasted that they needed to do very little in the way of monitoring the newspapers, since they practiced such excellent self-restraint.

Publications in foreign languages were surprisingly prominent in Tehran. There were two English- and one French-language daily papers, as well as one German-language weekly. The freedom allowed these publications was somewhat greater than that allowed Persian-language newspapers.

The effects of radio on the Iranian population were enormous during the postwar years. Inexpensive radio sets penetrated the villages throughout the country and served as an important communication link for the vast, remote, widely separated areas of the sparsely populated countryside. Radio was at the same time a controversial device, largely because of extensive broadcasts of popular and classical music. Under orthodox Islam, listening to music is highly disapproved of, on the theory that music provides the means for an individual to be transported to a plane of attention and consciousness that is outside the here and now of the mundane world. Thus to listen to music is in some sense to deny reality, which can be construed as blasphemous, since a denial of reality is a denial of God's creation. Although urban clerics would sometimes take a lax view of this prohibition, in rural areas public opinion has historically been quite clear that music is an improper human diversion. In rural areas of Iran, individuals buying radios would often claim that they were buying them only to listen to the news or to sports—not for music.

Nevertheless, it is clear that radio was a source for music listening throughout the country. In fact, Radio Iran became an important cultural institution, not for news but precisely for its controversial music. Rural areas possessed their own folk music, of course. This music, played at weddings and other celebrations, was an important aspect of rural life. The urban music played on the radio worked its way slowly into the folk repertoire until many urban melodies had become "folkloricised." As the national appetite for popular music grew, fed by radio broadcasts, writers began to look to the country for inspiration. Thus rural folk melodies became incorporated into urban music. The vital link between the two traditions, urban and rural, was chiefly radio. (For a more extensive discussion on this aspect of Iranian popular culture, see Beeman 1976, 1983.)

Radio was matched in its impact on Iranian life only by television, which hit the nation like a bomb in the late 1960s and early 1970s. Its effects were profound in every part of the nation. National Iranian Radio-Television, headed by a dynamic relative of Empress Farah and provided with an almost unlimited budget, embarked on a drive to bring television to every area of the nation by 1976.

The ambitiousness of this goal is only properly understood when one takes Iranian geography into consideration. The nation is uniquely vast and mountainous. Television signals, in order to penetrate the valleys and vault over the mountains of the country, had to utilize special technology. The system finally adopted was a microwave system, which worked fairly well but required a great deal of maintenance. As the coverage of the national television network spread, the public demand for the service became greater. Lack of electricity seemed to be no impediment. In even the most remote villages, the sound of portable kerosene or gasoline generators could be heard every evening as the inhabitants watched their favorite programs.

If radio was the means for urban culture to spread into rural areas of Iran, television became the Iranian villager's window on the world. The dark urban cinema, with its morally questionable fare, was heavily condemned by conservative religionists, but somehow television escaped approbrium. Some of the most conservative clerics went so far as to announce that they personally didn't watch television—a signal to their adherents that they should follow this example—but most religious figures remained neutral, saying only that popular music programs with "naked" (i.e., bareheaded, bare-armed) women should be avoided by the pious.

National Iranian Radio-Television generally did a reasonable job with television production. Like most of the world's television systems, however, it could not fill its entire schedule with home-produced fare. American and European syndicated programs became common. U.S. television star Lee Majors came to Iran in 1978 expecting to be able to rest and be anonymous for a short period when he was under some pressure in the United States. He was shocked to be mobbed by rabid fans who recognized him as the "Six Million Dollar Man," which was being shown every week on Iranian television at that time.

The cultural impact of television cannot be overestimated. The reality of the television screen was overwhelmingly impressive for many, creating a whole new set of images of modern life for traditional Iranians. In the smaller, more traditional towns, there was confusion and conflict between traditional local values and the more sophisticated ones being shown on the screen. Parviz Kimiavi, a prominent contemporary filmmaker, documented this poignantly in his film *The Mongols* (1973), in which the coming of television is likened to the Mongol invasion that destroyed Iranian society during the 12th century. (See Beeman 1983 for additional discussion of the effects of film and television on the Iranian public.)

The social life of small towns was likewise transformed by television. In the traditional coffee houses, storytellers who once entertained patrons were replaced by the television set. As in the United States, mealtimes were dominated by television programs, particularly the news, which coincided with the usual times for the noon and evening meals for the majority of Iranians. Television slowly took on the familiar role of a legitimizing device for much of the population. What one saw on television was not necessarily any truer than what one read in the papers or heard on the radio, but somehow seeing events directly made them more real for viewers.

National Iranian Radio-Television had a curious attitude toward its public mission. On the one hand it was a purveyor of much that was culturally foreign, vulgar, and low in quality. Nevertheless, it also saw as one of its missions the rescue and revival of Iranian traditional culture. To this end it spent enormous amounts of money bringing together and training traditional musicians. It supported playwrights, actors, and directors, and gave large grants for the production of films. Even *The Mongols* was produced with money from NIRT, which also sponsored live festivals and concerts, such as the annual Festival of Arts in Shiraz. These festivals were taped for later broadcast, but their cost was far greater than it would have been if the events had been produced for television alone. The results of all this activity were impressive. In the space of ten years a whole new generation of young artists had been developed through the good offices of NIRT, and the quality of their work was generally high. Some began to refer to NIRT as a "second Ministry of Culture," and indeed there was a great rivalry between the two bodies over authority and roles.

THE CHANGING FUNCTIONS OF THE MEDIA
IN THE IRANIAN REVOLUTION

The revolutionary events of 1978–79 demonstrated just how mutable the cultural role of the media can be during times of social and political stress. The news media, print, radio, and television all played a highly prominent role in the conduct of the revolution itself, leading many to comment that the Iranian Revolution may have been the first revolution conducted by the media. Because their original roles in society were so different, each of the media was affected in a different way by the revolution.

The first social protests that really stung the government began in the summer and fall of 1978. At that time the newspapers were somewhat at a loss as to what they were to print. When a confrontation between government troops and thousands of people took place on the streets, the papers couldn't simply ignore the fact. There were too many eyewitnesses to such events. In the early days some of the papers took to quoting foreign news sources, as if that would reduce the onus on them, although this was patently absurd. The BBC became one of the principal sources for print commentary. Some papers would print BBC reports along with government denials as a means of getting the news before the public by whatever means, however obtuse. The government became highly upset at the increased freedom being exercised by the newspapers, but it did not know how to handle the situation.

On August 27, 1978, Prime Minister Jamshid Amuzegar was removed from office and Ja'afar Sharif-Emami, an old-time Iranian politician, took over. He was faced with an immediate crisis, as government troops clashed with demonstrators in Jaleh Square in Tehran on September 7. Between 700 and 2,000 people were killed, depending on whom one wanted to believe. In a bid to quiet the restive population, Sharif-Emami introduced a number of reforms, including allowing the press to state for the first time that there were indeed social problems in Iran. This so-called "spring of freedom" was seized upon immediately by the press. The difference between the newspapers of August and September of 1978 was palpable.

The military was alarmed at the boldness of the newspapers and insisted on reinstating censorship to prevent them from inflaming the population further. The newspapers, having gotten one guarantee of freedom, took an uncharacteristically brave position and went on strike rather than publish under renewed control. For two weeks in October the major daily papers in Tehran refused to publish, but Sharif-Emami was able to prevail over the military authorities and the newspapers once again began to write freely about events as they took place in the capital. Part of the discontent of the newspapers was occasioned by Sharif-Emami's seemingly specific permission to write freely, given in a speech on October 4 to National Iranian Radio-Television. In this speech he said, "Why shouldn't we write about strikes? The people themselves know what is going on. . . . If our radio doesn't broadcast it, the BBC will." The government was forced to accept this situation, noting sourly that since the public was being misinformed by the international news media and the rumor mill anyway, they might as well get the story straight from Iranian sources.

Some citizens of Tehran wondered cynically how the newspapers, who had played such a subservient role for years, had suddenly become social revolutionaries. Nevertheless, for almost one year, until the fall of 1979, the newspapers experienced an almost unprecedented lack of regulation in their operations.

A second response to this new-found freedom was the revival of newspapers that had been closed years earlier under the force of the censorship of the shah. Marxist and other leftist publications, some dating from before World War II, were suddenly seen on every newsstand. The government itself tried to bring out one or two daily papers to present the standard official line, but these newspapers were quickly detected and avoided by the majority of the population.

Press freedom continued after the establishment of the Islamic Republic until approximately July of 1979, when the new government reinstated press censorship. Many of the editors and press executives who had survived the fall of the shah and continued their press activities were arrested, harassed, or otherwise forced out of their posts. The newspaper *Ayandegan*, which had published for decades, was suspended after being attacked several times by mobs inspired by Ayatollah Ruhollah Khomeini's statement, "I will no longer read *Ayandegan.*" In 1980, a number of other publications supported by moderate secularist politicians were also forced to close.

By 1981, the press situation was once more almost as it had been under the regime of the shah. Some leftist papers continued to be published in extremely mild versions as a kind of sop for the intellectual classes, but for all intents and purposes press censorship had been reimposed.

The national radio lacked the initial freedom of the newspapers during the course of the revolution. The last prime minister before the establishment of the Islamic Republic, Shahpour Bakhtiar, despite his general support of press freedom in principle, declared that since the national media were arms of the government, they naturally could not be allowed to broadcast antigovernment sentiments.

Nevertheless, in the period from August 27, 1978, when Ja'afar Sharif-Emami became prime minister, to the fall of Bakhtiar's government in February, 1979, radio broadcasts were far freer than ever before in the history of Iranian broadcasting. The radio occasionally broadcast opposition statements and tried to avoid contradicting the reports coming from foreign media during the period.

The Tehran-based FM radio station, Radio Tehran, played an interesting role for a few days between the time of the return of Ayatollah Khomeini from his exile in Paris on January 31, 1979, and the fall of Shahpour Bakhtiar on February 11–12. If the general population of Iran felt that radio was somewhat tainted as a medium, FM radio was the most suspect of all, since it leaned heavily toward the broadcast of foreign popular music and Western-style broadcast techniques. It was, moreover, aimed more at the middle and upper classes than at the traditional population. On February 3, 1979, during these final few days of secular rule, Radio Tehran opened its phone lines, allowing Tehran citizens to express their opinions openly and without censorship. Not surprisingly, given the composition of the listening audience, many expressed their misgivings about the nature of the revolution, aiming disparaging comments at "ultra-conservative" forces and suggesting that the revolutionary forces may have been more to blame for the violence in the streets than the government. The station was forced to close on February 6th by revolutionary supporters and striking radio employees.

The capture of National Iranian Radio-Television was one of the chief priorities of the revolutionary forces. When the government of Shahpour Bakhtiar resigned, the nation first heard the news over the radio waves. The first hint was given by the playing of a nationalist anthem, "Ey, Iran, Ey Marz-e Por Gohar (O, Iran, O Borders filled with Jewels)" instead of the familiar "Surud-e Shah-en-Shahi (Imperial Anthem)," and the announcement by radio staff of the success of the revolution. The rest of the day was given over to the reading of revolutionary bulletins and the playing of a whole spate of revolutionary songs and chants including one rousing march based on the Islamic call to prayer, "Allah-u akbar, la illa-he ila Allah (God is great, there is no god but God)," and the equally energetic "Khomeini, ey Imam! (Khomeini, O Imam!)." Among Western music used, a lush orchestral version of the popular song "Born Free" was played ad nauseam as background for readings of revolutionary literature.

Radio also underwent a rapid transformation as the revolution proceeded. From the first month, popular music was entirely banned, but the most popular commercial singers quickly began to write and record revolutionary songs that were barely different in form from the former Iranian top forty. It is noteworthy that during the revolution the Ayatollah Khomeini did not prohibit the playing of martial music and revolutionary songs. These, in contrast to the pop songs, did not transport individuals to a separate imaginary reality, but were permitted precisely because they allowed individuals to better concentrate on the reality at hand—namely, the revolution. The bulk of radio broadcasts were quickly given over to long ideological discussions and sermons from religious leaders. One important function of Radio Tehran was to release invective against the United States and other Western nations during times of stress. It is not clear whether these epithets and accusations represented the thinking of Iranian officials or merely the language of radio commentators, but they were certainly harsh. (For further discussion of the role of Radio Iran in presenting anti-American rhetoric, see Rubin 1980, Chapter 9.)

Nevertheless, even the most vicious and vituperative rhetoric becomes dull after long and steady exposure. Political commentary combined with sermons and ideological lectures became fairly wearisome for the general Iranian listening public, who offered some muted complaints, expressing the opinion that radio broadcasts should be diverting in some way. Despite these mutterings, the pattern has continued largely unchanged until the present. Some limited broadcasts of Iranian classical and folk music have been allowed from time to time, but the present regime is clearly uncomfortable with the official broadcast of music programs, even if they seem to be on a high cultural plane.

At present, Iranian radio, like so many other Iranian institutions, seems to be feeling its way carefully, trying to develop into something that will properly reflect the institutions and ideology of the new Islamic Republic. It still suffers from public complaints that it is tedious and dull. However, at present there seems to be no difficulty for the traditional classes who once wondered about the propriety of radio listening, who now listen to everything broadcast.

Television underwent a series of changes similar to that of radio during the course of the revolution. Under the regime of the shah there were three broadcast networks. The first and second networks had semi-separate management and production facilities. The third network was the "International Program," which broadcast primarily in English, with some limited broadcasts in French and German. This third network replaced the U.S. Air Force Television Station in the early 1970s, which had primarily broadcast old American situation comedies and adventure/crime shows.

The biggest controversy during the fall of 1978 raged over the broadcast of television news. The news programs were of varying lengths during this period, ranging from fifteen minutes to as long as an hour and a half. After Prime Minister Ja'afar Sharif-Emami's "liberalization" of news broadcasts, the television networks began to take a more daring attitude toward all programming. One highlight was the live broadcast of parliamentary debate. In this way, controversy in the country could be broadcast without subjecting the television executives to criticism. In November 1979, one important broadcast may have been more influential than any other in cementing public opposition against the shah. Television news carried pictures of Iranian troops firing at University of Tehran students from outside the closed gates of the university. Holding hands, the students advanced in a line toward the gates and were shown being gunned down. This documentary proof of the military's attacks on unarmed protestors delivered a violent shock to the population as a whole. The next day, crowds in Tehran went on a rampage, burning banks and government buildings in all sections of the city.

As had happened with radio, the television studios were captured almost as soon as the government fell. Television newscasters immediately began to reflect the new rhetoric and to provide readings of revolutionary literature interspersed with speeches from clerical leaders. On the day after the resignation of Bakhtiar, Ayatollah Ali-Akbar Hashemi-Rafsanjani, later to be speaker of Iran's parliament, went on the air to deliver an hourlong revolutionary sermon. The public was stunned into boredom, and the station was besieged by hundreds of calls demanding to know who had allowed such a person to speak.

Immediately after the revolution, the question of control of the airwaves became a political issue. During the first two days the television and radio stations both carried official notices from all groups who had taken part in the revolution. Then a government order declared that no more official notices from leftist groups, the Mujaheddin-e Khalq and the Fadayan-e Islam—later to come into more violent conflict with the Islamic authorities—were to be read over the air. The leftist groups were incensed. On February 14, just three days after the start of the new regime, an attempt was made to lay siege to the television studios. The announcer at the time made a quick appeal to the population at large to come and defend the studios, and people rushed from all parts of the city to battle the attackers. No official announcement was ever made as to the identity of the attackers, but many assumed that the disgruntled leftist groups were responsible.

Television quickly developed its own brand of revolutionary broadcasting. There were even children's shows for the first few days featuring pictures of five-year-old schoolgirls holding machine guns. One such program had the announcer telling children about proper revolutionary attitudes against the background of a giant bloody handprint. Once again, the phone lines were clogged with parents expressing their horror at such programming. Children themselves were upset at the removal of their favorite cartoon programs. One schoolyard chant took the revolutionary slogan: "Esteghlal, Azadi, Jomhuri-ye Islami! (Independence, Freedom, Islamic Republic!)" and converted it into "Esteghlal, Azadi, Palang-e Surati! (Independence, Freedom, The Pink Panther!)."

Television had a much harder time surviving as a pure conduit for ideology than radio. Some visually interesting programming eventually had to be planned. In the early days of the revolution, this consisted of "safe" programs dealing with nature and animal life. Interestingly, one American program survived the revolution. "The Little House on the Prairie" espoused enough in the way of acceptable moral values to be broadcast without censure.

Eventually, the television networks began to demonstrate their ideological differences. The third, "international" channel was immediately closed and never reopened after the fall of Bakhtiar's government. The first channel developed as the primary reflector of government attitude. The second channel, which had originally been established as a more intellectual and artistic programming conduit, kept a secular flavor. Sadeq Ghotbzadeh, the first director of television under the revolution, retained a degree of influence with the second channel even after the first channel was totally controlled by religious leaders. Ghotbzadeh eventually leveled some sharp criticisms at the Islamic Republic leaders in a forum broadcast over the second channel, an action that caused him to be imprisoned briefly.

The American hostage crisis lasting from November 4, 1979, to January 12, 1981, and the war with Iraq, which commenced on October 3, 1980, provided excellent opportunities for Iranian television to generate hours of documentary coverage. Iranian technical crews, often trained in the United States, performed work of high quality, and their locally broadcast coverage of these events, if it has been preserved, will provide an invaluable resource for students of the history of broadcasting.

IRANIAN MEDIA AFTER THE REVOLUTION

Since the Revolution, Iranian television has managed to stake out a role for itself that provides some balance between entertainment and ideology. In general, programming that reflects the righteous struggle of the oppressed against illegitimate authority is highly favored. Feature films such as *Z*, *The Battle of Algiers*, and *The Seven Samurai* have been screened regularly on television and are approved by government authorities. Some original programming has also been produced along the same lines. Nevertheless, television viewers still complain quietly to each other about the dullness of the television fare. One man, writing to relatives in the United States, said, "We all go to bed early these days, since there is nothing to do in the city, and we fall asleep in front of the television anyway, when we have to listen to these endless sermons and political discussions."

The New Medium — Tape Cassettes

One of the more remarkable aspects of the Iranian Revolution was the emergence of a new communication medium — the tape cassette — as a vital element in the political process that led to the revolution.

Iran was in many ways unique in its adaptation to recording technology. The phonograph record had limited use among the upper classes up until the sixties. Since phonograph records were mainly of music, it is not surprising that the traditional classes found little use for them. For this reason, the introduction of tape cassettes, and more importantly the combination radio-cassette recorder, launched a boom in the recording industry that totally bypassed the phonograph record. By the seventies, most popular music in Iran was recorded directly on cassettes, appearing in no other form. Even the traditional classes, who did not listen to popular music, found the cassettes useful. They were used to record the sermons of famous preachers who were invited to speak on religious holidays in the larger mosques, for considerable honoraria. Around the great shrines, cassette vendors selling recorded sermons of well-known clerics were common even years before the revolution. The religious chants performed during the mourning months of Moharram and Safar were also recorded extensively, even professionally, and the pious listened to them both for practice and for enjoyment.

The chief advantage of the cassette was that anyone possessing a recorder could duplicate it easily. Some cassette stores carried no stocks at all, only master tapes that were endlessly reduplicated for customers. Being portable as well, and easily hidden, the cassettes became the ideal medium for relaying revolutionary messages from government opposition leaders both at home and abroad. Radio signals could be jammed, and television appearances were out of the question for the opposition. Printed tracts and broadsides were not only easily confiscated because of their bulkiness, but they could also be counterfeited by government officials. A tract might be issued in the name of Ayatollah Khomeini, or one of the other leaders, but readers had no guarantee that the purported author of the statement was the true author. The tape cassette provided the opportunity for the listener to satisfy himself that the message or directive was genuine. This feature was particularly important during the final months of 1978, when revolutionary leaders were calling on individuals throughout the nation to strike or engage in work stoppages.

Ironically, the tape cassettes, which had been so useful during the revolution, returned to create problems for the new revolutionary regime once the Islamic Republic had been established. Popular music continued to be sold by the cassette tape stores in all large cities until late in 1979. Finally the government moved to close the stores and ban the sales of the music tapes despite the loud protests of the dealers.

Exiled former prime ministers Shahpour Bakhtiar and, later in 1981, Abol-Hassan Bani-Sadr, taking a page from the revolutionary handbook, taped exhortations to their followers inside Iran to resist the new Islamic Republic. These tapes were circulated widely within Iran, and the authorities of the Islamic Republic had as little success in stopping them as the shah's officials had before the revolution.

The Role of the International Broadcast Media

During the course of the revolution and afterward, international media played a profound role in Iran. The Iranian Revolution may have been the first major political upheaval in history to have been enacted almost directly before the eyes and ears of the world, and the Iranian revolutionaries knew very well the value of international press coverage and courted it at every possible opportunity.

The international press, radio, and television aided the revolution in several ways. First, they provided additional channels of information for individuals within Iran, effectively frustrating all attempts on the part of the government to control information on breaking events.

The giant among foreign broadcasters in terms of its influence on the Iranian people was the British Broadcasting Corporation. The BBC was the principal source of information for the Iranian people on the revolution for most of 1978 and 1979. Its prestige as a source was so great that persons who had never owned radios before purchased them solely in order to hear the BBC. Stores in the Tehran bazaar used this public interest as a selling point, and would tune radios to the BBC when customers bought them.

The BBC was far more than an information source, however. It also served as a conduit for revolutionary messages. Often the first news of an impending strike or the latest announcement from revolutionary leaders would be heard over the BBC Persian Service. Correspondent Andrew Whitley, who served as the principal relayer of information to the BBC London studios from his apartment in Tehran, faced an unending stream of telephone calls from all parts of the country telling him about clashes with military troops, strike actions, revolutionary deaths, and local political developments. He had to take his telephone off the hook at night sometimes in order to get any sleep at all.

The government of the shah was livid at the BBC, and seemingly tried to jam its broadcasts in a halfhearted way several times. The BBC was accused of fabricating stories, inciting the people to riot, and serving leftist factions. Paradoxically, after the establishment of the Islamic Republic, the BBC faced similar criticisms from the new regime, which didn't care for its continued reporting of arrests and executions by Islamic judges and local justice committees.

A different kind of information was provided by Radio Moscow, which operated Persian-language broadcasts on several levels. Official Radio Moscow maintained a somewhat neutral, but definitely anti-shah stand as the revolution progressed. The heavy propaganda was dealt out by a broadcasting station called the National Voice of Iran, operating from Baku in Soviet Azerbaijan just over Iran's northern border, but purporting to originate from inside the country. The chief purpose of this station seemed to be to convince the Iranian population that the United States was behind all of the excesses of the shah's regime and was continuing to plot against the Iranian people. During the period following the fall of the Bakhtiar government, this invective was particularly strong. In this period it was impossible to turn on a radio to either the AM or shortwave bands without encountering these messages, as they were being broadcast on dozens of frequencies all over the radio dial.

It is worth noting that the United States had no Persian-language broadcasts at all at this time. This is rather remarkable, since even such nations as Romania broadcast in Persian. In any case, Voice of America broadcasts in English were understood only by the middle and upper classes, who had little need to be disabused of the violent invective coming both from the USSR and Radio Iran. (For a brief additional discussion of Radio Moscow's role in Iran, see Beeman 1981.)

No matter what its political color, however, foreign media attention to the Iranian Revolution served another important purpose in that it served to legitimize the revolution itself in the eyes of the world. If the press had been prevented from covering these events, the revolution might conceivably have been smothered in a bloodbath, an outcome greatly desired by many of the shah's generals. As it was, the shah was conscious not only of his own image but the image of his nation, which he had hoped to make the equal of the European powers before the end of the century. As analyst Barry Rubin succinctly put it, ". . . he did not want to be regarded in the world's eyes as another Idi Amin" (Rubin 1980, 219).

Finally, the presence of the international media tended to render the revolution itself more acceptable to Iranians. In fact, the population became almost giddy with the orgy of media attention they were receiving, leading to statements like that printed in *Kayhan* on February 12, 1979, the day after the fall of the Bakhtiar government: "The Iranian Revolution is one of the greatest events in the history of the world."

Media coverage of Iran in the past tended to be inadequate. However, "By 1975 Iran was being better covered, receiving more attention than any other Third World country" (Rubin 1980, 346). This may well have been the case, but it does not speak well for U.S. press coverage of the Third World in general. The New York Times maintained a Tehran bureau for a brief period in the mid-seventies but, except for this, none of the major news reporting bureaus maintained anything much better than a system of stringers, usually Indian or Pakistani writers, who would do occasional day-to-day reporting. The usual coverage of Iran consisted of having a writer fly in from Beirut for a day or so, stay in the Hilton or Intercontinental, and interview upper-class, English-speaking Iranians. Predictably, much of the coverage was biased toward the interests of the upper classes, the financial, military, and foreign policy communities, and the throne. (See Dorman and Omeed 1979; Behnam 1979; Said 1980 for critiques of U.S. coverage of Iranian affairs.) Of course, truly spectacular events like the shah's self-coronation or the 2500-year celebration of the history of the Iranian monarchy received some media coverage, but in general the world's lack of attention tended to give Iranians a kind of inferiority complex. Iranians of all classes were inured to the idea that their nation was an unimportant backwater, about which the world cared very little.

The revolution changed all that, of course. Suddenly the focus of the world's attention was on Iran, and the Iranians liked this very much. They exclaimed proudly, even in the midst of the gunfire in the streets: "Now we won't have to explain to people where our country is." "We're on the map now," as one university student in Shiraz said, commenting on the international news teams filming a demonstration in which he was taking part.

The effect of international media on the American hostage crisis is a subject that has been covered at great length by media analysts. (See Rubin 1980, 356–64; also Beeman 1980a, 1980b; Quint 1980.) In general, the crisis as a media event had an astounding effect on both the American and

Iranian publics. Much of the hooplah around the American embassy generated by anti-American demonstrators was clearly produced for the benefit of the television cameras. The American viewing public failed to appreciate this fact and was simply appalled at the seeming virulence of the anti-American attacks. The hostage crisis, like the revolution itself, was shoveled into American living rooms as a media event, and the resulting negative attitude toward Iranians, even completely innocent ones, was expressed in a dismal record of public attacks on Iranian students, expulsions of Iranians from colleges and jobs, and failures of Iranian-owned businesses from lack of patronage.

At the time, the international media coverage served Iranian government purposes well. The attention provided by the world press, television, and radio helped the nation to accept the hostage crisis as something positive rather than something to be ashamed of. The result was increased support for the Islamic Republic and its policies. On the coattails of the hostage crisis, the clerical leaders of the new nation were able to easily win support for a highly controversial constitution, elect a slate of hand-picked candidates to parliament, and set up a government that featured clerical leaders in top posts.

Once the hostages had been released, however, the international media became troublesome. Continued stories of arrests and long imprisonment of members of the political opposition, reports on economic difficulties throughout Iran and the failure of the government to get Iranian industry operating again, led to government charges that the international media were engaged in a "Western plot to discredit the revolution," as one official in the Ministry of National Guidance put it.

One after another, the major wire services were expelled from the country for "inaccurate reporting." Only the French and Italian national news agencies were left among the European press by the end of 1981. The Indian and Japanese press remained as well, but as one reporter from the large Tokyo daily paper, *Yomiyuri*, said in January, 1982: "We have a staff in Tehran, but we don't dare write anything controversial. The Iranian ambassador in Tokyo combs the papers every day looking for some reason to expel us too."

MEDIA IN IRAN—A SHIFTING CULTURAL ROLE

At the beginning of this discussion I suggested that the media are first and foremost a cultural institution in any society. As such, a full understanding of the nature of their functioning, and the meaning they hold for the population as a whole, must be considered against the backdrop of the totality of other cultural institutions and social events in the society.

The functioning of the media on all levels during the Iranian Revolution of 1978–79 and after provides some interesting insights into how media function during periods of social stress. In looking at the Iranian case, it is impossible to avoid the conclusion that although the media underwent a fundamental change in their orientation and operations from October 1978 to July 1979, the essential quality and nature of their operations after the revolution, under the Islamic Republic, is functionally the same as it was under the regime of the shah.

Functionally, the press, radio, and television before the revolution were largely organs supporting the principal ideology of the state at the time— namely, Iranian nationalism as reflected in the institution of the monarchy and its extensions in the form of the Iranian government. Television and radio programming were largely dictated on the basis of the opinions of social and political leaders who felt they were providing the society with cultural materials that would ultimately prove beneficial. In this regard, seemingly contradictory events such as the financial support of films like *The Mongols*, which might even provide criticism of television itself, are subsumed under the general principle that the public must be exposed to advanced forms of culture and state communications institutions have the duty to provide this exposure.

During the revolution itself, the media turned to almost total opposition to the ideology represented by the monarchy as well as to the monarchy itself. The willingness to do this was accompanied by some genuinely courageous actions on the part of journalists and broadcast officials.

Nevertheless, once the Islamic Republic had been established, the media returned to their roles of supporter of the dominant state ideology. This time, however, the dominant ideology was that of the Islamic Revolution. Censorship, newspaper closings, arrests, and intolerance of critical opinion proceeded in a fashion nearly identical to that of the government of the shah.

Newspaper reporting, which used to be overwhelming in its sycophancy of the monarchy, is now replete in every issue with repeated glowing references to the "revolutionary clergy." It is a crime to insult a clergyman at present, and press reporters have been arrested for doing so. The pictures of the shah on the front page of every issue have been replaced with those of major religious/political figures. It is reported that individuals such as Ayatollah Rafsanjani complain to the newspapers when they are missing from the front page for several days running.

Moreover, much of the present press operation is carried out with a degree of public approval. At a public meeting just a few days after the resignation of Shahpour Bakhtiar, these sentiments were expressed at a rally on February 17, 1979, at the University of Tehran: "Whatever the leaders of the revolution do, it is for a good reason, so one shouldn't question it." "No one should be allowed to express opinions that will hinder the progress of the revolution." "Anyone who writes that television and radio are censored is obviously a supporter of the CIA and only wants to discredit the revolution."

Television and radio programming are likewise not geared to public tastes or desires any more than they were under the shah's regime. Formerly, the people got what was good for them in terms of culture and Westernized programming. Now they get what is good for them in terms of revolutionary ideology and religious values.

The foreign press, radio, and television were highly restricted in their operations under the shah, due in part to incompetence in the conduct of their operations. At present their operations are officially restricted. For better or worse, intentionally or not, their role in Iranian life occupies the same minimal space it did before the revolution.

Revolutions are extraordinary times in any society. They constitute the kind of events that anthropologist Victor Turner designates "social dramas" (Turner 1974). A social drama constitutes a disruption of social organization—a rupture that must eventually be healed. During the period of the rupture and the restoration process, however, the society enters a state which can be described as "liminal." During this period, the normal rules of society are suspended or, more often, totally reversed. In the words of the song, the society enters the state of "The World Turned Upside-Down."

In assessing the role of the media before, during, and after the Iranian Revolution, we see that their changing functions constitute an almost textbook illustration of the process of liminality and reversal during a social drama. The media reversed their functions for the short period of social disruption, but once the government had reestablished itself, the old cultural functions of the media were completely reinstituted, although in new ideological trappings.

ACKNOWLEDGMENTS

Much of the material contained in this chapter derives from my personal experience. During the period from 1976–79 I resided in Iran and was present in Tehran, Shiraz, and other cities during key political events of the revolution. Additionally, I served as research advisor to the Festival of Arts Center, a branch of National Iranian Radio-Television, from 1976–78. I wish to thank all of my Iranian colleagues for their help and support during those years, and express my sincere wish that the Iranian people will eventually realize their highest aspirations for themselves and their society.

REFERENCES

Beeman, William O. 1976. You can take music out of the country, but . . .:
The dynamics of change in Iranian musical tradition. *Asian Music*
7(2):6–20.

Beeman, William O. 1980a. Televised display of dead U.S. airmen—A horror show for Iranians too. *Boston Globe*, April 29.

Beeman, William O. 1980b. Why Iran negotiates through the media. *The
Press* 8(9):20.

Beeman, William O. 1981. War of words: Soviets are gaining. *Los Angeles
Times*, February 4.

Beeman, William O. 1983. Images of the Great Satan: Symbolic conceptions
of the United States in the Iranian Revolution. In *Religion and Politics in
Iran*, edited by Nikki R. Keddie. New Haven: Yale University Press.

Behnam, M. Reza. 1979. Misreading Iran through U.S. news media. *Christian Science Monitor*, March 12.

Dorman, William, and Ehsan Omeed (pseud. for Mansour Farhang).
1979. Reporting Iran the shah's way. *Columbia Journalism Review*, January–February.

Last, Jef. 1955. *Bali in de Kentering*. Amsterdam: C.P.J. Van der Peet.

Prakke, Hendricus Johannes. 1979. The socius function of the press. In
Entertainment: A Cross Cultural Examination, edited by Heinz-Dietrich
Fischer and Stefan Reinhardt Melnik. New York: Hastings House.

Quint, Bert. 1980. Dateline Tehran: There was a touch of fear. *TV Guide*,
April 5.

Rubin, Barry. 1980. *Paved with Good Intentions: The American Experience and
Iran*. New York: Oxford University Press.

Said, Edward. 1980. Iran. *Columbia Journalism Review*, March–April.

Turner, Victor. 1974. *Dramas, Fields and Metaphors*. Ithaca, N.Y.: Cornell
University Press.

CHAPTER 11

THE ROLES PLAYED BY THE NATIONAL AND INTERNATIONAL PRESS IN THE MANAGEMENT OF THE SRI LANKAN INSURRECTION OF 1971

Wimal Dissanayake

The Sri Lankan (Ceylonese)* Insurrection of 1971 was undoubtedly the most resolute attempt to capture power by force seen in Sri Lanka during the present century. One political scientist called it the most dramatic and agonizing test of the political order in modern times (Kearney 1973, 201). It has also been characterized as an uprising that produced "a convulsion of political violence on a scale previously unknown to the nation" (Kearney and Jiggeis 1975). The *Times of Ceylon* observed that "It used to be said (almost with regret or with satisfaction, according to the mood of the speaker) that the people of Ceylon got their freedom without the shedding of a drop of blood. ... In future, it will never be possible to claim that we preserved our freedom without the loss of blood. Ceylon's freedom has been sanctified by the blood of some of the brave security forces and the peace-loving law-abiding citizens who have been murdered by the treacherous attack of the terrorists" (April 6, 1971). A commentator in the British neo-Marxist journal, *New Left Review*, remarked, "In April 1971 a revolutionary insurrection exploded in Ceylon. Unanticipated by imperialism, and unexpected by revolutionaries elsewhere, sections of the rural masses rose in organized rebellion against the very government they had voted into power in the previous May. The upsurge marks a totally new phase in the hitherto relatively tranquil history of the Ceylonese state" (Halliday 1971, 55). A well-known political scientist commented that "What was most remarkable about the whole April 1971 rising was the failure of politicians with years of grassroots organizing to know what was going on among the youth of their own districts" (Jupp 1978, 297).

By all accounts it seems clear that the Sri Lankan Insurrection of 1971 was an armed rebellion against the government that was unanticipated,

---

*In 1972 the name of Ceylon was changed to Sri Lanka. Therefore the name Ceylon appears in all newspaper articles and other documents written before 1972.

terrifyingly violent, and had far-reaching political consequences. A study of the role played by the national and the international news media in the management of this conflict will enable us to gain a clearer understanding of the forces and mechanisms at work in comparable situations in the Third World in general.

THE SRI LANKAN INSURRECTION—WHAT HAPPENED?

The Sri Lankan Insurrection was an uprising of the youth against the government of the country. These youths, armed with homemade hand bombs and shotguns, attacked ninety-three police stations scattered throughout the island; some were destroyed and some were captured. The insurrection lasted for a few weeks. The combined might of the armed forces, with the generous help by way of military equipment received from the United States, United Kingdom, USSR, India, Pakistan, Egypt, and Yugoslavia, succeeded in quelling this rebellion. According to the official statistics released by the government, about 1,200 people were killed. Certain other informed sources, however, place the number at around 6,000 (Kearney 1973, 201).

The insurrection had profound consequences for the economy of the country. The then Minister of Finance N. M. Perera observed, "Not only the governmental machine, but the whole economy came to a grinding halt." This insurgency was ignited by a political organization called the Janata Vimukti Peramuna (Peoples' Liberation Front). The local press described it as a "Che Guevarist" movement. The members of the JVP were themselves of the opinion they were practicing a form of radical Marxism, drawing on the ideas of Guevara and Mao Tse Tung. The emphasis on armed revolution and the heavy dependence on rural youth were the hallmarks of this insurrection.

The JVP, which spearheaded this insurgency in 1971, came into existence in 1964. It made its first public appearance by coming out in the open to support the United Front government, which came into power in 1970. However, eventually the members of the JVP felt that the United Front government was not radical enough and was incapable of stemming the tide of public disenchantment resulting from joblessness, particularly among the youth, so it decided to capture power itself. The strategy was to attack simultaneously police stations scattered throughout the country and thus capture power in one stroke. The scenario was of a one-night revolution.

The government was clearly unprepared for an attack of this nature. Some of the police stations in the rural areas were captured; some localities were under JVP control for some weeks; a number of major highways were cut. However, due to the combined efforts of the army, the navy, and

Table 10. Nature and Characteristics of Broadcasting Media Systems

Nature of Media Systems	Examples	Characteristics
Centralized	USSR Cuba Pakistan	Media are voice of state. They legitimize and foreshadow government policy.
Fragmented	Iran Holland	Different voices competing for attention. Uncoordinated.
Highly regulated	Malaysia Philippines Sri Lanka	Legitimize action of government in times of crisis.
Moderately regulated	United States U.K.	Promote open discussion within obvious limits. Influence of state subtle.

the police, and the backing of the bureaucracy and the labor unions, the government succeeded in restoring order. This was indeed a national nightmare, of a kind not experienced in Sri Lanka before. For a country that had changed governments only five times in the twenty-two years since the establishment of parliamentary democracy through the ballot, the spectacle of an armed rebellion calculated to seize power by force was an unbelievably unnerving one. The scars of the insurrection remain visible even today in the collective psyche of the people.

DIFFERENT MEDIA SYSTEMS AND THEIR DIFFERENT ROLES

This insurrection affords us a wonderful opportunity to examine the role of national and international news media in the management of conflict. Broadly speaking, the media systems of the world can be put into four categories: controlled systems, fragmented systems, highly regulated systems, and moderately regulated systems, as shown in Table 10.

The controlled media systems are characterized by a high degree of control by the government. This type of system can be found in Communist countries as well as in rightist authoritarian societies. Fragmented media systems are characterized by the lack of a central controlling force. At times, although this is not necessarily the case, a measure of chaos goes hand in hand with this media system. The type of media system found in most developing countries is highly regulated, where an appearance of independence masks a high degree of governmental regulation. The media systems found in the United States and Great Britain can be described as moderately regulated systems. Some commentators seem to see them as free systems; however, this contention is not supported by the facts. Schlesinger points out that the "impartiality" and freedom from state restraint that supposedly characterize the BBC are more apparent than real (Schlesinger 1981, 90).

The media system in Sri Lanka can be described as highly regulated. Radio is totally in the hands of the government. The newspaper establishments are in private hands, but during times of national crisis, such as communal conflicts, a rigid press censorship is imposed and the newspapers disseminate basically what the government wants.

In this chapter, I will seek to examine the roles played by the national and international press in the Sri Lankan Insurrection of 1971, presenting my survey as a national case study. However, I believe that the broad discernible trends and the forces in operation are equally applicable to all those countries that have highly regulated media systems, and there is a substantial number of such countries in the Third World.

THE ROLE OF THE SRI LANKAN PRESS
DURING THE INSURRECTION

What was the role played by the local newspapers in the management of the Sri Lankan Insurrection of 1971? To examine this question, I selected two newspapers, the *Ceylon Daily News* and the *Times of Ceylon*. The three largest newspaper firms in Sri Lanka are the Lake House Group, the Times Group, and the Davasa Group. The *Ceylon Daily News*, a morning daily, belongs to the Lake House Group, while the *Times of Ceylon*, an evening daily, belongs to the Times Group. Although both newspapers were conservative in outlook, after the General Elections of 1970 in which a government with pro-Leftist leanings came into power, they decided to support the government. However, they were never controlled by the government in any formal sense. For the purpose of this study, I examined the *Ceylon Daily News* and the *Times of Ceylon* for a period of one month after the insurrection broke out. Despite sporadic violence here and there, for all intents and purposes the actual fighting during the insurrection was quelled in a matter of about ten days. Thus, examining the coverage over a period of one month seemed adequate to obtain an understanding of the role of the press during this conflict.

During the period of the insurgency, rigid press censorship was imposed. What was printed in the newspapers as well as what was broadcast over the radio had to be approved by the government. Hence, there was a remarkable uniformity in the news disseminated by the local media. Very often there were only government bulletins on the situation resulting from the uprising. The local press disseminated the bare minimum of information.

Under these circumstances, how did the local newspapers seek to cover this conflict? On the basis of a content analysis of the *Ceylon Daily News* and the *Times of Ceylon* during the study period, I wish to make the following observations:

1. There was an obvious attempt to withhold information and disseminate the bare minimum.
2. The severity and magnitude of the uprising was downplayed and the public was constantly reassured of a quick advance to normalcy.
3. Opposing viewpoints and interpretations of the insurgency were never given expression by the local press.
4. The police and the armed forces were regularly praised and their actions glorified repeatedly.
5. The insurgents were presented in the worst possible light, and the social and economic factors that may have prompted them to resort to this action were never adequately discussed.
6. It was constantly emphasized that the labor unions, the religious leaders, and the populace at large were unsympathetic to the cause of the insurgents.
7. The press saw its role as that of legitimizing the actions of the government.

The insurgency broke out on April 5, 1971. On the 6th, the *Ceylon Daily News* informed its readers that a dusk-to-dawn curfew had been imposed in five areas:

Last night the government decided to introduce a curfew in Colombo from 11 p.m. to 5 a.m. Since the announcement could not be made early the police enforced the curfew very leniently. Police hailers went about the streets announcing the curfew. . . .

Earlier a 7 p.m. to 5 a.m. curfew was clamped on five administrative districts—Kandy, Badulla, Amparai, Moneagala and Nuwara Eliya—last night after insurgents armed with bombs and guns killed two policemen and injured several others in an attack on the Wellowaya police station (p. 1).

On the same day the *Times of Ceylon* also informed its readers of the imposition of "an island-wide curfew from 6 p.m to 6 a.m." After this initial announcement, both papers were content with presenting minimal information relating to the insurrection.

THE ROLE OF THE INTERNATIONAL PRESS
DURING THE INSURRECTION

While the Sri Lankan newspapers were seeking to withhold as much information as possible, the foreign newspapers made every attempt to inform the world about what was happening in Sri Lanka during this turbulent period. The following headlines, selected at random from the *Hindustan Times* (India), the *London Times*, and the *New York Times*, reflect this phenomenon:

112 terrorists killed in Ceylon crackdown (*Hindustan Times*, April 9, 1971, p. 1)

IAF, Pak choppers help fight Ceylon rebels (*Hindustan Times*, April 13, 1971, p. 1)

Soviet pilots, planes to help Ceylon government (*Hindustan Times*, April 21, 1971, p. 1)

Ceylon revolt deaths may be near 1000 (*London Times*, April 13, 1971, p. 1)

Britain sells Ceylon six helicopters to combat insurgents (*London Times*, April 14, 1971, p. 1)

Captured rebels executed by Ceylon army (*London Times*, April 19, 1971, p. 1)

60 Russian instructors will train Ceylon pilots on MIG's (*London Times*, April 23, 1971, p. 1)

Rebels in Ceylon continue raids despite crackdown (*New York Times*, April 12, 1971, p. 1)

Ceylon gets aid to fight rebels (*New York Times*, April 14, 1971, p. 1)

The severity and magnitude of the rebellion were downplayed in the local press and the public was constantly reassured of the speedy progress the country was making toward normalcy. Three days after the insurrection broke out the local papers carried such headlines as:

Insurgents now in small pockets (*Ceylon Daily News*, April 8, 1971, p. 1)

Repel insurgents call by unions (*Ceylon Daily News*, April 8, 1971, p. 1)

Situation well under control (*Times of Ceylon*, April 7, 1971, p. 1)

Mass support for government (*Times of Ceylon*, April 8, 1971, p. 1)

The foreign newspapers were painting a somewhat different picture. For example, the *London Times* carried a news item on the front page under the headline "Ceylon insurgents may number 80,000": "The following dispatch from an Associated Press correspondent was telephoned to London, but the censor interrupted the call and refused to connect it again. A 24-hour curfew was ordered throughout Ceylon today as some sources estimated that the insurgents battling against the government had outnumbered the security forces by three to one" (April 10, 1971, p. 1).

Another report, which appeared in the *London Times* three days later, once again painted a picture radically different from that projected by the local press and radio:

"We'll be killed tomorrow," said a senior police officer in this district centre 40 miles from Colombo. His nervous chuckle showed he believed it.

The police front here was the only one in the district not burnt down or abandoned in the face of a Cuban-style insurgency by an estimated 80,000 activists.

Nearby a few officers rolled out a single strand of barbed wire to protect the post from a rice paddy over which officials said that they were sure an attack would come. Twelve policemen had already deserted. . . .

Villagers say that the insurgents are well fed by rural dwellers, either voluntarily or at gunpoint. Some say rebel leaders have raided villages, taking every youth between the age of 14 and 16 to join their ranks.

"They take our young girls" sobbed one bus driver at the police front. "Look at what is happening. Please do something" (April 13, 1971, p. 1).

This kind of report, both in substance and mode of presentation, stands in cutting contrast to the reports of the insurrection that appeared in the pages of the *Ceylon Daily News* and the *Times of Ceylon*.

Another interesting point that should be noted about the reporting as well as the commentaries and editorials that appeared in the Sri Lankan papers was the total absence of any attempt to present different viewpoints and interpretations regarding this calamitous event. The commentaries in the local newspapers did not evince any interest in examining the social and economic causes that precipitated this insurgency. An editorial in the *Times of Ceylon* was typical in this regard: "There is not the slightest doubt that all patriotic, law-abiding citizens, and they are by far the largest majority in the country, will be solidly behind the government now engaged in putting down terrorism and violence that a minority has unleashed upon the country" (April 7, 1971, p. 1).

On the other hand, the foreign newspapers were quick to raise a number of questions. For example, the *Hindustan Times* observed editorially under the title "Alarums Across the Waters":

There is much that still remains unexplained in the situation in Ceylon. What precisely is the extent of the armed revolution? Did it take such serious proportions in the past fortnight as to justify first, the government's decision to call out the troops, subsequently the declaration of emergency, and now the clamping down of an afternoon-to-dawn curfew throughout the island? Why has it been found necessary to adjourn parliament just when the need for consulting is more urgent? How is it that in spite of a rebel blueprint for seizure of power, which the government claims to have known in advance, including even the date and targets of attack and which ostensibly has forced the government to impose the latent countrywide curfew, all that has happened is some small-scale raids confined to the neighborhood of Colombo? . . .

It is, however, true that because of her economic difficulties and Mrs. Bandaranaike's poor record in grappling with these, there has been a marked disillusionment even among the Prime Minister's erstwhile supporters. Is she magnifying a minor law and order situation into a major conspiracy to silence what may in time grow into a real apparition? (April 8, 1971, p. 7)

The *London Times*, in an editorial entitled "Ceylon can learn from the shocks," observed that "It would be much better that the shock of insurrection and the state of emergency should help to sort out the priorities in Colombo and perhaps take some weight of dogma off the measures that are meant to control the economy" (April 21, 1971, p. 15). Five days later, in an article entitled "The danger signs Ceylon ignored," a commentator in the *London Times* remarked, "It was perhaps Mrs. Bandaranaike herself who inadvertently sowed the seeds of the present insurrection in Ceylon when during her first term of office as Prime Minister she barred horse racing in 1960. The huge grand stand of the Colombo Turf Club was converted into an open air university as part of Mrs. Bandaranaike's socialist policies of extending free higher education to the villagers" (April 26, 1971, p. 5). The commentator is referring to the educational policies of the government, which resulted in an army of unemployed and frustrated graduates, and he seems to be saying that this unfortunate situation was largely responsible for the uprising.

The *New York Times*, in an editorial entitled "Ultra-leftism in Ceylon," made the following observations:

Ever since the French Revolution and probably earlier than that, there has been a law of escalating extremism which guarantees that no matter how radical a group may be, it will soon run into more radical opposition once it assumes powers. . . .

Ceylon Prime Minister Mrs. Sirimavo Bandaranaike has encountered the same problem though her left-wing credentials seemed impeccable when she took office last year. But those attacking her democratically elected government are doing so with rifles and submachine guns, not mere words, and hundreds have already been killed in fighting which is by no means over. . . .

A fascinating aspect of this affair is the fact that Mr. Wijeweera [the leader of the insurrectionists] attended Patrice Lumumba University in Moscow and there are insistent rumors in Ceylon that the North Korean regime of Kim Il Sung provided clandestine backing for his movement. Last month the Mexican government arrested a group of young would-be revolutionaries who, it turned out, had attended Lumumba University and then gone to North Korea for training in terrorism and guerilla warfare. . . .

The Soviet Government has always maintained that the function of Lumumba University was to train engineers, doctors and other technical personnel for the developing countries. In the light of developments in Mexico and Ceylon, the security forces of developing countries are likely to pay more attention to returned graduates from the Moscow "friendship" university, especially those who made side trips to Pyongyang (April 13, 1971, p. 38).

The result of the local press following a policy of supplying readers with the minimum of information, downplaying the intensity of the insurgency and purveying the views and opinions of the government, was to make people look to other sources of information—All India Radio, BBC, VOA broadcasts, and the international newspapers. (During this period, a columnist in the *Ceylon Daily News* questioned whether the BBC, the VOA, and All India Radio were vying for popularity with Ceylon's radio listeners.) Another result of the information vacuum created by the local press was that rumor mills were operating in full swing. The government had to warn repeatedly that those who spread rumors would be dealt with severely, and, in point of fact, quite a few people were taken into custody for spreading unfounded "information." The *Ceylon Daily News* remarked: "The arrest of three persons a few days ago for spreading false and malicious rumours would have brought a lot of blabbermouths to their senses. We hope the example made of these three people will be sufficient to make every one of us realize that this is not the time to talk foolishly, let alone false and maliciously" (April 12, 1981, p. 6).

During this period, it was evident that the local press as well as radio made a concerted effort to praise the police and the armed forces. The radio beamed special broadcasts in honor of those in the forces. The *Ceylon Daily News* remarked that "It takes a crisis to bring out the best in man, and those privileged to look on have a duty to applaud the fine human qualities that emerge in these times of national stress and strain. Everybody will take special pride in the loyalty, devotion to duty and what is basically a sense of patriotism of the police and armed services these days. Already reports have come in of exceptional courage too" (April 8, 1971, p. 4). . . . "All credit to the security forces who are doing such a magnificent job to retain law and order. From the word go, they have given their best to their country in its hour of need. Human beings forget, but nobody is likely to forget the superb bravery of the policemen when the terrorists launched the first night of their bombs and bullets. The armed forces took their places beside their police colleagues and together they have chalked up a bright record of service to their country" (April 20, 1971, p. 4).

At the same time, the insurgents were presented in the worst possible light. It was constantly reiterated that they did not enjoy the support of the people and that desertions from their ranks were rampant. Headlines such as these were frequently encountered:

Repel insurgents call by unions (*Ceylon Daily News*, April 8, 1971, p. 1)

People will assist services, police (*Ceylon Daily News*, April 11, 1971, p. 1)

Many desertions from terrorists (*Ceylon Daily News*, April 11, 1971, p. 1)

Shun violence says Cardinal to youth (*Ceylon Daily News*, April 11, 1971, p. 3)

Buddhist, Hindu, Christian, Muslim leaders appeal stop violence (*Ceylon Daily News*, April 12, 1971, p. 1)

Insurgents running short of food (*Ceylon Daily News*, April 14, 1971, p. 1)

Mass support for government (*Times of Ceylon*, April 8, 1971, p. 1)

Terrorists turn to kidnapping (*Times of Ceylon*, April 13, 1971, p. 1)

The general impression created by the local press during the time of the insurrection was that it was firmly resolved to support the actions of the government. The rebellion itself was put down by the combined effort of the armed forces. The role played by the national press in this conflict was to secure legitimation for the course of action embarked upon by the government. An editorial in the *Times of Ceylon* was typical in this respect:

Thanks to the courage of the armed services and the police the venture of the insurgents is doomed to failure. The government has announced that the insurgents seem to be avoiding contact with the security forces. We have no doubt that the latter will seek out and exterminate all pockets of resistance. . . . Meanwhile, every citizen, however humble he may be, can make a contribution to the restoration of law and order by scrupulously obeying the curfew, by refraining from purveying rumours and by undergoing as cheerfully as possible such inconveniences and hardships as are unavoidable under the present circumstances (April 11, 1971, p. 1).

Whenever a foreign newspaper commented favorably on the actions of the government, the local papers were quick to report it. For example, the *Times of Ceylon* wasted no time in reporting on the favorable comments offered by the *Pakistan Times* under the caption "Pakistan paper says: PM's role aims to save democracy":

The *Pakistan Times* Rawalpindi commenting on the current situation in Ceylon has observed that one cannot but feel the deepest sympathy for Mrs. Bandaranaike in her present crisis. In an editorial entitled 'Storm in Ceylon' in its issue of April 17 the newspaper says Mrs. Bandaranaike's sole aim is to save democracy and the future of socialism in her little island which has a proud record of nearly a quarter century of parliamentary democracy (*Times of Ceylon*, April 20, 1971, p. 1).

LOCAL VS INTERNATIONAL COVERAGE OF THE INSURRECTION: SOME CONTRASTS

Because the role of the national press in the management of the Insurrection of 1971 was one of legitimizing the actions of the government, and local papers were allowed to publish only those items of news, opinions, and viewpoints approved by the government, the press forfeited a large measure of credibility in the eyes of the public.

What was the role played by the international press in the management of this conflict? The international newspapers sought to disseminate as much information as they could from all available sources, official and unofficial. As a result, many of the locals were also able to gain a clearer understanding of what was taking place. The *New York Times* reported that "In at least nine areas of the countryside covering hundreds of square miles, the rebels maintained control uncontested by government forces" (April 25, 1971, p. 2).

According to *Le Monde*, "There is no doubt that the villagers are sympathetic to the young rebels. They were all received in a friendly fashion by the local people" (April 30, 1971, p. 4).

The *Hindustan Times* observed that "The Indian Air Force helicopters began hovering over their makeshift bases at services football grounds here and fanned out to various parts of Ceylon to fight the insurgents held up in hills and hideouts (April 14, 1971, p. 1).

The *London Times* stated that "A senior officer told reporters: 'Once we are convinced prisoners are insurgents, we take them to the cemetery and dispose of them.'" Ten had been shot already and another 12 were to be executed in the next 24 hours. He added that 200 rebels had been killed in battle last week (April 19, 1971, p. 1).

The *London Times* also carried news stories about hundreds of bodies of insurgents floating in the Kelani River (April 26, 1971, p. 5). The *International Herald Tribune* reported that an army officer said, "We have learnt too many lessons from Vietnam and Malaysia. We must destroy them completely" (April 20, 1971).

The *Washington Post* carried an item claiming that a senior officer in the army had even welcomed the insurrection. "We have never had the opportunity to fight a real war in this country. . . . All these years we have been firing dummies, now we are being put to use" (May 9, 1971, p. A.4).

These are only some of the news stories that appeared in the foreign press, but not in the local press. Similarly, the BBC was broadcasting reports of certain activities that were never covered by the national press and radio. The foreign correspondents made a strenuous effort to gather as much information as possible from as many sources as possible. Consequently, there were times when their reports were distorted and somewhat off the mark. The *London Times* news item that there were 80,000 insurgents involved in the uprising (April 10, 1971, p. 1), or the remark in the *Hindustan Times* that the rebellion consisted of "some small-scale insurgent raids confined to the neighbourhood of Colombo" (April 8, 1971, p. 1) are examples of this kind of distortion. The point is, however, that the international press, in contrast to the national press, sought to disseminate as much news as possible.

As previously mentioned, there was very little analysis in the national press of the conditions that led to the rebellion and the different interpretation one could place on it. The international press, on the other hand, did attempt to examine the rebellion's meaning and potential ramifications. Both the *London Times* and the *Hindustan Times* saw the uprising in terms of the frustration among jobless youth and the poor performance of the economy. In a similar vein, the *Sydney Morning Herald* commented that "Stern action by the Armed Forces against Ceylon's youthful 'Che Guevarist' People's Liberation Front seems to have brought the rural districts which it was beginning to terrorise under control again. Unfortunately, the economic and social problems which nourished the movement are by no means under control. Some observers fear that the potential threat to parliamentary democracy is by no means quelled. . . . The PLF may be broken up, but the disillusion of educated rural youth with parliamentary democracy cannot be cured so simply or quickly" (April 14, 1981, p. 1).

The *New York Times* observed that "An insurrection by radical youths, apparently Communist-led, has plunged Ceylon into a bloody civil war that has had a shattering effect on the beautiful tropical island. . . . The situation is a strange mixture of generation gap, ideologies run wild, massive popular discontent, foreign intrigue and incredible political muddle and naivete on the part of the government" (April 15, 1981, p. 1). The British *Daily Telegraph* remarked bluntly that "It seems absurd in many respects that Britain should be supplying arms for Mrs. Bandaranaike's irresponsible and bankrupt government . . . if she has not learned her lesson it must be hoped that the people of Ceylon have done so" (April 14, 1981).

Some interpretations of the insurrection seemed wide of the mark. For example, the Pakistani newspaper, the *Dawn*, under the heading, "Ceylonese coup was Indian-inspired," editorialized:

> To what extent the militant People's Liberation Front which instigated the revolt in Ceylon was supported by India is still unclear. Several Indian newspapers and political factions have, however, lately been vocal in their support of the Front and other opponents of the government in Ceylon" (April 9, 1971, p. 1).

Thus, while the Sri Lankan newspapers were preoccupied with legitimizing the course of action embarked upon by the government, the international press was interested in examining and commenting on the insurrection from different viewpoints and in relation to the larger picture. The center of gravity of discussion shifted from the local arena to the international arena. The elite of the country, if not the common mass of people, were increasingly tuning in to the BBC, VOA, and All India Radio, and were trying to obtain a fuller picture of what was occurring in the country through the international media. This practice was so widespread that at times the government was compelled to step in and comment on these foreign reports through the voice of the local press. "There has been a BBC and Associated Press report saying that captured insurgents are being shot by the army. This is completely false. On the contrary, the government has appointed a special Ministerial committee to ensure the rehabilitation of captured and detainees" (*Ceylon Daily News*, April 20, 1971, p. 1).

The news items and commentaries appearing in the international press had an impact on the government, the media institutions, and the people of Sri Lanka. They no doubt had an effect on the governments of the other countries as well (see Figure 3). The armed forces may have quelled the insurgency, but the government was sensitive to the observations of the foreign newspapers, especially of those countries that were sending military aid to Sri Lanka during the crisis. More importantly, the commentaries in the international press had a palpable impact on the course of events immediately after the quelling of the uprising, encouraging the speedy release and rehabilitation of the prisoners. As the Amnesty Mission to Sri Lanka observed:

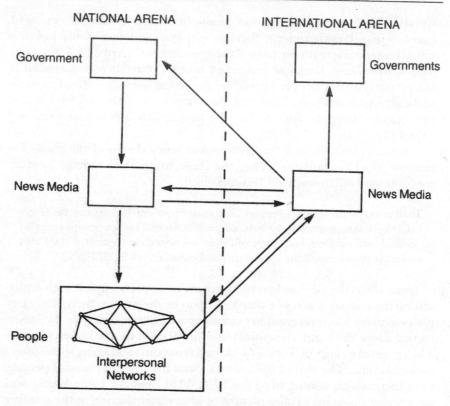

Figure 3.   The role of the media during the Sri Lankan insurrection.

In the months following the uprising, bitter fighting ensued, during which atrocities were committed on a large scale, and summary executions were widely reported to have taken place, which the Sri Lanka government has not denied. . . . The government arrested a total of 18,000 persons, but adopted at an early stage plans for the release and rehabilitation of prisoners. Already in her statement of 20 July 1971 before parliament, the Prime Minister stated that a special investigation unit had been set up: "The task of this unit is to go into each one of these 14,000 cases and to categorize them according to the degree of involvement of these persons, and to release those who in the opinion of the investigators, need not be detained any longer." Although the government has been criticized for the slow implementation of its release program it should be noted that only 2,000 persons remained in prison at the time of the Amnesty International Mission—January 1975—out of a total of 18,000 taken into custody (amounting to a release rate of 89%) (Report of Amnesty International Mission 1976, pp. 11–12).

What were the roles played by the national and international press in managing the Sri Lankan Insurrection of 1971? The local newspapers saw their role as one of supporting the actions of the government. In the circumstances under which the media system operated, there was in a sense no other option open to it. The international press, on the other hand, sought to widen the field of discourse regarding the insurrection by investigating as much as possible and by seeking to examine the situation as deeply as the available information would permit. The international press had an impact on the governments of the countries in which they operated, and these governments had close links with the Sri Lankan government. The international press also had an impact on the local media system, as well as the people of Sri Lanka. In other words, we observe the phenomenon of the international press taking the center stage and the local press being relegated to the wings (Figure 3).

REFERENCES

Amnesty International. 1976. Report of an Amnesty International Mission to Sri Lanka, January 9–15, 1975, pp. 11–12. London: Amnesty International Publications.

Ceylon Daily News. April 6, 8, 11, 12, 14, 20, 1971.

Daily Telegraph. April 14, 1971.

Dawn. April 9, 1971.

Halliday, Fred. 1971. The Ceylonese insurrection. *New Left Review* 69:55 (September–October).

Hindustan Times. April 8, 9, 13, 14, 21, 1971.

International Herald Tribune. April 20, 1971.

Jupp, James. 1978. *Sri Lanka—Third World Democracy.* London: Frank Carr.

Kearney, Robert N. 1973. *The Politics of Ceylon (Sri Lanka).* Ithaca and London: Cornell University Press.

Kearney, Robert N., and Janice Jiggers. 1975. The Ceylon insurrection of 1971. *Journal of Commonwealth Political Studies* 13:40 (March).

Le Monde. April 30, 1971.

London Times. April 10, 13, 14, 19, 21, 23, 26, 1971.

New York Times. April 12, 13, 14, 15, 25, 1971.

Schlesinger, P. 1981. Terrorism, the media and the Liberal-Democratic state. *Social Research* 48(1):90.

Sydney Morning Herald. April 14, 1971.

Times of Ceylon. April 6, 7, 8, 11, 13, 20, 1971.

Washington Post. May 9, 1971.

CHAPTER 12

JOURNALISTIC "PARADIGMS" OF CIVIL PROTESTS: A CASE STUDY IN HONG KONG

Joseph Man Chan
Chi-Chuan Lee

THE RISE OF CIVIL PROTESTS IN HONG KONG

Hong Kong has been called an "administrative no-party state" (Harris 1978, 11) or a "colonial city-state" (King 1975). While Hong Kong has no political party of its own, it is embedded in China's party system, dominated by the Chinese Communist Party (CCP) and the Chinese Kuomintang (Nationalist) Party (KMT). Because they are unregistered with the Hong Kong government, both parties work underground or behind the veils of legitimate institutions. The interparty disputes, which spilled over from the Civil War period and culminated in a political riot in 1956, continue up to the present (Miners 1979, 32). Between China and Taiwan, the Hong Kong government tries to maintain some kind of balance and to play one against the other, giving itself room to maneuver. All groups, rightist or leftist, are permitted to organize trade unions, publish newspapers, distribute propaganda, and operate other activities as long as they do not break the law.

The colonial government of Hong Kong cannot be voted out of office, and it is unlikely that the local population would seek to overthrow the government and put itself under Communist rule. Therefore the Hong Kong government, in theory, can have its own way regardless of public opinion, but this is not the case in reality. On the contrary, the government is sensitive to, and tolerant of, public opinion. It must take this position to consolidate its ruling legitimacy in the postwar era of national liberation. Moreover, the government has to head off the outburst of severe riots, such as occurred in 1967, that may threaten Hong Kong's lifeline—foreign investment. The Hong Kong government then can claim to be a government "for the people," if not necessarily "by the people." Administratively, the government has absorbed a number of elites into its machinery (e.g., through advisory committees) to tap their technical know-how and to gain their consent to government rule (King 1975). Ironically, the 1967 riot, aimed by the Communists at toppling British rule, boosted the self-confidence of the Hong Kong government because the local population forcefully demonstrated its determination not to "rock the boat." After the riot, the government, while still keeping a watchful eye on Communist infiltration, has taken steps to smooth its channels of communication with the public (Miners 1979).

Along with such improved communication channels, protest gradually became a means of airing grievances by various groups, especially the underprivileged. This action at first seems ironic. But the fact is that the propensity to protest has existed for some time, and the underprivileged have been resentful of being neglected (e.g., they are not represented in the legislative and executive councils). They had refrained from taking their anger to the streets for fear of ruining social stability. They are now aware, however, that a civil protest would not tear apart the social fabric but would effectively make their feelings known and contribute toward problem solving. This latent propensity to protest has been actualized by the government's efforts to improve communication, by the mobilization of socially conscious pressure groups, and by the media's prominent coverage. Once the appetite is whetted, protest can be an irreversible trend.

The drastic change in Hong Kong's demographic structure that occurred in the past decade has a significant implication for political culture. For the first time, the first-generation Chinese—locally born, educated, and below 30—comprise 60 percent of the population. They differ from their parents in several important respects. First, although being committed to Chinese culture, they have accepted Hong Kong as their given life space and thus are much more concerned with local public affairs. Their parents, mostly refugees and immigrants from China, while appreciative of Hong Kong, are apathetic to local affairs (Hoadley 1973). Second, the young are less paranoid about civil protests, perhaps partly because they did not witness the kind of social turmoil that their parents experienced. Lau (1978) discovered that the younger people are much less inclined than their parents to place familial interests above the interest of society. The gradual erosion of parental authority, the diminution of social control exercised by the families, and the awakening of social consciousness all make people increasingly assertive about their rights and interests. They are ready to protest if their grievances through formal channels do not produce expected results. Conflicts of interest multiply across social strata, as well as between government and the people, as Hong Kong society rapidly modernizes and expands.

Furthermore, pressure groups such as trade unions and professional, religious, and social organizations interested in promoting not only the cause of their own members but also what promises to be for the communal good have emerged in the past decade. In 1970 an unprecedented movement to legitimize Chinese, along with English, as an official language scored a remarkable success. Subsequently, a 1973 teachers' strike resulted in the government's fulfillment of their demand for higher pay. Now leaders of pressure groups, many formerly radical student leaders in the late 1960s or the 1970s, have become self-appointed spokesmen for the underprivileged with unorthodox outspokenness and occasional militancy. The government's attitude toward the proliferation and eminence of pressure groups is one of ambivalence. On the one hand, it argues against the feasibility and desirability of instituting political parties or a universal electoral system in Hong Kong and prefers to tolerate the role of pressure groups as a "useful and sometimes timely safety valve" (SCOPG 1980, Annex B). On the other hand, the government is guarding closely against the Communists infiltrating these groups and is plagued by the activities of some groups that may tarnish its image. This concern is intensified by the tendency for pressure groups to form coalitions in their dealing with the government. Early in 1981 speculation about the government's possible approval for a bus-fare increase led to an allied boycott campaign by some 300 groups representing 2.5 million people. The bus companies, the government, and leaders of pressure groups all engaged in a fierce competition for media resources. It is unlikely that the coalition movement of these groups will evolve into a political party of some sort, but there is no doubt that protest gradually has been legitimized as an important means of public opinion expression.

POLITICAL IDEOLOGY AND A JOURNALISTIC "PARADIGM" ON CIVIL PROTESTS

Political Parties and the Press Structure

Seymour-Ure (1974) observes that in Europe and the Third World, a close "parallelism" exists between the press system and the party system; the press is linked to political party organizations, is loyal to party goals, and caters to partisan audiences. This parallelism is strongest in one-party systems, followed by multiparty systems, but weaker in two-party systems. In no-party systems the press typically is left to private ownership with governmental "supervision."*

In the administrative no-party state of Hong Kong, this press-party parallelism is unique in that it grows not out of local politics but is a residual extension of modern Chinese politics. For the past century the media system in Hong Kong has been intensively involved in Chinese politics; it tried to effect political changes in China on the one hand and was influenced by them on the other. Since the era of the rift between revolutionaries and constitutional monarchists in the late Ching dynasty, Hong Kong has served as a key listening post and propaganda base for Chinese politics, with many dissident journalists and politicians taking refuge in Hong Kong to advocate their doctrines (Lee-Hsia 1974). In particular, the protracted KMT-CCP struggle has made Hong Kong's press system a residual microcosm of yesterday's China. The British have been tolerant of partisan political journalism as long as it does not disrupt social order or ruin their vital ruling legitimacy. In a sense, the British are content with keeping control of the game, and under this premise they are willing to grant a wide scope of press freedom.† Therefore even today there are papers directly financed from Peking (notably *Wen Wei Pao* and *Ta Kung Pao*) and Taipei (*Hong Kong Times*), and still others, though not directly financed, are clearly identified with either party in goal orientation. According to Taiwan sources (Tseng 1966, 739), among the forty-nine Chinese-language newspapers and magazines that existed in 1963, only five were Communist controlled, with eight others sympathetic to the Communist cause, while thirty-six were classified to be pro-KMT or neutral.

Against this large backdrop, it was not until a decade ago that "centrist" newspapers, which are primarily loyal to Hong Kong and critical of both Peking and Taipei, began to emerge and prosper. They, being profit motivated, are beneficiaries of Hong Kong's rapidly expanding economy and its formidable advertising industry. While devoting significant coverage to Chinese politics, they appear to focus more on local issues and the immediate concerns of Hong Kong citizens at large. Notable examples include *Ming Pao* (for intellectuals), the *Oriental Daily*, and *Sing Pao* (for mass publics).

---

* This parallelism is generally valid up to the present (Hoyer et al. 1975). Since the end of the Second World War, however, party loyalists have declined substantially in many advanced capitalist or democratic countries. In the developing world, the "neutral" commercial press has surfaced because of expanding economies, but party orientation undoubtedly remains a significant feature (Omu 1978).

† The International Press Institute (IPI) in 1977 ranked Hong Kong as having the second highest degree of press freedom, surpassed only by Japan, in Asia. The granting of newspaper licenses is extremely lenient, requiring only a safety deposit of US$2,000 and an annual registration fee of US$20, which has resulted in the growth of some 100 newspapers, of which seventeen were classified as major ones with a combined circulation of 1.2 million copies (Slimming 1979, 24).

The Journalistic "Paradigm" Concept

The absence of representative politics and the small geographical size combine to make the role of Hong Kong's press unique. The press, as one government official puts it, are "very useful pointers to the mood and intensity of public opinion" (Slimming 1979, 25). This role is far more salient in Hong Kong than elsewhere and especially manifest in the event of social upheaval. Surveys have shown that Hong Kong citizens are prepared to defend social stability almost at any cost,* and it would be suicidal for any political organization to defy this norm. The leftists, miscalculating mass opinion, rioted in 1967 as a spin-off of China's Cultural Revolution and almost defeated the fragile stability of Hong Kong. They have been suffering the consequences of that unpopular riot ever since. The phenomenal growth of civil protests in the last ten years, therefore, must *not* obscure the fact that both the Hong Kong government and protest groups always have taken great pains to ensure that these protests are conducted in the framework of social stability. Civil protests in Hong Kong, in short, are reform minded, gradualist, and piecemeal.† Violation of this basic premise would sever any groups, exogenous political parties included, from grass-roots support.

Nevertheless, it should not be assumed that rightist, centrist, and leftist newspapers would "see," "explain," and "map" civil protests objectively. They do not. The practices of newspapers across the full political spectrum are conditioned by different sets of "paradigms." We use Kuhn's (1970) concept of "paradigm" in a rather loose way to mean a "metaphysical" world view or a gestalt that defines the entities of concern, indicates to journalists where to look (and where not to look), and informs them about what to discover.** In Britain, Marsh (1977), for example, found that people's party identifications were significantly related to their propensity to engage in protest activities, as well as the propensity to use suppressive measures to end a protest. We will argue that newspapers reflect such

---

* For example, Lau (1978, 13) found that 87 percent of the population in Hong Kong preferred social stability to economic prosperity. Furthermore, in reply to a hypothetical question, 41 percent indicated that they would be willing to remain in a stable society even if it does not have much social justice.

† Gusfield (1970, 86–87) says: "What characterizes reform is its gradualist and legitimate status. Operation within the institutional structure for conflict regulation, the 'rules of the game,' is a major form of reformist action. What is sought are usually changes in specific institutions rather than general shifts in major social values or in the forms of authority. In these respects reform contrasts both with the episodic and sometimes illegal nature of protest and with the general and also immediate demand of revolutionary action."

**This "paradigm," in the language of Berger and Luckmann (1967), is a socially constructed consciousness. More concretely, Altheide (1976) uses "news perspective" to mean those personal and organizational factors that may affect newsmaking. We prefer the concept of "paradigm" to that of "news perspective" because of the former's holistic nature.

party-linked propensities in the manner events are reported. The function of political ideology in structuring such journalistic "paradigms" can be observed most clearly in ambiguous protest movements. Psychologically speaking, Fensterheim and Tresselt (1953) argue that the less well defined the stimulus, the greater the contribution of the perceiver. Analogously, Hall (1970, 1974) pointed out that the role of the media in the labeling process is at its maximum in situations that are unfamiliar or ambiguous. The mass media, in Hall's words,

> . . . do have an integrative, clarifying, and legitimating power to shape and define political reality, especially in those situations which are unfamiliar, problematic, or threatening: where no "traditional wisdom," no firm networks of personal influence, no cohesive culture, no precedents for relevant action or response, and no first-hand way of testing or validating the propositions are at our disposal with which to confront or modify their innovatory power (1974, 277).

In this chapter we concentrate on the case of the Golden Jubilee School Affair—a protest movement whose motivations and causes were ambiguous, at least during the initial period—to see how rightist, centrist, and leftist papers used different sets of journalistic "paradigms" to uncover and interpret social conflict.

Journalistic "Paradigms" of Civil Protests

Journalistic "paradigms," as determined by political ideologies, make newspapers attribute different cause-and-effect relationships to civil protests and assign varying degrees of support to protesters. As a rule, the leftist journalistic "paradigm," although endorsing social stability in Hong Kong, tends to lend a more sympathetic ear to civil protests even if these are nonpolitical in nature. Conversely, the rightist journalistic "paradigm" is constantly antagonistic to civil protests, fearing that these activities are conspiratorial and Communist initiated. The centrist journalistic "paradigm," standing somewhere in between, displays a less consistent pattern and can be for or against civil protests, with each case being weighed on its own merits.

The leftists' high propensity to support civil protests derives from a number of reasons. First, Maoist ideology puts a premium on social conflict. As Schram (1974, 25) succinctly remarks, "For Mao, contradictions are not merely, as for Hegel and Marx, the motor of change; they are the very stuff of life and reality." This ideology has made a penetrating imprint on the "paradigm" of Communist politics and press (Lee 1980, 203–19). Despite the post-Mao criticism of Mao's "errors," leaders of the current regime—the majority of whom had fallen victim to the Mao-engineered

Cultural Revolution—still painstakingly uphold his image and ideology. Second, the CCP has had a glorious past of manipulating the press to organize and agitate civil protests in its struggle with the KMT. It would be out of character for the CCP to give up any opportunity in which the media can be mobilized in its favor. Third, leftist newspapers in Hong Kong deliberately sympathize with civil protests, especially those which purport to articulate the interests of the underprivileged in order to cultivate the image of championing social justice for the underdog. While leftist newspapers enthusiastically may endorse civil protests outside of China, they advocate mercilessly crushing any outbreak of similar actions inside China.*

The rightist journalistic "paradigm" represents a mirror image of its leftist counterpart. Since the KMT came to power, it has long declared Confucianism as its official ideology and embraced social order and stability as the highest value. Therefore it cannot condone civil protests in which the low rises against the high, or the young against the old. Its bitter experience with student demonstrations and social movements during the interparty struggle against the CCP seems to have left a permanent scar on its view of civil protests. The progressive May Fourth Movement of 1919 has been accused of paving the way for Communism (Yang 1959, 153), and Taiwan students studying overseas are discouraged from involving themselves in political activities. This ill feeling about civil protests is acute especially in Hong Kong where the CCP, because of geographical proximity and economic connections, has a greater capacity than the KMT to make trouble. The memory of the 1967 Communist riot is forever vivid. As a result, the KMT-linked papers are constantly suspicious of Communist plots behind any civil protests, even those aimed at local issues. Any efforts to frustrate the Communists from making propaganda strides can be viewed as a reverse victory for the KMT and its sympathizers, so it is not surprising that the rightist journalistic "paradigm" has stood closer to the status-quo-minded policies of the Hong Kong government.

As a product of the market economy in Hong Kong, centrist newspapers belong to Hong Kong rather than to China. They focus primarily on local issues but also reserve a significant proportion of space for reporting, deciphering, and criticizing the mysteries of Chinese politics because, in the final analysis, these are of salient concern to Hong Kong citizens. Centrist newspapers, however, neither owe allegiance to the KMT or the CCP nor

---

* Leftist Press (and Marxism for that matter) in the West and the Third World is a critical force in the established capitalist system, but in the Communist societies it becomes a tool to uphold the existing power structure (Brzezinski 1970). Just recently the Chinese Communist Party suppressed a Hong Kong newspaper and a monthly journal, both of which were originally established with the indirect financial aid of Peking but are now found to be too "right" (because of their critical discussion of China's internal problems) for China's leadership (*Far Eastern Economic Review*, August 7, 1981, p. 34).

take much interest in being engulfed in interparty conflict. Without ruling out their international variations, it is possible to characterize them as a group slightly right of the center—again, not out of loyalty to the KMT necessarily but a reflection of the mainstream consciousness of Hong Kong citizens. In spite of constant intellectual criticisms of their low professional quality, these newspapers thrive on boasts of journalistic objectivity and editorial independence. What would they do in the face of civil protests, which have different aims, involve diverse segments of the society, and acquire varying degrees of radicalness and militancy? Centrist newspapers would be primarily in strong support of a *mild* civil protest participated in by a *large* segment of potential readership with a *clearly just* cause. They are less likely to support a radical protest perceived to be out of touch with reality or incompatible with public tolerance.

THE GOLDEN JUBILEE SCHOOL AFFAIR: A CASE STUDY

The Case

A journalistic "paradigm" can be best revealed in an ambiguous civil protest movement; therefore, we have chosen the Golden Jubilee School Affair as an illustration. In brief, the nature of this civil protest was initially unclear and was open to conjectures. Teachers and students in one of the traditionally conservative and obedient Catholic schools rebelled against their principal. Their anger was directed subsequently toward the Catholic Church and the government of Hong Kong. They staged sit-ins, sleep-ins, demonstrations, petition drives, and press conferences. They appeared so well organized and disciplined that some people suspected a Communist plot. Others reasoned, however, that since the protesters were so consistently serious about their goals they could not be troublemakers. Long and relentless efforts cleared up the ambiguity of the event, and no political motive was found.

The Jubilee Secondary School was founded in 1973 by the Catholic Precious Blood Order under the principalship of Sister Leung Kit-fun. All went well until 1977, when teachers, through a series of incidents, discovered that the school authorities had been systematically defrauding and profiteering. Failing to get a satisfactory reply from the school authorities and the Catholic Church, the teachers brought the matter to the Hong Kong government's Independent Commission Against Corruption (ICAC), but ICAC refused to take any action. The teachers then filed a memorandum of the financial irregularities with the Education Department, which turned the case over to the Commercial Crime Bureau.

In June 1977 the teachers were asked to sign new contracts that gave the school authorities the arbitrary power to dismiss teachers. The Student Union learned of the corruption and asked the principal and the Education Department for a clarification, but to no avail. They were sternly upbraided and ordered to return to their classrooms. Students began to stage a sit-in and were joined later by their teachers. The sit-in resumed the next day, but no reply was forthcoming. On the same day, the teachers signed the new contract.

On June 17 when classes had already resumed for a week, the Director of Education issued letters to all thirty-five teachers warning that any repetition of such defiant behavior would result in cancellation of teachers' registration. On August 1, 1977, Bishop John Wu appointed Hilda Kwan as the new school principal. The aftermath of the financial scandal lingered, however, and conflicts within the school continued to develop.

After former principal Sister Leung was convicted by the Commercial Crime Bureau on ten charges of false accounting, the student body and a number of pressure groups repeatedly asked, in vain, that the Director of Education rescind the thirty-five warning letters that had been issued to the teachers and give a full disclosure of the investigation. In April 1978, the new principal, Miss Kwan, sent seven letters to teachers warning against their "behavior." Meanwhile, four students were suspended from school for two weeks and another three were given warning letters for having "infringed the principal's personal freedom." To make matters worse, on May 3, some students were said to have been physically assaulted by the school staff. When a number of teachers and students asked to see the principal, she sent for the police, claiming that she was intimidated.

On May 7, the students' parents, with the help of the Professional Teachers' Union, revealed the details of the principal's high-handed measures to the media. The principal, with the full support of the Education Department, denied all the charges. On May 9, about 400 students, twenty parents, and sixteen teachers petitioned the Bishop and the governor of Hong Kong to dismiss the principal. The Bishop remained silent. Teachers slept in that night and sat in outside the cathedral the following day.

Amidst the calls of some prominent educational groups for protesters to stay calm, the Education Department abruptly closed the school. It also announced that the school would be reopened under a new name, St. Teresa's, in the coming September with the same board of management and principal, but that the sixteen protesting teachers' contracts would not be renewed. On May 16 the executive council unanimously endorsed the Education Department's decision. At the same time, an Enquiry Committee was established to "recommend measures aimed at preventing a recurrence of the problems besetting the school."

A series of protests, petitions, sit-ins, and press conferences took place. The debate about the closure of the school dominated the media and became "the talk of the town." Under a united front of pressure groups, support of the protesters finally culminated in a mass rally attended by 10,000 people on May 28. It was followed by numerous petitions by the victims and their supporters, countermoves by the Education Department, and meetings between the teachers and the Enquiry Committee. On June 26, two teachers took off for England to petition members of the Parliament and the Office of Home Affairs for support.

The scenario quieted down briefly until July 7, when some protesters went on a hunger strike demanding rapid reopening of the school. On July 9 a mass demonstration was organized by the United Front for the reopening of the school.

The Jubilee School Affair virtually came to an end when, on July 15, the official Enquiry Committee published its report, pinpointing the school authorities' corruption as the major cause of the conflict. As a remedy, the committee recommended that a new school be established to accommodate the sixteen teachers and those students who would not want to return to their old school. The warning letters issued to the teachers were rescinded, implying that the Director of Education had made a mistake.

Research Methodology

Supplemented by in-depth reading and interviews, this study is mainly a content analysis of eight Hong Kong newspapers located along a continuum of right-left political ideology. Rightist papers in the sample include *Hong Kong Times*, *Kung Sheung Daily*, and *Sing Tao Daily*; centrist papers include *Sing Pao*, *Ming Pao*, and *South China Morning Post* (an English-language paper); while leftist papers include *Ta Kung Pao* and *Wen Wei Pao*. Rightist papers are registered with Hong Kong and Taipei governments. They identify with the Republic of China, celebrate its national birthday on October 10, and adopt its calendar (i.e., 1911 as the first year of the Republic). Also, they refer to the Peking regime as "Mainland China," "the Mainland," or "the Communist Chinese," but never as "the People's Republic of China." Conversely, leftist papers are registered with Hong Kong and Peking governments. They identify with the People's Republic of China, celebrate its national birthday on October 1, and follow Peking's practice to adopt the Western calendar. They refer to Taiwan as "Taiwan province," "the Taiwan authorities," or "the Chiang clique," but call Peking "our country," "our government," or "China." Centrist papers are registered only with the Hong Kong government, adopt the Western calendar, call Taipei "Taiwan" and Peking "Communist China," "Mainland China," or "China."

These papers were chosen on the basis of their representativeness and influence.*

We sampled dates for analysis in three stages according to the development of the Golden Jubilee School Affair. The first stage unfolded with the exposure of financial irregularities on February 1, 1977, and ended with the closure of the Jubilee School on May 14, 1978. During most of this period the interactions among protesting teachers, the school principal, and the government did not gain substantial media coverage. Two student sit-ins on June 9 and June 10, 1977, attracted some media attention, so papers published on the following two days (June 10 and 11) were chosen for analysis. In addition, every other day between May 1 and May 14, 1978, was sampled. The second stage spanned from the Education Department's closing of the Jubilee School on May 14, 1978, to the mass rally held in support of protesting teachers and students on May 28. This period was densely dotted with protests and prominently covered by the media. Every other day was sampled from May 15 onward. The third stage stretched from the May 28, 1978, mass rally to July 14, 1978, when the government's Enquiry Committee released its interim report. Since the mass rally, joined by some 10,000 people, was believed to have had a decisive impact on the course of the development, every other day during this week was sampled—namely, May 29, 31, June 2, 4, 6, 8, and 10. Three other dates—July 8, 10 and 15—were added to the sample because significant events had occurred on the preceding days.

We developed a priori thematic statements relating to the Jubilee case around three theoretical hypotheses and coded the presence or absence of these thematic statements in the news, headlines, and letters to the editors that found their way into the eight newspapers on the given sample days. All editorials throughout the entire period, sparsely spread, were carefully examined for the same sixteen thematic statements.†

Hypotheses and Findings

Our first hypothesis was that the rightist journalistic "paradigm" is more likely than the centrist, and even more so than the leftist counterpart, to

---

* The *Oriental Daily*, the best-circulated centrist paper, was not included for practical reasons. Catering to lower-class readers with explicit sex and violence content, it is not on the collection stock of any public libraries, and our request to use the *Oriental Daily*'s in-house library was not approved. Fortunately, *Sing Pao*, its chief rival, is very compatible in content and audience, so the *Oriental Daily* could be excluded without serious loss of generality.

† We gratefully acknowledge the able research assistance of Lee Yuet-lin and Kwok Tatchun, among others.

favor the maintenance of the status quo and, by implication, to support the government's suppressive measures to end a civil protest.

This hypothesis was measured by the presence or absence of seven thematic statements: (1) The government's measures were necessary for maintaining school peace, social order, and the dignity of education; (2) The government's measures to deliver warning letters to protesting teachers and to close the Jubilee School was "timely;" (3) The government's measures were "fair" and "well thought out;" (4) The protesters were disrupting social peace and social order; (5) The spark of protest could kindle a prairie fire and should be stopped before it spreads; (6) The government's determined policies could teach potential protesters in other schools a lesson; and (7) The government should prevent recurrence of similar incidents.

The results of the content analysis are summed up in Table 11. Hypothesis one clearly drew very strong confirmation in the areas of editorials and letters, despite their relatively small number of items.* This is less apparent in news and headlines, partly because they are supposedly "neutral" factual reporting and partly because our a priori thematic statements are not sophisticated enough to tap whatever subtle differences might be embedded. The pattern was stable across the three stages of sampling.

Leftist papers also carried some letters that dissented from their editorial dogma and supported government policies; this did not occur in news, headlines, or editorials. According to one anonymous leftist editor whom we interviewed, this strategy was carried out deliberately to project the impression of being objective and impartial, an impression that leftist newspapers needed in times of a civil protest such as this because they have not recovered from the credibility gap caused by the 1967 riot and the ensuing Cultural Revolution. But this strategy could not be overused as to create a reverse effect, so the supportive letters were rather few in number.

Qualitatively, regarding the closure of the Jubilee School, the rightist Kung Sheung Daily (May 24, 1978, editorial) praised the Education Department's decision as "far-sighted and in the interest of the people" which ought to be "supported by all responsible citizens"—because, it said, "the existing campus 'anarchy,' if left undeterred, might develop into a social uproar." In contrast, the leftist Ta Kung Pao (May 15, 1978, editorial) charged the Education Department with "setting a bad precedent," doubted that closing the school could effectively resolve the conflict, and urged that the interests of students and their parents be given utmost consideration.

Hypothesis two was that the rightist journalistic "paradigm" is more likely than its centrist, and even more so than its leftist, counterpart to

---

* The two leftist newspapers in the sample carried fewer editorials relating to the Jubilee case than the three rightist newspapers. This discrepancy partly can be accounted for by the leftist newspapers' tradition of carrying no editorials unless significant events occur and of calling for "official" comment.

Table 11. Percentage of References Made by Newspapers of Different Political Ideology to Maintain Social Order and Support the Government's Measures for Ending the Protest

Thematic Statements	News			Headlines			Editorials			Letters		
	R^a	C^b	L^c	R	C	L	R	C	L	R	C	L
Government's measures necessary for keeping social order	4	4	4	2	2	0	16	13	0	33	2	4
Government's "timely" decisions	3	3	3	0	1	0	18	13	0	22	2	8
Government's measures "well thought out"	6	2	5	5	0	0	21	0	0	56	5	8
Protesters disrupt social order	12	5	1	4	1	0	40	6	0	33	5	2
End protest before it spreads	2	1	0	0	0	0	11	0	0	11	5	0
Discourage potential protesters	1	0	1	0	0	0	13	0	0	11	0	8
Prevent further recurrence	9	2	3	6	1	1	18	13	0	0	2	4
TOTAL NUMBERS	(104)	(148)	(95)	(104)	(147)	(92)	(38)	(16)	(5)	(9)	(41)	(24)

[a] R denotes 3 rightist papers.
[b] C denotes 3 centrist papers.
[c] L denotes 2 leftist papers.

politicize a civil protest. Here, by "politicization," we mean the tendency to define a civil protest in political perspective, to liken it to other similar political events (similar in form, perhaps) in the past, and to attribute it to external manipulation rather than a spontaneous reaction to internal social-structural deficiencies. This politicization was measured by the presence or absence of any of six thematic statements: (1) that the school had been infiltrated by the Communists or activists; (2) that the event had a "political background;" (3) that the event was connected with the local Trotskyist "Revolutionary Marxist Union;" (4) that the behavior of the protesters resembled that of radical rebels in the 1967 riot and the Chinese Cultural Revolution; (5) that protesting teachers were selfishly motivated (for example, to take over the school); and (6) that protesting students were used as "blind followers."

Table 12 shows that hypothesis two was strongly supported in the areas of editorials and letters, but less so in news and headlines, perhaps for the reason cited in the discussion of hypothesis one. The pattern remained stable for the three stages of sampling. Qualitatively, the rightist *Hong Kong Times* (June 19, 1978, editorial) discredited protesting teachers as a small subversive group "with political and organizational background," whose aim was "to coopt other teachers, deceive students, control the school, and finally to break up the whole educational system and uproot a free Hong Kong society." On May 19, 1978, the same paper even more explicitly published an editorial entitled "Don't Forget 1967," warning that "rioters are still there, only with a different face." Conversely, the leftist *Wen Wei Pao* (May 26, 1978, editorial) viewed the protest as nothing more than "a dispute between two kinds of educational philosophy" and a reaction "to the dominant, traditional 'duck-stuffing' or rote-learning methods."

Hypothesis three was that the rightist journalistic "paradigm" is more likely than its centrist, and even more so than its leftist, counterpart to define a civil protest as defying traditional morality. Since rightists are more tradition-bound, deviation from traditional morality implies unorthodoxy and thus unacceptability. This defiance was measured by the presence or absence of three themes: (1) that the protesting teachers and students were defying hierarchical order, and the low should respect the high; (2) that teachers and students teach and learn, end the protest, and return to classroom; and (3) that the protesters should learn good codes of behavior from traditional Chinese culture.

Table 13 reveals that hypothesis three was strongly supported in the areas of editorials and letters, but less so in news and headlines. The rightist journalistic "paradigm" is best represented by an editorial carried by *Kung Sheung Daily* (May 11, 1978), which compared the protest to the Cultural Revolution and denounced it as violating the "gentle, non-aggressive, and respectful Chinese intellectual traditions."

Table 12. Percentage of References Made by Newspapers of Different Political Ideology to Politicize the Jubilee Case

Thematic Statements	News			Headlines			Editorials			Letters		
	R[a]	C[b]	L[c]	R	C	L	R	C	L	R	C	L
Communist infiltration	0	0	0	0	0	0	34	0	0	0	0	0
"Political background"	3	0	0	0	0	0	36	0	0	22	2	0
Local Trotskyists involved	1	0	0	0	0	0	16	0	0	0	0	0
Comparable to Cultural Revolution	0	0	0	0	0	0	13	0	0	33	0	0
Teachers selfishly motivated	6	2	1	4	0	0	42	6	0	22	12	0
Students were "blind" followers	3	6	5	5	1	0	42	13	0	44	15	0
TOTAL NUMBERS	(104)	(148)	(95)	(104)	(147)	(92)	(38)	(16)	(5)	(9)	(41)	(24)

[a] R denotes 3 rightist papers.
[b] C denotes 3 centrist papers.
[c] L denotes 2 leftist papers.

Table 13. Percentage of References Made by Newspapers of Different Political Ideology to Define a Civil Protest as Defying Traditional Morality

Thematic Statements	News			Headlines			Editorials			Letters		
	R[a]	C[b]	L[c]	R	C	L	R	C	L	R	C	L
Teachers and students disrespect hierarchical order	8	3	4	3	0	0	29	13	0	11	7	0
Teachers and students should end protest and return to classroom	3	0	0	0	0	0	3	13	0	0	0	0
Protesters should learn from Chinese traditional culture	5	3	3	1	1	0	10	25	0	22	10	0
TOTAL NUMBERS	(104)	(148)	(95)	(104)	(147)	(92)	(38)	(16)	(5)	(9)	(41)	(24)

[a] R denotes 3 rightist papers.
[b] C denotes 3 centrist papers.
[c] L denotes 2 leftist papers.

To recapitulate, the case of the Golden Jubilee School took a "radical" form of protest (such as sit-ins, sleep-ins) that led many groups, including the government and most extreme rightist papers, to suspect Communist involvement. The suspicion was especially strong when the goal of the protest was rather ambiguous, at least to outside observers. When the real cause — exposure of a school's financial corruption—was discovered, all parties sighed with relief. As the rightist *Hong Kong Times* later confessed in an editorial of May 12, 1978, the form of the protest was so radical for such "insignificant" causes that the paper had been led to "smell a rat." Even leftist editors were shocked by the radicalness of the generally conservative Catholic school students and therefore restrained themselves from siding with either party. But, after some investigation, they decided to support protesting teachers and students while blasting the establishment's reluctance to right the wrong. Confused by the ambiguity and radicalness, centrist papers also waited and remained silent for a period. *Sing Pao*, for example, said in an editorial of May 18, 1978: "From the beginning we have been urging the government to release all the facts about this conflict, because we feel that the extraordinary event warrants explanation. A fair judgment by the citizens requires an understanding of the reality." *South China Morning Post*, another centrist English-language daily, initially was an ardent supporter of the government's action in closing the Jubilee School. But later, when it found that the Education Department had deliberately released incorrect information to discredit the protesters, it urged accuracy and fair dealing, wondering "whether there are other aspects of the case that have been presented to the public as undisputed facts which will have to be qualified or corrected in the future" (May 19, 1978, editorial).

SUMMARY AND DISCUSSION

While all political forces now respect the existing political framework, they nonetheless hold different journalistic "paradigms" on civil protests. The rightists, characterized by a political suspicion of radical civil protests, read party politics into the Jubilee Affair. They politicized, stereotyped, and attributed the cause to external Communist conspiracies. Their high propensity to advocate suppressive measures to end the protest was correlated with a strong support for the government's policies and harsh criticisms of the protesters. Their tolerance of social conflict was relatively low, while their concern for social order was very high. In contrast, the leftists were more supportive of the protesters. Condemning the Hong Kong government's suppressive policies, they tended to attribute the occurrence of protest to internal social-structural deficiencies. Centrist papers, on the other hand, appeared to be more moderate and diversified in their outlook.

Besides the sixteen a priori thematic statements organized around the three hypotheses, we also developed another thirteen mirror-image statements pointing in the opposite direction as an effort for negative crossvalidation. We hypothesized that:

1. The leftist journalistic "paradigm" is more likely than its centrist, and even more so than its rightist, counterpart to favor social reforms and, by implication, to support civil protests; and

2. The leftist journalistic "paradigm" is more likely than its centrist, and even more so than its rightist, counterpart to depoliticize a civil protest.

In some exceptional cases, since the KMT-linked newspapers also exploited protests to embarrass the Communist Party (such as the 1956 riot caused by rightists, and the rightist Wanderers Association protesting the Hong Kong government's decision to expel illegal immigrants from Mainland China), one is then justified to ask whether political ideology is a spurious cause of journalistic "paradigm" on protest. The Golden Jubilee is a good test case to establish the credibility of political ideology as the major determinant of journalistic "paradigm" for three reasons. First, the leadership in the Jubilee Affair was in the hands of neither KMT nor CCP. A few teachers were rumored to be Trotskyists from the local Revolutionary Marxist Union but the Education Department denied any political complications. No evidence had been produced to suggest that they were affiliated with the Communist Party. Second, the protest was directed not to either external political party, but to the Jubilee School authorities, the Catholic Church, and the Hong Kong government—actors that do not ordinarily get involved in the KMT-CCP polemics. Third, such issues as school corruption and the government's mismanagement also had little to do with China's interparty politics. Had party politics been involved in the Jubilee School Affair, the government's Enquiry Committee would not have placed the burden of the blame on the school authorities, credited the teachers for exposing the corruption, reversed its suppressive policies, and rescinded the warning letters issued to rebels. In short, despite the possibility that political ideology may interact with the target at which a protest is aimed, the former remains unequivocally as a strong independent determinant of journalistic "paradigm" rather than a surrogate of other variables.

To push our case further, we might cite two other protests. First, in 1967 a militant riot led by local Communists, as a spin-off of the Chinese Cultural Revolution, broke out and put the social fabric at stake. This impending danger, plus partisan politics, sharply polarized the press with progovernment centrists and rightists on one side and leftists on the other. Rightist and centrist newspapers instantly became an integral part of the government's "ideological apparatus" to discredit the protesters. Meanwhile, leftist newspapers became the propaganda machine for China, modeling after Lenin's and Mao's conceptualization of a press to agitate, to organize, and to combat. The three hypotheses as presented in this chapter were confirmed in this case (Lee 1981).

The other case concerned an anti-bus-fare-increase campaign led by some 300 social groups (including "radical" pressure groups and many religious groups) in early 1981. Obviously its purpose was definitely nonpolitical, its scale was relatively mild, and the issue was not so explosive as to disrupt Hong Kong's stability. While the press unanimously supported the protesters, intensity varied: rightists were more reserved, while leftists and some centrists were much more outspoken.

REFERENCES

Altheide, David L. 1976. *Creating Reality: How TV News Distorts Events*. Beverly Hills: Sage.

Berger, Peter, and Thomas Luckmann. 1967. *The Social Construction of Reality*. Middlesex: Penguin.

Brzezinski, Zbigniew. 1970. *Between Two Ages: America's Role in the Technetronic Era*. New York: Viking.

Far Eastern Economic Review. 1981. August 7.

Fensterheim, Herbert, and M. E. Tresselt. 1953. The influence of value system on the perception of people. *Journal of Abnormal and Social Psychology* 48: 93–98.

Gusfield, Joseph R. 1970. *Protest, Reform and Revolt: A Reader in Social Movement*. New York: John Wiley and Sons, Inc.

Hall, Stuart. 1970. Watching the box. *New Society*, no. 411 (August 13): 295–96.

Hall, Stuart. 1974. Deviance, politics and the media. In *Deviance and Social Control*, edited by Paul Rock and Mary McIntosh. London: Tavistock Publications.

Harris, P. B. 1978. *Hong Kong: A Study in Bureaucratic Politics*. Hong Kong: New Kwok Printing Press Co. Ltd.

Hoadley, J. S. 1973. Political participation of Hong Kong Chinese: Patterns and trends. *Asian Survey* 13(6):604–16.

Hoyer, Svennih, Stig Hadenius, and Lennant Weibull. 1975. *The Politics and Economics of the Press: A Development Perspective*. Beverly Hills: Sage.

King, Ambrose Yeo-chi. 1975. Administrative absorption of politics in Hong Kong: Emphasis on the grass roots level. *Asian Survey* 15(5):422–39.

Kuhn, Thomas. 1970. *The Structure of Scientific Revolutions*. Chicago: The University of Chicago Press.

Lau, Shui-kai. 1978. Utilitarianistic familism: The basis of political stability in Hong Kong. Monograph, Social Research Center, Chinese University of Hong Kong.

Lee, Chin-Chuann. 1980. *Media Imperialism Reconsidered*. Beverly Hills: Sage.

Lee, Yuet-lin. 1981. The role of the press in the 1967 riot in Hong Kong. Undergraduate thesis, Department of Journalism and Communication, Chinese University of Hong Kong (in Chinese).

Lee-Hsia, Hsu Ting. 1974. *Government Control of the Press in Modern China: 1900–1949*. Cambridge: Harvard University Press.

Marsh, Alan. 1977. *Protest and Political Consciousness*. Beverly Hills: Sage.

Miners, Norman. 1979. *The Government and Politics of Hong Kong*. Hong Kong: Oxford University Press.

Omu, Fred I. A. 1978. *Press and Politics in Nigeria, 1800–1937*. Atlantic Highlands, New Jersey: Humanities Press.

Schram, Stuart. 1974. *Mao Tse-tung Unrehearsed*. Middlesex: Penguin.

SCOPG (Standing Committee on Pressure Groups). 1980. Information paper for chief secretary's committee monitoring of pressure group activities. Home Affairs Branch, Hong Kong Government.

Seymour-Ure, Colin, 1974. *The Political Impact of Mass Media*. Beverly Hills: Sage.

Slimming, John. 1979. Government and the mass media. *Journal of Journalism and Mass Communication*, Department of Journalism and Communication, Chinese University of Hong Kong.

Tseng, Hsu-pai, ed. 1966. *The Press History of China*. Taiwan: National Chengchi University, Graduate School of Journalism (in Chinese).

Yang, Yin. 1959. *History of China's Recent Revolution*. Taiwan: Construction Press (in Chinese).

CHAPTER 13

MEDIA EVALUATIONS AND GROUP POWER

George A. Donohue
Phillip J. Tichenor
Clarice N. Olien

Media-event strategies such as press conferences, picket lines, protest demonstrations, and other forms of confrontations may be viewed as forms of information control (Donohue et al. 1973). Such events are vital to a group for gaining or maintaining social control and establishing organized strength. Information in newspapers and television reports may draw attention to an issue, provide alternative views of a social problem, raise questions about the positions of adversarial groups, give visibility to new leadership groups, or contribute to an increased membership base of a group. These aspects of information control have consequences for the balance of power among interest groups within a community, and for the relative power position that the group and community may occupy in the total social system.

Confrontation over social issues such as location of high-voltage power lines, disposal of hazardous wastes, the values of the "moral majority," and coverage of the Middle East crises all highlight the use of media strategies for gaining and maintaining social power. Criticism of the media for "blowing an issue out of proportion," whether valid or not, indicates the value of media strategy for organized social action.

Media coverage is not available equally to all groups in society. Success of a group's media strategy depends on its organizational strength and on its strength relative to other groups (Tichenor et al. 1980). Such dependency may seem ironic to interest groups when they realize that they must first possess organized strength to gain power through media. The group's subsequent growth in power and scope is influenced in part by the design and results of the media strategy.

THE HYPOTHESIS

This chapter is concerned with the outcome of media coverage of social conflicts from the viewpoint of the groups involved. The specific question is if, through media coverage, the interest groups achieve what they consider to be helpful or harmful results. One hypothesis is that among the various groups and organizations that receive media coverage, those that occupy more established and dominant power positions will evaluate media coverage as more favorable to their collective ends than will groups and organizations with less established power positions. This hypothesis is based on the assumption that mass media, like all social agencies, constitute a segment of the society they serve and are not a separate or distinct group external to the system. This position holds that media do not operate as an independent "fourth estate" apart from society and are structurally incapable of doing so.

The tendency for the media to be responsive to the dominant power centers of the social system has been illustrated in a wide range of social science literature. If a community is small and depends primarily on a single industry, public decisions tend to be made in ways based on tradition and consensus; these traditions and consensual processes will be reflected and reinforced in the local newspaper (Olien et al. 1968). In a more pluralistic urban structure, decision-making processes must be based on the differing and conflicting interests of the multiplicity of power centers of that structure. Decisions based on conflict and involving representatives from different groups such as city councils, school boards, government agencies, and business groups are more likely to be reflected in the urban newspaper. Thus, the small-town paper mirrors a small-town outlook and the urban paper mirrors an urban outlook; sociologically, the name "Mirror" for a newspaper may be more realistic than the name "Sentinel" or "Guardian," to the extent that the latter two names symbolize an independent surveillance function.

Community differences in portrayal of an event or crisis are clear especially when the interests of a particular small town conflict with those of a larger urban center that dominates the region containing the small town. As an example, weekly newspapers in small towns near the Boundary Waters Canoe Area of northeastern Minnesota reflected the local view on multiple use of that area that would include logging, mining, and motorized recreational traffic. Daily newspapers in Duluth and the Twin Cities, however, were more likely to stress restrictions on motorized transportation and the maintenance of a state of wilderness, a view that is particularly characteristic of metropolitan areas, which view the boundary waters primarily as a recreational resource.

Further evidence that media coverage is generally supportive of established groups is provided by a number of other empirical studies. In their case study of a city council, Paletz, Reichert, and McIntyre (1971) found that newspaper reporting consistently supported local government authority when challenges occurred from citizen groups (Paletz and Entman 1981). Molotch and Lester (1974) found that newspaper coverage around the nation was heavily dominated (more than nine to one) by events concerning oil companies and federal agencies, rather than by events involving local conservationists and other local groups. Sigal (1973) found that nearly 60 percent of the sources of the *New York Times* and *Washington Post* for national and international news could be classified as "routine" contacts with legislative bodies or government agencies. Only 25 percent reflected "reporter initiative"; Sigal concluded that the routine character of newsgathering provides a mechanism for official dominance of national and foreign news in both papers. His conclusion is similar to that of Schudson (1978), who finds, historically, that marginal interest groups, lacking resources and organizational skills, fall "outside the news net," and do not make conventional news. Tuchman (1978) concludes that lower status groups, in particular, are unable to gain access to the media as a resource unless they develop linkages with higher status groups that have media access. One empirical indicator of how lower status groups may be excluded from papers is a study by Lemert and Larkin (1979); they found that nearly 50 percent of the individuals who succeeded in having their letters published were active in four or more community activities. By comparison, less than 20 percent of those whose letters were rejected and 10 percent of those who did not write to the editor were active to the same extent. Furthermore, a newspaper policy of restricting letters to the editor to discussion of issues and prohibiting "mobilizing information" appeared to reinforce existing power interests. This means that coverage of mediaevent strategies will tend to be confined to news columns written by reporters whose news selection criteria typically include the established strength of the group concerned.

Three additional studies document specific dependence of media upon positions of structural power. Shepherd (1979), in an extensive study of the sources of information used in press reporting of the marijuana controversy, found that among the most heavily publicized ten authorities on marijuana, seven had never done any recognized marijuana research at all but were influential primarily as administrators of prestigious health research centers or federal agencies. Weaver and Wilhoit (1980) found that coverage devoted to individual U.S. senators could be traced not only to their organized political activity within Congress itself, but also to the more basic "opportunity structure," as they termed it, which provides a "base from which to attract national media exposure, especially for Republicans." The key elements of this "opportunity structure" include population of the state the senator represents and senate staff resources. In a Minnesota study, public understanding of science news articles was higher for those news articles that depended upon editor assignment, rigid organizational policy in research agencies for mass media reporting, and administrative power position of the scientist quoted. These results may be interpreted as indicating that press roles are organized so as to respond most efficiently to positions of power in the source groups (Tichenor et al. 1970).

METHODS AND PROCEDURES

Data for this analysis were taken from three studies of news sources conducted in Minnesota from 1978 to 1980. The first study was a survey of thirty-five news sources in two communities, both in the same county—St. Cloud, a regional urban center with a population of 30,000, and Paynesville, an agricultural business and service center of 2,000. St. Cloud is served by a daily newspaper and Paynesville by a weekly. Sources of news articles about local issues, which appeared during a two-month period in early 1978, subsequently were interviewed. These sources included thirteen elected officials, sixteen agency and school officials, and six leaders of recently organized citizen groups concerned about such issues as street and bridge repair and drug abuse problems, which had been the topics of the news articles.

The second study was conducted in 1979 among news sources quoted in newspaper articles about the second tractorcade demonstration by the American Agriculture Movement (AAM) in Washington, D.C. The AAM had generated a large-scale media event in which thousands of tractors were driven to Washington in an attempt to dramatize problems of costs, prices, and low net profit in agriculture and to seek political remedies. The newspaper articles selected for study had appeared in newspapers in Minneapolis and St. Paul and in southwestern Minnesota, the area of concentrated organizational activity when the AAM was first formed a few years earlier. News sources interviewed in the study included twenty-eight AAM members and eleven officials in such established groups as city government, chambers of commerce, state and federal agricultural agencies, and older farm organizations.

The third study, conducted in 1980, was a comparison of news source reactions in four communities selected to represent sharp differences in size and structural pluralism—St. Paul, a city of 280,000 served by a daily; Cottage Grove, a St. Paul suburb of 16,870 served by a weekly and within the circulation area for the St. Paul daily papers; Red Wing, a regional city of 13,000 served by a daily; and Zumbrota, a community of 2,300 in a predominantly farming area, served by a weekly. In each community, sources quoted in local newspaper articles about the three most heavily covered local issues were selected for interview. These sources included a total of fifty-one elected and appointed agency officials and business group leaders who were classified as part of the established power groups of the communities, and twenty-three others, including students at an energy center and individuals who were either quoted as individual citizens or who wrote letters to the editor about the local issues.

The questions asked of the news sources were the same in all three studies. Sources were asked whether any particular newspapers or particular television or radio stations "have been especially helpful to your organization or agency," and whether any of these media "have been especially harmful to your organization or agency."

FINDINGS

Findings are generally supportive of the hypothesis that among the various groups and organizations that receive media coverage, those that occupy more established and dominant power positions in society will evaluate media coverage as more favorable to their collective ends than will members of groups and organizations with less established power positions.

This conclusion is apparent in the data in Table 14 from St. Cloud and Paynesville, studied in 1978. While a small number of cases is involved, none of the thirteen elected officials interviewed in that study mentioned any medium as harmful, while five of the six citizen group leaders mentioned at least one newspaper or broadcast station as harmful to their groups. Harmful media or media acts were named by three of the sixteen agency and school officials, while ten saw all media as helpful and none as harmful. If the elected and appointed officials are considered as a group, only three saw one medium or more as harmful. By comparison, five of the six citizen group leaders did see harm, with complaints ranging from editorial opposition to charges of news slanting by reporters. The complaints that did occur were largely about newspaper activity; an example is the leader of a neighborhood group, protesting a bridge project, who contended that the local newspaper was unsympathetic toward the problems of citizens inconvenienced by a plan to widen the bridge and increase traffic through their neighborhood.

Support for the hypothesis is especially strong in the findings in Table 15, from the 1979 interviews with sources quoted in news stories about the American Agricultural Movement (AAM) and its second tractorcade protest. Although the tractorcade was widely publicized, there is a sharp difference in media evaluations, in the hypothesized direction, between the

Table 14. Evaluations of Media for Organizational Purposes among News Sources in Two Communities

Response	Elected Officials	Agency and School Officials	Citizen Groups Leaders
All media seen as helpful, none harmful	11	10	1
Media seen as neither helpful *nor* harmful	2	3	0
One medium or more seen as harmful	0	3	5
TOTAL	13	16	6

AAM members and news sources who represent such established groups as older farm organizations and federal agricultural agencies. Only two of the eleven sources from the more established groups mentioned one medium or more as harmful to their interest. This evaluation compares with twenty-one of the twenty-eight AAM news sources who saw harm being done by at least one medium.

Again, the criticisms that appeared were directed primarily toward newspapers. In their individual responses, thirteen AAM members mentioned Twin Cities newspapers and six mentioned national newspapers as harmful to their organization. Nearly all of the AAM sources mentioned local and regional media (i.e., in southwestern Minnesota) as helpful to their organization, and only one mentioned a local paper as harmful.

None of the eleven sources from the established groups associated with the AAM tractorcade issue saw newspapers in the Twin Cities or Washington, D.C., as harmful. The two mentions of harmful media, made by sources from these established groups, included a single small-town weekly and a national paper sold largely through supermarkets and newsstands.

Evaluations of media by dominant or challenging power groups depend upon the context and the issue (Tables 14 and 15). In the context of St. Cloud, Paynesville, and their community issues, the local media are perceived as more supportive of the established local power groups than of citizen groups that may be challenging established agencies. In the context of the national tractorcade media strategy and challenge raised by the AAM, the national media are perceived as more supportive of the established powers than the challenging AAM source. The AAM had established itself as a group dealing with an agricultural problem of general concern to the region that includes rural southwestern Minnesota. As an organized advocate of local interests seeking a political resolution of agri-

Table 15. Evaluations of Media for Organizational Purposes among News Sources from Established Groups and the American Agriculture Movement

Response	Established Groups	American Agriculture Movement
All media seen as helpful, none harmful	7	6
Media seen as neither helpful *nor* harmful	2	1
One medium or more seen as harmful	2	21
TOTAL	11	28

cultural problems, the AAM was reported in the local media in a way seen as positive by the AAM itself. The functional utility of rural weekly papers from the viewpoint of the AAM is in serving as an organizational resource for mobilizing local public opinion favorable to the position of AAM (Tichenor et al. 1980).

Newspapers in the metropolitan areas, such as the cities of Minneapolis-St. Paul and Washington, D.C., structure their reporting from the perspective of a different power mix than do rural papers. Much of the reporting of conflict in both areas involves selective labeling of acts in a way that has ramifications for the legitimacy and, therefore, power of the groups involved. Reference to powerline protest acts as "vandalism," as occurred in another Minnesota controversy, has consequences similar to referring to politically motivated groups on the international scene as "terrorist." Such labels serve to withdraw legitimacy from the groups and give a negative connotation to the behavior of the actors. Applying such labels of marginality or deviancy to groups with marginal power status is only one of several mechanisms by which interests of established power centers may be supported in media reports. Errors of omission, deliberate or not, as well as errors of commission with respect to the information, are other techniques through which particular perspectives are favored in the reporting process.

MEDIA EVALUATION AND COMMUNITY STRUCTURE

The third study, conducted among four communities of varying size and structure in 1980, makes it possible to examine further the differences in media evaluations between established group sources and other sources, and to examine these evaluations according to structural differences between communities as well.

In communities where there is a diversity of power sources, one would expect the reporting of conflictual issues to be accepted as a normal and regular occurrence by leader groups. Political roles in a large metropolitan center or at the state or national level require a conflict orientation and a socialization that recognizes the role of media in reporting diverse views about intense controversies. Even in such cases, however, the media would be expected to reflect the power distribution through selective reporting and definition of issues. The implication is that evaluations of media by established power sources in these pluralistic structures would be favorable to the extent that coverage does not appear to threaten the existing balance-of-power relationships. Coverage of formalized conflicts, such as legislative procedures that leave power relationships intact, would not be expected to elicit negative reactions from incumbents of established power positions. On the other hand, if a controversy is such that it raises serious questions about existing power relationships and creates uncertainty and confusion about where power lies, media coverage reflecting that confusion would be expected to draw negative reactions from established leadership groups who now find their power status in doubt and regard media coverage as a contributory factor.

While evaluations of media performance in more pluralistic systems would be expected to vary according to whether press coverage reflects confusion about the balance of power, evaluations in more homogeneous systems depend more on an absence of controversy entirely. In such systems as small rural communities, the power concentration is such that the media are generally controlled by a power elite. To the extent that the media in these communities support the rural system's consensus model of operation, they will generally be viewed favorably by the leadership group for that performance.

Control of media performance may be especially problematic in communities that are transitional. If a community is growing and diversifying in a context that emphasizes changing linkages between the community and the rest of society, strains over media coverage may be especially intense. The conflictual nature of the emerging decision processes may require the reporting of conflict, and if the concentration of the power base is undergoing modification, a newspaper might well be expected to be confused and to reflect confusion about where control lies. If the leadership structure itself is in transition, newspapers cannot respond to leadership as they can when power is stabilized. One might expect, in a transitional situation, that confusion over lines of control might exist not only in the community as a whole but also in the substructure called the "press." The question becomes, quite literally, to whom does the press respond?

The four communities in the third study represent the kinds of differences suggested here. St. Paul is an older center city and state capital, with a long tradition of the kind of open debate over political, economic, and other social issues characteristic of such a community. Zumbrota is a small community in a rural area, with high dependence on agriculture, that typifies the most homogeneous type of community. Cottage Grove is a rapidly growing suburb that today has more than three times the population it had twenty years ago and has encountered a variety of developmental problems typical in suburban communities. Red Wing is an older regional trade center, with some state institutions and small-scale manufacturing, about 45 miles from St. Paul and therefore within the sphere of influence of the expanding metropolitan area.

Data from these four communities generally support the central hypothesis of this study, that media evaluations will be more favorable among established power groups than among less established groups. The differences, as indicated in Table 16, are not as sharp as in the first two studies. Adding across all four communities one finds, in the right-hand columns of Table 16, that fewer than a fourth of the sources in established groups in these communities saw media as harmful to their own organizations, compared with a third of the nonestablished groups. Again, most of the criticisms of media were about newspaper performance. Among the nineteen sources who stated some harm from media, fifteen mentioned newspapers *only*, and only four mentioned television as harmful to their own organizations. All four of these criticisms of television were from established group sources.

Media evaluations differ according to community. There were few criticisms of media among the sources in St. Paul, where only two of the twenty sources saw any medium as harmful. The stories in which these sources were quoted dealt with highly publicized and, in at least two cases, highly controversial issues. They were not, however, controversies that were crucial to the power distribution of the community, either for the established power centers or special interest groups. One topic was a proposed "people mover" transit system that involved questions of legislative support and federal funding. The other topic was introduction of cable television in St. Paul, a subject related to a recent debate over cable contracts that had occurred in adjacent Minneapolis. The third topic was the mayor's energy conservation program, a project that involved voluntary audits of energy saving in individual homes. Sources quoted in these stories included a number of professional politicians such as state legislators and council members, heads of agencies, and attorneys for various interests.

Also, no media were seen as harmful by sources quoted in the Zumbrota stories, suggesting that the consensus nature of this community is recognized by the sources who are in the news there. There is an absence of controversy in the press reports from this community, rather than report-

Table 16. Evaluations of Media for Organizational Purposes among News Sources in Four Communities

Response	St. Paul Elected and Agency Officers	St. Paul Individual and Citizen Leaders	Cottage Grove Elected and Agency Officers	Cottage Grove Individual and Citizen Leaders	Red Wing Elected and Agency Officers	Red Wing Individual and Citizen Leaders	Zumbrota Elected and Agency Officers	Zumbrota Individual and Citizen Leaders	Total Elected and Agency Officers	Total Individual and Citizen Leaders
All media seen as helpful, none harmful	8	3	7	3	9	6	4	1	28	13
Media seen as neither helpful *nor* harmful	5	2	3	0	1	1	3	0	12	3
TV seen as harmful	0	0	0	0	4	0	0	0	4	0
Newspapers *only* seen as harmful	2	0	2	2	3	5	0	0	7	7
TOTAL	15	5	12	5	17	12	7	1	51	23

ing of controversy and a balancing of power centers. This finding is consistent with the idea that small communities generally operate on a consensus model. The Zumbrota newspaper, a weekly, gave less coverage to any social issues topic during the period of study than any other paper in the four communities, and none of the reports in the Zumbrota weekly indicated much local controversy. The Zumbrota topics included a question of financial help for heating homes in the county and local opposition to a uniform building code passed by the state legislature. Both questions concerned acts of bodies external to Zumbrota, and the newspaper reported the topics without any indication of local difference on either topic. The third topic in Zumbrota was about a city street development project, and the newspaper reports mentioned decisions and future construction with minimal attention to differing views about these decisions.

The most frequent mention of media harm—by twelve of twenty-nine sources—among the four communities was in Red Wing, which, as indicated above, is a community in transition. The issues there reflect a changing set of power relationships, with attendant confusion over lines of control. One of the topics under study there, the nuclear power plant, raised complex questions of local vs nonlocal control. The national question of nuclear plant safety was being acted out in a local context, amid a variety of unanswered questions about control of and responsibility for safety monitoring, warning and evacuation systems, and storage of radioactive waste. The study was conducted about six months after an accident at the power plant led to some release of radioactivity. This accident and attendant questions of safety had been discussed in local and statewide media in the context of the nationally publicized Three Mile Island accident in Pennsylvania that had preceded the accident at the plant near Red Wing by about half a year. Another issue in Red Wing concerned a student and citizen challenge to the leadership of an energy education center at an area vocational technical institute, a regional facility. Questions were raised about technical and staffing adequacy of the school in a way that questioned directly the officials in charge of the institute. The third issue in Red Wing revolved around a question of preserving or tearing down a set of old houses, which symbolize a nineteenth century ethnic tradition in the community. This issue involved a procedural and legal confrontation between groups favoring traditional landowner control over razing and development and groups seeking to restrict that control in favor of preservation policy.

The three topics in Red Wing had been subject to more stories in the local paper than had been reported in any other local paper on any issue during the study period. The relatively high rate of negative evaluations of media in that community, including television, may reflect strains that occur in a community faced with a variety of conflicts and a power transition. The structure produces conflicts and requires media reporting of them. All three controversies produced uncertainties in power relationships. This structurally originated power confusion appears to have led to a stalemate and to negative evaluations of the media for reflecting those conditions.

Next to Red Wing, the most frequent mention of harmful effects by media, expressed by four of seventeen sources, is in Cottage Grove where there were also questions of control over community processes. The issues involved a highly disputed question of annexing an area to that community over the objection of resident groups—a controversial street-parking ordinance that raised questions of property rights, powers of law enforcement agencies, and a rural development plan.

MEDIA EVALUATION AND ESTABLISHED POWER

Each of the three studies here involves a small number of cases. However, it should be pointed out that the differences across the studies are sharp. By aggregating the findings from all three studies, one finds that only 18 percent of the ninety-one sources representing established groups saw harmful effects for their organizations in one medium or more. That compares with 58 percent of the fifty-seven sources from the less established and therefore less powerful groups who perceived such harm. The difference between these two proportions is significant at the .001 level, and if one treats perception of harmful effects in media as a dichotomous variable, the contingency coefficient between power status of the source and perception of media effects (corrected for a 2-by-2 table) is .55. In these studies as a whole, sources from the less established groups were more than three times as likely as established sources to perceive harmful media effects for organizations they represent.

Most of the criticisms were directed toward newspapers rather than television. This finding suggests the possibly distinct role of television in reporting issues, and it appears that further analysis is needed of the joint roles of newspapers and television in coverage of social issues.

CONCLUSION

Data from three studies in Minnesota support the hypothesis that media coverage generally is evaluated as more favorable among those groups and organizations that occupy more established and dominant power positions, compared with members of groups and organizations with less established power positions. The findings also suggest that such criticisms may be associated with community structure, in that negative evaluations may be especially frequent in transitional community structures that face a growing number of social issues that raise questions of uncertainty about lines of control and distribution of power within the system. An implication of these findings is that any groups designing media strategies must be fully aware of the distribution of power and its consequences for media control. These data, as well as literature cited earlier, challenge the notion of the media as a fourth estate and suggest that the media, if they are a fourth estate, are controlled by the other three.

REFERENCES

Donohue, G. A., P. J. Tichenor, and C. N. Olien. 1973. Mass media functions, knowledge and social control. *Journalism Quarterly* 50:652–59.

Lemert, James B., and Jerome P. Larkin. 1979. Some reasons why mobilization information fails to be in letters to the editor. *Journalism Quarterly* 56:504–12.

Molotch, Harvey, and Marilyn Lester. 1974. News as purposive behavior. *American Sociological Review* 81:235–60.

Olien, C. N., G. A. Donohue, and P. J. Tichenor. 1968. The community editor's power and the reporting of conflict. *Journalism Quarterly* 45:243–52.

Paletz, David L., and Robert N. Entman. 1981. *Media Power Politics.* New York: Macmillan.

Paletz, David L., Peggy Reichert, and Barbara McIntyre. 1971. How the media support local government authority. *Public Opinion Quarterly* 35:80–92.

Schudson, Michael. 1978. *Discovering the News: A Social History of American Newspapers.* New York: Basic Books.

Shepherd, R. Gordon. 1979. Science news of controversy: The case of marijuana. *Journalism Monographs* 62, August.

Sigal, Leon. 1973. *Reporters and Officials.* Lexington, Mass.: Heath.

Tichenor, Phillip J., George A. Donohue, and Clarice N. Olien. 1980. *Community Conflict and the Press.* Beverly Hills: Sage.

Tichenor, Phillip J., Clarice N. Olien, Annette Harrison, and George Donohue. 1970. Mass communication systems and communication accuracy in science news reporting. *Journalism Quarterly* 47:673–83.

Tuchman, Gaye. 1978. *Making News.* New York: Free Press.

Weaver, David H., and G. Cleveland Wilhoit. 1980. News media coverage of U.S. senators in four congresses, 1953–74. *Journalism Monographs* 67, April.

CHAPTER 14

THE MEDIA MIX: TV AND SOCIAL CONFLICT

Phillip J. Tichenor
George A. Donohue
Clarice N. Olien

In the structural frame of reference, mass communication media constitute an interdependent subsystem of the total social system. Holistically, any one medium must be understood as part of the overall media subsystem, which further must be analyzed in terms of its linkages with the other subsystems—economic, governmental, legal, religious, and educational—that constitute the total system.

This perspective differs from the McLuhanite view that "the medium is the message," in that it would be more appropriate to say that "the medium *as organized and integrated into the media mix* is *part* of the message" (Paletz and Entman 1981). It would be incorrect to attribute public opinion or any aspect of social change solely to television or any other medium. The impact of television must be interpreted as part of the total flow of communication on any topic in a particular community or region and at a particular point in the development of an issue.

As the mass media system has evolved since World War II in the United States, television has developed a highly visible role in social action as well as in popular entertainment. The potential of television for social power was recognized early, with televised coverage of political conventions and election debates widely regarded as a crucial part of media strategies by parties and candidates during the past twenty-five to thirty years. Television, along with newspaper coverage, figured strongly in the strategies of groups involved in civil rights, antiwar protests, and environmental movements (Palmgreen and Clark 1977). It became increasingly clear to these interest groups that as the media mix changed, they had to take television into account as well as newspapers and other media.

While acknowledging the role of television in major social issues, students and critics have also stressed television's primary orientation to national and

217

metropolitan news as contrasted with news about local communities (Patterson and McClure 1976, Bagdikian 1971, Williams and Larsen 1977). There is persistent doubt as to whether television's superficial coverage of local or nonlocal issues contributes to citizen understanding and, therefore, to a level of citizen involvement that a participatory democratic society appears to require. Evidence cited by these critics includes the limited attention to political processes and to local topics generally provided by TV coverage compared with newspapers (Shaw and McCombs 1977, Tipton et al. 1975, McLuhan 1964). An interesting hypothesis, which is often stated but not substantiated, is that television might have an even more pronounced narcotizing effect than other media, in the sense of creating a belief by the citizenry that they are informed when in fact they are not.

THE MEDIA MIX

Emphasis of U.S. television on nonlocal topics, rather than on the range of local topics presented in weekly and daily newspapers, may be traced to the way television has developed. At the outset, this medium was nationally organized and nationally controlled, following the organizational model established for radio and based on the concept that air waves were public and seen as a scarce national resource and therefore requiring national control (Bagdikian 1971, Hirsch 1981). Local stations needed not only a nationally controlled license to operate, but also an affiliation with a major network if they were to have the programming to command a major market share. The advent of television altered the national role of radio in local and nonlocal news reporting. Television did not displace radio; radio has proliferated in numbers of both AM and FM stations and has taken on a specialized function in an increasingly pluralistic system. In television, the national focus has become apparent in virtually every aspect of programming—sports, performing arts, talk shows, religion, education, and network news. With the development of cable television, it appears that television is proliferating as radio did earlier, to serve specialized interest groups. This development may be expected to have some implications for the configuration of media for news and information.

The national, or systemwide, orientation of television organization is not unique to this medium but reflects the general development of the system. Much as thousands of communities today find their manufacturing firms, retail stores, schools, and churches increasingly controlled by centralized authority, they find the content of television increasingly controlled by and oriented toward the larger system.

In sports, entertainment, and news, concentration on a high degree of professionalism requires a national organization for recruitment and training. The use of local TV stations as training grounds for reporters and anchor persons closely resembles the "farm club" system of other professions and industries. For television news personnel, this system of career advancement and socialization emphasizes the importance of being familiar and conversant with the more general concerns of society.

The configuration and orientation of news on television differs from that of newspapers. The smaller amount of television news, compared with newspapers, is often noted; in addition, television coverage tends to be more cosmopolite, rather than localite, in comparison with newspapers. Metropolitan television is controlled not only by the local power structure but also by national power centers through network affiliations. Even metropolitan daily newspapers tend to be less cosmopolitan in their coverage than television, and dailies in small regional cities and weekly papers of even smaller communities are the most localite of all. When an issue develops, television reports it in terms of what it means to the nation or region; the weekly paper reports it in terms of what it means to the community.

While newspaper wire services also represent a national system of news origination and delivery, these wire services are structured in a way that differs from television network news. The newspapers' national wire services might be described as a cafeteria offering of news items from which individual newspapers select a diet, whereas network news provides a more specific menu for local viewers to digest with little or no intervening selection by the local station.

This chapter looks at the role of television within the media system as currently structured, specifically, whether the use of television for local and nonlocal news, as contrasted with newspapers, varies predictably according to structure; whether the contribution of television to citizen knowledge, in comparison with other media sources, varies according to the phase of a social controversy; and whether television's contribution to knowledge varies with community type. Data are from community studies in Minnesota, including a longitudinal study of an intense conflict over an energy facility.

DATA SOURCES

Data for this analysis are taken from three groups of studies in Minnesota. One is a study of media uses for local and nonlocal news conducted in 1978, in communities that included St. Paul, suburban Cottage Grove, an outlying regional city (St. Cloud), a small town (Paynesville), and the surrounding rural area. A second group of studies, conducted in 1980, includes samples in St. Paul, suburban Cottage Grove, a regional city (Red Wing), and a small rural community (Zumbrota). In both of these groups of studies, two questions were asked to measure use of media for local and nonlocal news. The first was: "Between television, radio and newspapers, which one do you feel gives you the most local news?" The second was the same, except that "local" was replaced with "state, national, and international"; this item is used as a measure of use of sources for nonlocal news.

The third data set is from a longitudinal study of a controversy involving a high-voltage power line across central Minnesota. Organized protest developed against a proposal of utility cooperatives to establish a 400 kilovolt (DC) line through primarily agricultural areas to transmit electric power from generators near North Dakota coal fields to substations near the Twin Cities. The organized protests were directed toward the exercise of control over community conditions by external agencies, including the use of eminent domain procedures for siting the lines, and toward questions of safety and health for human beings and farm animals. This study involved samples in rural Paynesville in Minnesota's Stearns County and in a metropolitan suburb, near Minneapolis, where the line was initially sited and eventually built. Different but comparable citizen samples were interviewed in fall 1975, winter 1976, winter 1977, and again in late winter and early spring 1978. This period was characterized by two different phases. The first, including the period of summer 1975 through winter of 1976, was a bureaucratic confrontation phase, during which the principal events were governmental and judicial-type procedures for determining line location. The second was a construction confrontation phase marked by confrontation and increasingly intense conflict. Confrontation strategies included demonstrations and picketing, in an attempt by citizens to gain support for the views of the opposition groups.

TV AS A SOURCE OF LOCAL NEWS

The structural frame of reference holds that relative use of television and newspapers for local and nonlocal news will vary according to community structure. As a corollary to this, newspapers would be expected to be used more frequently than television as principal sources of local news because of the greater structural identification of newspapers with their communities. Television news coverage is oriented more toward activities of individual interest groups that relate to more generalized system concerns. Hence, one would expect television to be more frequently mentioned as a source of nonlocal news than newspapers. To a lesser extent, one would also expect metropolitan newspapers to be used more for this purpose than weekly papers.

It would also be hypothesized that relative use of television for nonlocal news, compared with newspapers, would be greater in smaller, more homogeneous communities than in larger, more pluralistic communities. This expectation is based upon the orientations of newspapers as well as television in different kinds of communities. The daily newspapers of larger communities reflect the multiple concerns of those communities and the larger systems in which they exist; this means a combination of local and nonlocal news. In smaller, more homogeneous communities, newspapers tend to concentrate on local news and are often the only source of such news.

FINDINGS

Data from the 1978 and 1980 studies indicate that newspapers are mentioned most frequently as giving the "most local news," with television running a close second in the metro areas and third after radio in the outlying communities. Television is clearly first for nonlocal news in all communities; the *relative* use of television for nonlocal news is clearly greater in smaller, more homogeneous communities than in the metropolitan area communities (Table 17).

The data show a sharp difference among communities in sources for both local and nonlocal news. In 1978, use of newspapers over television for local news is greater in the outlying communities of St. Cloud and Paynesville than in Cottage Grove or St. Paul. In 1980, the difference is greater for the outlying communities of Red Wing and Zumbrota than in St. Paul or suburban Cottage Grove.

The communities also differ as expected in the pattern for nonlocal news. The margin of television over newspapers is greater in the outlying communities of St. Cloud and rural Paynesville in 1978 than in Cottage Grove or St. Paul, and greater in Red Wing and Zumbrota than Cottage Grove or St. Paul in 1980. These findings provide support for the structural hypothesis and suggest that the functions of the different media are more clearly delineated in the outlying communities. Local news in the outlying city is the more exclusive province of a daily paper, as in St. Cloud and Red Wing, and in small towns it is provided by weeklies, as in Paynesville and Zumbrota. In the metropolitan communities, a combination of local and nonlocal news is provided by both television and newspapers, with television the first-ranked source for nonlocal news and newspapers first for local news.

Results for both 1978 and 1980 indicate the strong role played by electronic media in the media mix. Radio was the second most frequently named source for local news in all four outlying communities. When radio and television were considered jointly, they accounted for more than half of the mentions of media for local news in Minneapolis and for 43 percent

Table 17. Percent of Respondents Mentioning Newspapers, Television, or Radio as Giving Them Most Local News or Most State, National, and International News

Most Local News

Information Source	1978				1980[a]			
	St. Paul (n=159)	Cottage Grove (n=110)	St. Cloud (n=100)	Rural Paynesville (n=120)	St. Paul (n=247)	Cottage Grove (n=249)	Red Wing (n=250)	Zumbrota (n=253)
Newspapers	50	53	62	46	51	55	79	72
Television	30	29	7	23	30	31	7	9
Radio	15	13	30	28	17	12	13	17
DK, no response	5	5	1	3	2	2	1	2
TOTAL	100	100	100	100	100	100	100	100
Difference, NP[b] > TV	+20	+34	+55	+23	+21	+24	+72	+63

Most State, National, and International News

Information Source	1978				1980[a]			
	St. Paul	Cottage Grove	St. Cloud	Rural Paynesville	St. Paul	Cottage Grove	Red Wing	Zumbrota
Newspapers	42	36	20	19	29	36	20	22
Television	46	51	73	67	59	55	73	69
Radio	9	7	7	9	11	9	6	6
DK, no response	3	6	0	5	1	—	1	3
TOTAL	100	100	100	100	100	100	100	100
Difference, TV > NP[b]	+4	+15	+53	+48	+30	+19	+53	+49

[a] Number of cases reflects a pooling of two different but equivalent samples interviewed in each of the four communities in winter and spring, 1980.

[b] NP = newspapers

or more in both St. Paul samples and in suburban Cottage Grove. Radio was mentioned less frequently for state, national, and international news, however, reflecting a far different role for radio in the media mix than one would have found thirty-five or forty years earlier.

There were other differences among communities in local and nonlocal sources in addition to those mentioned previously. These include: (1) the outlying communities studied in 1980 showed higher use of newspapers for local news than those studied in 1978; (2) rural Paynesville in 1978 had a different media mix than Zumbrota, a community similar in size and rural character, had in 1980; and (3) St. Paul had higher use of television in 1980 than in 1978. A full interpretation of these findings would require additional studies of local factors and is beyond the scope of this analysis.

Media Sources and Knowledge

Television and newspapers have predictably different utilization patterns for local and nonlocal news in different types of communities. That is, one would expect newspapers to contribute more to knowledge of local issues than television, and one might expect this difference to be greater in small, more homogeneous communities having newspapers that concentrate more on local news than larger, more pluralistic communities having newspapers that cover a wider range of topics, both local and nonlocal.

Data relevant to this question include correlations between the measured amount of media use and accurate knowledge about topics (Table 18). These correlations are presented for local topics, which were different for each community, and for the power-line topic, which was a statewide issue in 1978 when these data were gathered.

These data indicated that the correlations between TV news-watching and knowledge of local topics tended to be low in all communities. The highest correlations with local knowledge were for the type of newspaper that serves the particular community. In rural Paynesville and the six metropolitan suburbs, the local paper is a weekly, and the correlations between local knowledge and reading a local weekly were higher, as expected, than between local knowledge and daily newspaper reading. Conversely, in St. Cloud, Minneapolis, and St. Paul, where the local paper is a daily, the correlations between local knowledge and daily newspaper reading were higher than between local knowledge and use of television or a weekly. It should be noted than in St. Paul, the correlation between daily newspaper reading and knowledge of local topics was only slightly higher (.21 vs .20) than for weekly newspaper reading and local knowledge.

One might expect, given the nonlocal orientation of TV news and the nonlocal nature of the power-line issue, that TV news-watching in the met-

Table 18. Correlations between Use of Media Sources and Knowledge of Topics in Different Communities, 1978

Media Source and Topic	Rural Paynesville	St. Cloud	Minneapolis	St. Paul	Average of Six Suburbs
Correlation of knowledge of three local topics with					
TV news watching	.11	.10	.00	.00	−.015
Local weekly reading	.42	.02	.26	.20	.33
Daily newspaper reading	.05	.23	.46	.21	.12
Correlation of power-line knowledge with					
TV news watching	.07	.09	.19	.02	−.03
Local weekly reading	.41	.09	−.02	−.02	−.025
Daily newspaper reading	.06	.33	.14	.18	.09

ropolitan area would have been more highly correlated with knowledge of the power line than with knowledge of local topics. This was not the case. Minneapolis was the only community in which the correlation between TV news-watching and knowledge of the power-line topic was greater than .10. In fact, except for rural Paynesville and St. Cloud, none of the correlations between level of newspaper *or* television use and power-line knowledge was particularly high. In rural Paynesville, the correlation between use of the local weekly and the power-line issue was .41; in St. Cloud, the correlation between daily newspaper reading and power-line knowledge was .33. In both of these communities, the power line was a local as well as a statewide issue; the line was directly relevant to the concerns of Paynesville and the surrounding rural area. For St. Cloud, the county seat for the county in which Paynesville is located, the issue was a regional one. In the metropolitan communities, none of the three measures of media use was strongly correlated with power-line knowledge.

Media Sources and Stage of a Conflict

An additional question for analysis is whether television, in comparison with other media, makes its strongest contribution to knowledge at a particular phase of a controversy. One might hypothesize that, given the current definition of the medium, with its coverage of social action and focus on systemwide issues, its contribution to knowledge would be greatest at points of high conflict intensity. This is not to say TV is inherently limited to this function; its usage might well change with an increase in use of cable TV and related technologies.

One would also expect that at any given time, TV and newspapers would both be more highly correlated with information-holding in a more pluralistic community, which by its nature depends more on secondary communication, than in a less pluralistic community that depends more on primary forms of communication. Television news dramatizes the confrontation stages of conflicts and, therefore, the issues underlying those conflicts. Television does not perform this function apart from newspapers; highly intense conflicts are likely to involve media strategies directed toward print as well as broadcast media. In the case of the power-line controversy, the principal coverage during the bureaucratic phase, including the hearings over corridor location and line location, was from newspapers. Media strategies that would have involved television were not employed at that particular stage. As a result, metropolitan television channels provided little visual coverage of the conflict until summer 1976, when preliminary construction activities began and protest groups organized confrontations with construction survey crews. These confrontations were intense, with widely recognized potential for violence. From that point on, through winter of 1978, the power-line issue was a major TV story.

In the four interviewing waves of the power-line study, respondents were asked to state specifically which source, or sources, provided them with information about the issue. Newspapers were the primary source in both of the first two waves of the study, with television being used with equal or greater frequency as a source in both communities in the third and fourth waves. This was during the construction and social action phase, to which television coverage is particularly suited given the current definition of the medium.

The partial correlations between use of specific sources and knowledge of the power-line issue indicated that the relative contribution to knowledge of the different media varied, as hypothesized, both by community and phase of the controversy (Table 19). In the suburban area, there was a steady decline in the strength of the partial correlation between accuracy of knowledge and the use of newspapers from the first through the third waves, with the partial correlation continuing to be low (.22) in the final wave. For television, the partials were low in the first two waves but high (.48) in the third wave; then they declined to .09 in the fourth wave.

In the rural area, there was a decline in the partial correlations between accuracy of knowledge and use of newspapers as a source through the third wave of interviews, dropping from .45 in the first, to .30 in the second, and to .26 in the third. The correlation between accuracy of knowledge and use of newspapers as a source in the rural area increased to .33 in the fourth wave.

Table 19. Partial Correlations between Information Sources and Knowledge of the Power-line Issue in Two Communities and at Four Times[a]

	Suburban				Rural			
Information Source	1[b] Sept. 75	2 Winter 76	3 Winter 77	4 Winter 78	1 Sept. 75	2 Winter 76	3 Winter 77	4 Winter 78
Newspapers	.74	.52	.19	.22	.45	.30	.26	.33
Radio	.12	.17	.13	.25	.04	.14	.17	.16
Television	.28	.15	.48	.09	.14	.05	.33	.30
Other persons	.42	.39	−.07	.01	.18	.16	−.17	−.19
Percent perceiving issue as conflict	19	30	65	52	40	45	75	67

[a]Each partial correlation is calculated with the other three media source variables held constant.
[b]Numbers designate study waves.

The partial correlation between accuracy of knowledge and use of television in the rural area was .14 in the first wave, .05 in the second wave, and then increased to .33 in the third wave, dropping slightly in the fourth wave. The patterns of partial correlations from the two sample areas were similar in that the highest relationship between use of newspapers and accuracy of knowledge occurred in the first wave of interviews in September 1975, and the highest correlation between use of television and knowledge occurred in the third wave, when the proportion of respondents in each community regarding the issue as conflictive was highest. These data indicated the role of newspapers as principal sources of information in the early phase of the controversy, with television playing a particularly strong role in the media mix, at the point of most intense conflict.

The low correlation between television and knowledge in the suburban area in the fourth wave does not reflect a decline in TV coverage. Television attention to the issue was higher in the months preceding the fourth wave of interviews than at any other point in the controversy. By the time of the fourth wave, however, the line construction itself was nearing completion and the opposition groups were viewed as engaging in a "last ditch stand." In such a situation, with a conflict winding down, even high television attention to such circumstances appears to make relatively little contribution to public knowledge.

Radio was generally not a strong contributor to knowledge. At only one point, in the fourth wave in the suburban area, did the partial correlation between use of radio and accurate knowledge surpass .17 (Table 19).

In each of the first two waves, the partial correlations between accurate knowledge and use of newspapers were higher in the more pluralistic suburban area than in the rural area. In the third wave, television was the strongest contributor to knowledge and the correlation was higher in the suburban area than in rural areas. This difference was in line with the expectation that in a more pluralistic structure, such as a suburb with a multiplicity of interest groups, mass media are generally depended upon to a greater extent for knowledge than would occur in a less pluralistic community.

SUMMARY

This analysis of media use indicates that relative use of television and newspapers and their relative contributions to knowledge varies as hypothesized from a structural perspective according to type of content, type of community, and phase of a controversy.

Newspapers are generally rated higher than television as sources giving "most local news," and the differences between the two media, for local news, are greater in small, more homogeneous and nonmetropolitan communities than in larger, more pluralistic metropolitan cities. Television is rated higher than newspapers as a source of nonlocal news, and this difference is also greater in smaller, more homogeneous nonmetropolitan communities than in metro centers.

The level of knowledge of local issues is generally correlated to a lower degree with the amount of TV viewing than with the amount of newspaper reading. Data on a statewide issue, the power-line controversy, indicated that correlations between use of a medium as a specific information source on that topic and having accurate knowledge were higher for newspapers than for any other source in the early stages, before the controversy had reached maximum intensity. The correlations between use of TV as a source and having knowledge about the power-line issue tended to be higher, as expected, at the stage where level of conflict intensity was highest. The analysis as a whole reinforces the structuralistic view that the effect of television, as with any other communication medium, must be understood in terms of its linkages with other components of the media mix and the role played by media generally in social processes in the system as a whole.

It should be noted that television, as a source of knowledge, is not dependent upon the ability to read, and its distribution may lead to more availability of information to all socioeconomic groups, especially as cable television develops. As changes in distribution of television occur, there could be changes in amount of knowledge distributed and in the particular points in action phases at which television is most effective. In view of its nondependence on reading, television in the near future might experience a great increase in its use as a source of knowledge. This potential raises the possibility of a rapid change in knowledge patterns in lesser developed countries.

REFERENCES

Bagdikian, Ben H. 1971. *The Information Machines, Their Impact on Men and the Media.* New York: Harper and Row.

Hirsch, Paul M. 1981. Public policy toward television: Mass media and education in American society. In *Reader on Public Opinion and Mass Communication,* 3rd ed., edited by Morris Janourty and Paul Hirsch. New York: Free Press.

McLuhan, Marshall. 1964. *Understanding Media: The Extension of Man.* New York: McGraw Hill.

Paletz, David L., and Robert M. Entman. 1981. *Media Power and Politics.* New York: Free Press.

Palmgreen, Philip, and P. Clarke. 1977. Agenda-setting with local and national issues. *Communication Research* 4:435–52.

Patterson, Thomas, and Robert McClure. 1976. *The Unseeing Eye: The Myth of Television Power in National Politics.* New York: Putnam.

Shaw, D., and M. McCombs. 1977. *The Emergence of American Political Issues: The Agenda-setting Function of the Press.* New York: West.

Tipton, Leonard, R. D. Haney, J. Basehart, and W.R. Elliott. 1975. Media agenda-setting in a state election campaign. *Journalism Quarterly* 52:15–22.

Williams, Wenmouth, Jr., and D. C. Larsen. 1977. Agenda-setting in an off election year. *Journalism Quarterly* 54:744–49.

CONCLUSION

CHAPTER 15

THE NEWS MEDIA AS THIRD PARTIES IN NATIONAL AND INTERNATIONAL CONFLICT: DUOBUS LITIGANTIBUS TERTIUS GAUDET

Andrew Arno

THE REALIST APPROACH TO CONFLICT AND THE NEWS MEDIA

The underlying assumption of the realist approach to international conflict is a durable one. There is a strong common sense appeal to the idea that nations have basic vital interests that they pursue in rational, self-serving ways. Violence or the threat of violence, then, can be seen as something calculated and—from a strictly instrumental, amoral point of view—reasonable. The intrinsic appeal of such a view is twofold. From the academic perspective, the assumption that there is a basic core of rationality to conflict processes means that they can ultimately yield to systematic analysis (cf Snyder and Diesing 1977) and be fully understood, just as the stable, law-conforming character of nature makes physical science possible. From the humanistic point of view, the idea that intelligible interests are being pursued rationally in international conflict leaves open the possibility that nonviolent means can be found for the adjustment of interests. A rational actor, in other words, can be persuaded that certain extreme forms of international or national violence are actually inefficient and self-defeating. Unfortunately, it is evident that the strategic, game-playing perspective of classical political realism encourages a mental set that can also lead to ingenious, intricately argued justifications of war as an instrument of policy (e.g., Kahn 1965).

As Tehranian remarks in Chapter 5, standard realist theory—in which incompatible interests are seen as the real basis of conflict—discounts the importance of the symbolic dimensions of international conflict. What is said in international conflict is mere rhetoric, propaganda, or false justification that hides the real issues from view. But Coser (1956) has shown that conflicts over symbolic issues can actually be harder to control than those over more realistic, material points of contention. Interests, therefore, must be defined to include symbolic, subjectively defined goals as well as those that can be objectively determined.

In understanding the rational aspects of conflict, account must be taken of *perceived* interests, and such perceptions grow out of symbolic exchange within and among nations. Communication about conflict, including both what is said and the conceptual categories within which issues and strategies are understood, therefore must be moved to the center of conflict analysis. The U.S.-Iran conflict, described from the international point of view by Tehranian (Chapter 5) and Mowlana (Chapter 3), and from the internal Iranian perspective by Beeman (Chapter 10) illustrates the problems that can arise when each country has difficulties in understanding the interests of the other.

Coser's point in Chapter 2 is well taken, however, and clearly, more and better communication would not help resolve conflict in every case and would exacerbate and create conflict in some cases. The meaning and function of noncommunication must also be taken into account, and even here cultural differences may be important. Silence can be a strategy in conflict behavior, and the meanings of strategic moves are as problematic as the definition of objectives and interests in intercultural and conflict situations.

The U.S.-Iran conflict demonstrates how perceptions of excess and restraint in language and nonverbal communication can become an obstacle to resolution of conflict. Vigorous theatrical demonstrations by crowds and a satisfying level of rhetorical hyperbole on one side may be interpreted as hysteria by those outside the cultural tradition, and what the other side intends as measured and reasonable restraint may be interpreted by the other as implacable hostility and recalcitrance or as an expression of contempt. The cultural meanings of apology as a conflict strategy clearly became an issue between the U.S. and Iran, and it also might be argued that there were differences in strategic bargaining concepts as well.

The basic, structurally defined national interests taken into account by political realist theory are important fundamentally, but culturally defined interests and the meanings attributed to conflict behavior patterns are becoming more and more critical as the kinds of technological advances described by Dordick in Chapter 4 bring publics of different nations into contact. One way of interpreting the situation is to say that increased international and intercultural communication through the news and other mass media have increased the scope of possible conflicts over symbolic issues in world politics. As people share in symbolic systems, they have more and more things about which to disagree. But while communication can create such problems, it also lies at the heart of their control and resolution. Whichever side of the coin one chooses to look at — mass communication as cause or cure of conflict — there is no doubt that the media are no longer peripheral players, and the ebb and flow of international conflict is taking on more of the character of social drama and becoming less of a simplified, culturally independent game of strategy.

Another, related factor that suggests a need to modify the classical realist approach is the proliferation of actors relevant to international conflicts. As the means of communication across national boundaries improve, the opportunities for the development of cross-cutting interest groups and dispersed communities linked by agreement or contention over special symbolic issues increase, and nation-states cease to be the only players. Rummel's (1983) finding that libertarian states are less likely than nonlibertarian ones to engage in international violence is highly relevant to this point. Rummel defines a libertarian state as one in which there is a high level of domestic diversity and pluralism, based on individual political and economic freedom, and he argues that the resulting checks and balances among multiple political elites make it hard to get the necessary support for a war — especially a war against another libertarian state. It is not that there are no conflict issues among such states, but such conflicts as do arise are being managed or resolved short of violence. From the perspective of international communication, libertarianism translates into freedom to make use of mass and person-to-person media and the density of ties thus formed would be especially great between states that enjoyed similar degrees of free access.

Among the vast array of entities, formal and informal, enduring and ad hoc, that can become involved in public conflicts within and among nations, the one constant, whose very existence is defined by conflict participation, is the news media organization. It is essential therefore, in attempting to understand national and international conflict processes, to take into account the nature and behavior of the news media. In Chapter 1, I argued that the news media, as storytellers, have to be studied within particular cultural contexts. But it is just as important to look at the structural positions that news media occupy in a generalized, cross-cultural account of conflict scenarios.

Characterizing the news media organizations metaphorically as storytellers gives an idea of the way they express themselves, but it does not deal with the more fundamental issue of their structural relationships to the other relevant actors. If news is conceptualized as largely conflict, it makes sense to narrow the examination to the structural properties of conflict situations. More specifically, because a news media organization itself is seldom a primary party to the conflict reported, I am most interested in the structural logic of third parties. This can be called, after Simmel (1950), "the sociology of three, when two are in conflict."

THE MEDIA AS THIRD PARTIES

According to the general usage of the term, a third party either "provides good offices" or serves as a mediator, an arbitrator, or an adjudicator (Schellenberg 1982, 236). When the third party provides good offices, it simply makes communication between the parties easier, usually by functioning as a go-between and shuttling messages back and forth when the principals do not want to or cannot approach one another directly. A mediator gets more deeply involved in the conflict process by participating in discussions between the parties, summarizing arguments, making suggestions, and asking questions. Still, the mediator, like the go-between, is mainly a facilitator of communication. In arbitration, on the other hand, the third party has the power to make a decision, and in some cases the parties may have agreed beforehand to accept that decision as binding on them. And while arbitrators are invited into disputes to serve as third parties and help settle the issues, adjudicators can intervene as a matter of right. The adjudicator's power, in other words, is derived from an independent, higher source, and the parties must accept his decision.

Whichever of these roles the third party plays in helping to manage or resolve conflict—and in some circumstances the roles may be combined with one another—there is an underlying assumption that he or she must be fair and unbiased. Autonomy is the critical issue, therefore, because the third party tied to either side may be prejudiced. But the built-in paradox of the third-party situation is that, in the complexity of actual societal organization true autonomy is impossible. Freedom from the bias that results from ties, obligations, and common interests between the third party and one side or the other is an ideal, but generally the real question is simply at what level the bias will surface or how it can be countered with sufficiently powerful countervailing forces.

The theme of press autonomy—its presence or absence—runs through all of the case studies in this book, and in general the authors have pointed out the difficulties that news media would have in performing the role of the third party in national or international conflict. In Chapter 13, Donohue, Tichenor, and Olien directly attack the notion that the U.S. press operates, as it claims to, as an independent "fourth estate." They did find that television news was less tied to the established powers than were the newspapers, but it might be argued that this result is more the product of an illusion than reality. Pictures, perhaps, are more ambiguous than words and can be perceived as supportive by partisans, such as the Minnesota respondents, who might find it hard to estimate the impact on the uncommitted.

In the U.S.-Iran conflict (Chapters 3, 5, and 10) the issues of autonomy and objectivity were squarely raised. When a news organization's own country is involved in conflict with another country, at some point it will be called upon to place national interests above journalistic ones. In internal conflicts too, news media may be controlled tightly by the government in times of crisis, as in the Sri Lankan Insurrection (Chapter 11), or they may be subordinated to the government at all times, as the *People's Daily* is in China (Chapter 9) and as the Iranian press was under the shah and the revolutionary regime as well (Chapter 10). In the Hong Kong case study by Chan and Lee (Chapter 12), newspapers were seen to be tied to political parties and to reflect political ideologies in their reporting, which is yet another way in which the press can be tied to special interests and under their control.

Despite all this support for the proposition that the news media do not and cannot operate as effective third parties, I would still argue that they can and do. In the first place, it is striking that the idea of the news organization as objective and uncontrolled should be so strong, even in political contexts in which it is difficult for them in fact to be so. Out of deference to such expectations, the Hong Kong newspapers, for example, made it a point not to print only letters to the editor representing their own position. In the China case too, the *People's Daily* surprisingly kept a steady course in its anti-U.S. orientation rather than doing an about face to keep in alignment with changing government policy. All this indicates that autonomy, as illusion if not fact, is important to the logic of the news reporting enterprise. And when structural conditions allow it, the forces, or the structural logic, that support press autonomy and opposition to control will assert themselves. The Indian case study shows an example of a press playing the role of supplying information to reader whether or not that information supports government positions. In Iran, the government of the shah as well as the revolutionary government had to exercise continual surveillance and pressure to keep the news media in line, even given their captive tradition. In the liminal state described by Beeman as coming into existence in Iran as the old order crumbled and the new one was not yet in place, the news media asserted their independence almost as an automatic response. The liminal state was one in which normal restraints were thrown off, and when that happened the press could revert to type.

The problem, then, is not to detail the circumstances in which the news media are repressed by political situations in which they operate, but to explain the strong tendency that they display to act as if they were free agents. I believe the most satisfactory answers will be found through exploring the nature of the news media's third-party role, but it is clear that the usual catalog of third-party patterns is too lacking in subtlety to serve. When we ask if a newspaper or television news organization operates like a good judge or even a disinterested go-between, the answer must be no, in most cases. But there are other ways of looking at third parties and understanding their goals and motivations.

Media actors fit into the category of third parties that Simmel (1950) labeled the *tertius gaudens*, the third who rejoices. In many cases, a third party profits from the conflict of two others, and this is especially true of news organizations. Were it not for such conflict, in fact, they would not even exist. Newspapers or television stations could serve other purposes, such as education, national integration, or entertainment. In order to function as news media, they need the conflict of others.

If A and B, each an entity, are in conflict with one another, and M, a newspaper or broadcasting organization, is totally identified with the interests of and under the control of either A or B, there are only two parties, not three. When parties to conflict have identical interests, they coalesce, in the structure of the conflict situation, and neither can act as a third party to the dispute. From this point of view it appears that a news medium, if it does have the character of the *tertius gaudens*, cannot operate if it is firmly tied to one of the parties to conflict. In practice, this seems to be so. If A is a national government that owns and controls a newspaper or radio station M, and if A is in conflict with B, a rival faction within the country for example, M will not be a credible source of information about the conflict—it will not function as a news medium—for supporters of either A or B, or indeed for any other observers. B's media organization, if any, would be in the same position. The people of that country might turn to outside sources of news, as for example happened in the Sri Lanka crisis described by Dissanayake (Chapter 11) or in Iran (Beeman, Chapter 10). This does not mean, however, that M would necessarily be totally discredited as a news source. If the news concerned a conflict in another place, and if neither A nor B had any special interest in it, M could well function as a news medium. M's role as the *tertius gaudens* then, is situational and depends on the issue being reported. It is probably also the case that the status of M as such is not an all-or-nothing one but is graduated with the relative degree of interest that it, through its controlling agency, has in the conflict at hand.

To be the third party in a conflict situation is to be in a position of power, and, to the *tertius gaudens*, one of potential profit as well. Both power and profit are strong motives in the sphere of human conduct, and they might affect the actions of the social actors under consideration here also. In accord with my metaphorical line of argument then, I will credit news media organizations with a desire to maximize both power and profit, and I would argue that this assumption allows one to go beyond a description of the media's structural position and account to some degree for the dynamics of their behavior.

The power of a third party to influence the course of events derives solely from his* position, and he may have little or no power base aside from that. In the absence of conflict, or if he allows himself to be permanently attached to one of the parties, he loses all of his power. The relationship between the third party and the two parties in conflict is symbiotic; he needs them—and their state of conflict—and they also need him. The two parties each want the third in some cases as an ally, and in some cases they need him as a nonpartisan mediator. In the latter instance, they are unable to deal with one another directly, and they need his offices to allow communication that can lead to accommodation. The first kind of position, that of the courted ally, can sometimes evolve into the more prestigious role of mediator, and eventually the sacred authority of the adjudicator may be attained. Simmel (1950) cites the historical example of the early bishops of Rome, who made it a practice to side with any bishop who, in a conflict with another bishop, asked for their support. To protect themselves, both parties found it necessary to petition the Roman bishop, and his authoritative role in conflict management was established.

It is often said that the mass media in the contemporary United States enjoy enormous power. In particular, they are often cited for their influence in the political processes of the nation, and it is possible to read that power as deriving from a *tertius gaudens* position. Certainly, politicians court the media, and the media do provide support that can mean victory in a particular election. The value of media support, however, would evaporate if one party were to gain actual control of it. The third-party position would be gone, and with it its power. Applying this kind of logic to the history of the news media in the United States, the emergence of objective, fair, informative newspapers and broadcast news from the beginnings of special interest propaganda sheets would seem to owe as much to the structural path toward self-aggrandizement offered by the role of the nonpartisan third party as to any free press ideology. Press freedom in the constitutional sense might well engender a plethora of competing, ideologically distinct media organizations, but it does not account for a growing centralization of print and broadcast news in the hands of profit-oriented corporations without any coherent political ideologies. As the news media become more expert in their jobs and less obviously partisan on issues, their prestige and authority increase, and correspondingly, their power as third parties grows. Politicians need and seek them more, which again enhances their role.

The news media have not by any means reached the point, beyond that of being a sought-after ally in conflict, of having enough authority and prestige in their own right to act as agents of dispute settlement. In the

---

*The use of the masculine pronoun to refer to the third party throughout this chapter is for convenience only.

international arena, however, in the absence of any stable political order, they do seem at times to take on the role of mediator. If they were to become genuinely internationalized, as some industries have, and if they were able to retain autonomy with respect to issue, they might achieve even more important and powerful roles as third parties to conflicts. In this regard, the contrast between the roles that the media organizations are able to fulfill within the political context of a stable nation, like the United States, and in international conflict is illuminating. In the United States, with regard to most important public issues, there is no lack of conflict management agencies. Among the legislature, the administrative bureaucracy, and the judiciary, political and much social conflict can be taken care of through mediation, arbitration, and adjudication. Still, there probably are areas of conflict not covered by government agencies that can be said to be mediated by the U.S. press. In international affairs, however, conflict management structures are still embryonic, and the mass media, if they can preserve a stance of disinterest and maintain a high level of integrity, could emerge as an important factor. In early European history, the church, being the most stable and respectable international actor, was called upon in the disputes of minor princes and other rulers and thereby became more and more powerful. Perhaps in the coming, secularized, information age, the media will flourish in a similar way.

When one considers the way the media might actually carry out their third-party roles, discussion of the media's structural position as the *tertius gaudens* leads back again to the notion previously introduced of the news media as storytellers. Media organizations as social actors must be considered together with their audiences. It is the media's relationship with the audience that gives force to their actions as a third party. In a way, it is ultimately the people who are reached by the media who are being sought when politicians or others in conflict appeal to the press, but this does not detract from the importance of the media or indicate that it is the audience that constitutes the true third party. The audience, as such, does not exist without the specific medium. The people exist, but they are not organized and accessible to the parties in conflict as the media organizations are. The practical priority, therefore, is clear; it is the news media that are effective third parties. They act, and their action has a predictable impact on the audience. At least that is the operating theory of those involved in the conflict scenarios. The chain of causation is complex, and it is ultimately the audience that will exert effective influence on the conflict.

THE PUBLIC'S EFFECT ON CONFLICT

Many researchers in the area of international conflict resolution and the media have discounted the impact the public can have on actual issues. Davison (1974), for example, assumes it is the leaders and decision-making elite who are the primary actors in international conflict, and public opinion can have only a rather indirect and remote influence. There is a good deal of truth in this from a certain perspective, and in some instances it is quite accurate. In general, however, I think this kind of argument seriously underestimates the power of the mass media audiences, and the reason for it is too simple a model of the dynamics of international conflict.

Nation-states are not necessarily the most appropriate entities on which to base an analysis of international conflict. It is not the nation as a whole that has relations with other nations, and it is not the nation as a whole that gets involved, in the first instance at least, in conflict situations. Countries are complex combinations of mobilized groups, and nations are not normally homogeneous but extremely varied and fragmented in their interests. Certain structural centers of interest are extensive in their influence, and others are quite restricted. Because they vary among lines of topic— religion, automobile manufacturing, trade unionism, for example—as well as being differentiated in geographical and social class terms, there is great potential for overlap as well as competition among them. In conflicts between countries, it is often more a matter of strained relations between centers of interest than whole countries. Deutsch (1966) conceptualizes international relations in terms of aggregate interaction, but an issue focus is necessary for analyses of conflict situations. If the auto industry in the United States is unhappy about its relations with its counterparts in Japan, it may well be the case that other sectors of the United States are quite pleased with the state of U.S.-Japan relations. Centers of interest are, in communication terms, also centers of persuasion and message generation, and a powerful group such as the auto and auto-related industrial and labor complex must exert itself to get its view of the international crisis accepted. The elected leaders of the country and those charged with foreign relations are often more like the spokesmen for particular clients within their own nation than actors in their own rights.

The mass media come into play internally in the struggle among centers of interest and persuasion to build consensus for a foreign policy action, and they can also reach across national boundaries from both directions, and influence internal support for a country's foreign relations positions. It is also the case that the media can reach across national boundaries to influence the purely internal affairs of a country, and here again the complex nature of multiple interest centers and their far-flung relationships provides the opening. The new communications technology has so far improved international communications that dispersed multinational interest groups are more than just a possibility. The labor union crisis in Poland is a good example of the appeal to the mass media by a party to conflict within a nation. The Polish labor movement used the international news media to get their messages across to trade unionists all over the world, most significantly in the United States. At least two dispersed interest groups were involved, ethnic Poles and trade unionists, and both responded by applying political pressure on their own government. It is the mass media, with the new technologies such as satellite-transmitted television at their disposal, that make such multicountry interest groups viable in conflict situations.

In summary, then, the identity of news and conflict is not a problem to be solved, but a fact to be recognized so that the operations of the news media can be understood better. It is essential also to look at the media themselves as important actors in conflict situations at both the national and the international levels. Professionalism and the values associated with new technology tend to enhance the autonomy of the media, but the necessary link with the audience ties them to cultural differences and prevents homogeneity. In order to function in intercultural contexts, the media must confront the limitations imposed on them by their roles as storytellers within given social contexts. In any case, in conflict the position of the news media as the third party who profits and grows powerful is important in explaining the dynamics of relations between the press and society.

REFERENCES

Coser, Lewis A. 1956. *The Social Functions of Conflict*. New York: The Free Press.

Davison, W. Phillips. 1974. *Mass Communication and Conflict Resolution*. New York: Praeger.

Deutsch, Karl. 1966. Power and communication in international society. In *Conflict in Society*, edited by Anthony De Reuck and Julie Knight. CIBA Foundation Symposium. Boston: Little, Brown.

Kahn, H. 1965. *On Escalation: Metaphors and Scenarios*. New York: Praeger.

Rummel, R.J. 1983. Libertarianism and international violence. *Journal of Conflict Resolution* 27(1):21–71.

Schellenberg, James A. 1982. *The Science of Conflict*. New York: Oxford University Press.

Simmel, Georg. 1950.*The Sociology of Georg Simmel*, edited by Kurt H. Wolff. New York: The Free Press.

Snyder, Glenn H., and Paul Diesing. 1977. *Conflict Among Nations: Bargaining, Decision Making and System Structure in International Crises*. Princeton: Princeton University Press.

ADDITIONAL READINGS

Adams, William C., editor. 1982. *Television Coverage of International Affairs.* Norwood, New Jersey: Ablex.

Barrett, Marvin, editor. 1982. *Broadcast Journalism 1979–1981: The Eighth Alfred I. duPont/Columbia University Survey.* New York: Everest House.

Boyd-Barrett, Oliver. 1980. *The International News Agencies.* Beverly Hills: Sage.

Burton, John W. 1969. *Conflict and Communication: The Use of Controlled Communication in International Relations.* New York: Free Press.

Choucri, Nazli, and Robert C. North. 1975. *Nations in Conflict.* San Francisco: W. H. Freeman.

Cohen, Stanley, and Jack Young, editors. 1973. *The Manufacture of News.* Beverly Hills: Sage.

Desmond, Robert W. 1982. *Crisis and Conflict: World News Reporting Between Two Wars 1920–1940.* Iowa City: University of Iowa Press.

Diamond, Edwin. 1978. *Good News, Bad News.* Cambridge, Mass.: Massachusetts Institute of Technology.

Edgar, Patricia. 1980. *The News in Focus: The Journalism of Exception.* Melbourne: The Macmillan Company of Australia.

Elliott, Philip, and Peter Golding. 1971. *The Mass Media and Foreign Affairs.* Leicester: University of Leicester.

Fishman, Mark. 1980. *Manufacturing the News.* Austin: University of Texas.

Gelfard, Donald E., and Russell D. Lee. 1973. *Ethnic Conflicts and Power: A Cross-National Perspective.* New York: Wiley.

Golding, Peter, and Philip Elliott. 1979. *Making the News.* New York: Longman.

Halloran, J., P. Elliott, and G. Murdock. 1970. *Demonstration and Communication.* Hammondsworth: Penguin Books.

Halmon, P., editor. 1969. *The Sociology of Mass Media Communication.* Sociological Review Monograph No. 13. Keele: University of Keele.

Jackson, Ian. 1971. *The Provincial Press and the Community*. Manchester: Manchester University Press.

Lent, John A., editor. 1978. *Asian Newspapers: Reluctant Revolutionaries*. Ames: Iowa State University Press.

Manekar, D. R. 1979. *Media and the Third World*. New Delhi: Institute of Mass Communication.

Miller, G. R., and H. W. Simons. 1974. *Perspectives on Communication in Social Conflict*. Englewood Cliffs: Prentice-Hall.

Nordenstreng, Kaarle, and Herbert Schiller, editors. 1979. *National Sovereignty and International Communication*. Norwood, New Jersey: Ablex.

Richstad, J., and Michael H. Anderson, editors. 1981. *Crisis in International News: Policies and Prospects*. New York: Columbia University Press.

Rummel, Rudolph J. 1975. *Understanding Conflict and War*. 2 vols. New York: Halsted Press.

Schiller, Dan. 1981. *Objectivity and the News: The Public and the Rise of Commercial Journalism*. Philadelphia: University of Pennsylvania.

Schlesinger, Philip. 1978. *Putting "Reality" Together: BBC News*. London: Constable.

Schramm, Wilbur, and L. Erwin Atwood. 1981. *Circulation of Third World News: A Study of Asia*. Hong Kong: Press of Chinese University of Hong Kong.

Smith, Anthony. 1980. *Geopolitics of Information: How Western Culture Dominates the World*. London: Faber and Faber.

Sussman, Leonard R. 1977. *Mass News Media and the Third World Challenge*. The Washington Papers No. 46. Beverly Hills: Sage.

Tiffen, Rodney. 1978. *The News from Southeast Asia: The Sociology of Newsmaking*. Singapore: Institute of Southeast Asian Studies.

Tunstall, J. 1971. *The Media are American*. New York: Columbia University Press.

Tunstall, J., editor. 1970. *Media Sociology*. London: Constable.

CONTRIBUTORS

Elie Abel is Chandler professor of communication, Institute for Communication Research, at Stanford University. Formerly he was dean of the School of Journalism at Columbia University, and he was the American representative on the MacBride Commission. Professor Abel is also a distinguished journalist with many years of experience in print and electronic news media.

Andrew Arno is a research associate with the East-West Communication Institute. Trained as a lawyer and as a social anthropologist, Dr. Arno's published writings have explored problems in legal anthropology from a communication perspective. His current research centers on the mass media in legal and political conflict control.

William O. Beeman is assistant professor of anthropology at Brown University. Dr. Beeman is a specialist in Iranian culture, and he appeared several times on the McNeil-Lehrer Report, NET, as an expert commentator during the U.S.-Iran hostage crisis. He also writes for the Pacific News Service, and his articles have appeared in many U.S. newspapers.

Joseph Man Chan is a Ph.D. candidate at the University of Minnesota. He was previously with the Social Research Center of the Chinese University of Hong Kong. He engaged in extensive communication research in Hong Kong.

Lewis A. Coser is professor of sociology at the State University of New York at Stony Brook. One of the world's leading sociologists, Professor Coser is especially well known for his work on conflict. His books include *The Social Functions of Conflict* and *Continuities in the Study of Social Conflict*. His current interests include the sociological analysis of the publishing industry in the United States.

241

Wimal Dissanayake is a research associate at the East-West Communication Institute. Formerly, he was chairman of the Department of Mass Communication at the University of Sri Lanka, and he has been a visiting Fulbright research scholar at the University of Pennsylvania. He is a trained broadcaster and has worked as a newspaper journalist in Sri Lanka.

George A. Donohue is a professor of sociology at the University of Minnesota. Together with P. J. Tichenor and C. N. Olien, he has written numerous scholarly articles concerning the mass media, knowledge, and social control. One of the most recent books produced by this distinguished research team is *Community Conflict and the Press*.

Herbert S. Dordick, trained as an engineer and for many years a researcher and consultant in various areas of communication technology, is director of the Center for Communications Policy Research at the Annenberg School of Communications, University of Southern California. His most recent book is *The Emerging Network Marketplace*.

S. K. Jagadeswari, a professional associate with the East-West Culture Learning Institute for 1980–81, is a writer from India.

Chi-Chuan Lee is associate professor of journalism and mass communication at the University of Minnesota. He is the author of *Mass Media Imperialism Reconsidered* and two books in Chinese on mass communication. He previously taught communication at the Chinese University of Hong Kong.

Hamid Mowlana is professor of international relations and director of international communication studies at the School of International Service, The American University, Washington, D.C. He was editor-in-chief of Kayhan Newspapers in Tehran, Iran, and has worked as a foreign affairs analyst in the United States media. Among his books are *International Communication, Social Communication in Iran*, and *Watergate: A Crisis for the World*. He is an editor of *Journal of Communication* and *USA Today*.

Clarice N. Olien is professor and extension rural sociologist at the University of Minnesota. Her research and publications in the area of conflict and communications, in collaboration with George Donohue and Phillip Tichenor, are widely recognized.

Sripada K. S. Raju is a senior fellow with the East-West Culture Learning Institute. He has published numerous papers on communication and social science knowledge dissemination.

Majid Tehranian is professor of political economy and international communication at the University of Hawaii. He is the author of some ten books and forty-four articles in scholarly journals. An expert on the communication media in Iran, he has held policy positions, including director of the Prospective Planning Project of National Iranian Radio and Television, president of Iran Communications and Development Institute, and program specialist at the Division of Development of Communications Systems, UNESCO.

Phillip J. Tichenor is a professor of journalism and mass communication at the University of Minnesota. With George Donohue and C. N. Olien, he has published many books and articles on the mass media and community conflict. Their research team is well known, among other things, for its pioneering explorations of the "knowledge gap" concept in communication research.

Georgette Wang is a professor at the Graduate School of Journalism, National Chengchi University, in Taipei, Taiwan. She has worked as a research associate with the East-West Communication Institute, at universities in Hong Kong, and has been a feature writer for one of the largest private newspapers in Taiwan. She has published several articles in the area of media and intercultural communication.

NAME INDEX

SUBJECT INDEX

Access to media, 205
Autonomy of news media, 14, 15, 90, 133, 205, 232

BBC, 170
 role in international conflict, 13
 role in Iranian revolution, 152, 153, 159, 160

Centers of interest in conflict process, 237. *See also* Pluralism
Cinema in Iran, 151, 152
Civil protest
 leftist, rightist, and centrist perspectives on, 188–190
 as political action in Hong Kong, 184
Communication
 and conflict, 1, 3
 and conflict management, 3
 distorted, 19
 international. *See* International communication
 interpersonal, 30, 32, 142, 143, 144
 limitations in conflict processes, 25. *See also* Ignorance in conflict situations
 in Marxist theory, 18
 open, 17, 18
 role in global symbolic systems, 33, 47
Communist countries, press in, 134
Conflict
 definition of, 13
 distinguished from "crisis," 80
 international, role of media in, 11
 management of, definition, 3
 as news, 2, 133
 as product of communication, 1
 scenarios, in cultural context, 9
 social usefulness of, 9
 worldwide processes, 10

Conflict of interests in Hong Kong society, 184
Crisis, definition of, 80
Cultural patterns in conflict management, 4, 5
Culture, impact on technology, 38

Development, theories of, 30
Diplomacy and media in U.S.-Iran conflict, 81, 82
Disclosure in social interaction, 21, 22

Educational systems as communication channels, 31
Ethics
 code of, 34, 35
 in communication, 30, 33

Foreign correspondent system, decline in TV news, 67

Gallegos, Corp., interview with, 86–87

Hostage crisis, 48
 background of, 50, 51
 as media event, 43, 44, 50, 58, 161, 162
Hostages, U.S., in Iran
 negotiations for release of, 55, 56
 rescue attempt, 56
 return as media event, 8, 57

Ignorance in conflict situations, 20–25
Image making in international politics, 45
Image politics, 44
Indo-Pakistan conflict
 background of, 102–106
 mass media roles in, 103–104